GUEST MANAGEMENT

GUEST MANAGEMENT

R.K. ARORA

A P H PUBLISHING CORPORATION
4435-36/7, ANSARI ROAD, DARYA GANJ
NEW DELHI-110 002

Published by
S.B. Nangia
A P H Publishing Corporation
4435-36/7, Ansari Road, Darya Ganj
New Delhi-110002
Ph. 23274050
Email : aphbooks@vsnl.net

2011

Printed at :
Balaji Offset
Navin Shahdara,
Delhi-32

Preface

Guest is a person who patronizes a hotel, restaurant, etc., for the lodging, food, or entertainment it provides. In the contemporary world, hospitality is rarely a matter of protection and survival, and is more associated with etiquette and entertainment. However, it still involves showing respect for one's guests, providing for their needs, and treating them as equals. Cultures and subcultures vary in the extent to which one is expected to show hospitality to strangers, as opposed to personal friends or members of one's in-group. The hospitality service industry includes hotels, casinos, and resorts, which offer comfort and guidance to strangers, but only as part of a business relationship. The terms hospital, hospice, and hostel also derive from "hospitality," and these institutions preserve more of the connotation of personal care. Hospitality ethics is a discipline that studies this usage of hospitality. In India, hospitality is based on the principle *Atithi Devo Bhava*, meaning "the guest is God." This principle is shown in a number of stories where a guest is literally a god who rewards the provider of hospitality. From this stems the Indian approach of graciousness towards guests at home, and in all social situations. Today, guest management and reservation software have been designed for use by bed and breakfast innkeepers.

This book titled, "Guest Management" gives its readers an introduction to guest and hospitality management. Focus lies on Mehmaan Khana, Haveli, hotel, motel, hostel, resort and restaurant. Considerable reflections are made on hotel amenities, guest rooms and other facilities. Special focus has been laid on guest house facilities, amenities and functionalities. The related elements of tourism, tourist attraction, tourist destination and tourist holidays are covered. Focus is also laid on relevance of couch surfing, hospitality service and social networks. Important related elements of guest management are described with focus on role of hotel manager, general manager and receptionist. To make this publication more user-friendly, an annotated bibliography and detailed index are provided.

—Editor

Contents

1

Introduction to Guest and Hospitality Management

HOSPITALITY

Hospitality is the relationship between guest and host, or the act or practice of being hospitable. Specifically, this includes the reception and entertainment of guests, visitors, or strangers, resorts, membership clubs, conventions, attractions, special events, and other services for travelers and tourists.

The word *hospitality* derives from the Latin *hospes*, which is formed from *hostis*, which originally meant "to have power." The meaning of "host" can be literally read as "lord of strangers." *Hostire* means "equalize or compensate."

Contemporary Usage

In the contemporary West, hospitality is rarely a matter of protection and survival, and is more associated with etiquette and entertainment. However, it still involves showing respect for one's guests, providing for their needs, and treating them as equals. Cultures and subcultures vary in the extent to which one is expected to show hospitality to strangers, as opposed to personal friends or members of one's in-group. The hospitality service industry includes hotels, casinos, and resorts, which offer comfort and guidance to strangers, but only as part of a business relationship. The terms hospital, hospice, and hostel also derive from "hospitality," and these institutions preserve more of the connotation of personal care. Hospitality ethics is a discipline that studies this usage of hospitality.

Global Concepts

Pakhtuns

The Pakhtun people of South-Central Asia, pre-dominant in the Khyber Pakhtunkhwa province of Pakistan and Afghanistan have a strong code of hospitality. They are a people characterized by their use of *Pakhtunwali*, an ancient set of ethics, the first principle of which is *Milmastiya* or Hospitality. The general area of Pakhtunistan is also nicknamed *The Land of Hospitality*.

Biblical and Middle Eastern

In Middle Eastern Culture, it was considered a cultural norm to take care of the strangers and foreigners living among you. These norms are reflected in many Biblical commands and examples. The obligations of both host and guest are stern. The bond is formed by eating salt under the roof, and is so strict that an Arab story tells of a thief who tasted something to see if it was sugar, and on realizing it was salt, put back all that he had taken and left.

Classical World

To the ancient Greeks and Romans, hospitality was a divine right. The host was expected to make sure the needs of his guests were seen to. The ancient Greek term *xenia*, or *theoxenia* when a god was involved, expressed this ritualized guest-friendship relation.

Celtic Cultures

Celtic societies also valued the concept of hospitality, especially in terms of protection. A host who granted a person's request for refuge was expected not only to provide food and shelter to his/her guest, but to make sure they did not come to harm while under their care.

India

In India, hospitality is based on the principle *Atithi Devo Bhava*, meaning "the guest is God." This principle is shown in a number of stories where a guest is literally a god who rewards the provider of hospitality. From this stems the Indian approach of graciousness towards guests at home, and in all social situations.

Cultural Value or Norm

Hospitality as a cultural norm or value is an established sociological phenomenon that people study and write papers about. Some regions have become stereotyped as exhibiting a particular style of hospitality. Examples include:

- Minnesota nice
- Southern hospitality

LODGING

Lodging (or a holiday accommodation) is a type of residential accommodation. People who travel and stay away from home for more than a day need lodging for sleep, rest, safety, shelter from cold temperatures or rain, storage of luggage and access to common household functions. Lodgings may be *self catering* in which case no food is laid on but cooking facilities are available. Lodging is done in a hotel, hostel or hostal, a private home (commercial, i.e. a bed and breakfast, a guest house, a vacation rental, or non-commercially, with members of hospitality services or in the home of friends), in a tent, caravan/camper (often on a campsite). In addition there are make-shift solutions.

Sleeping is typically done lying in a bed, or more generally on a soft surface, such as an air mattress, a couch, etc. Some trains have sleeping cars. Sometimes people sleep sitting, because lying is not possible, such as in a train (if not in a sleeping car), a bus, a seat in a waiting room or a bench on the street or in a park. Inclinable seats allow something between sitting and lying. Whether lying on a row of seats is possible and comfortable depends on the presence of arm rests, and whether they can be moved up. In some public places, lying would be possible, but is not permitted.

HOMESTAY

Homestay is a form of tourism and/or study abroad programme that allows the visitor to rent a room from a local family to better learn the local lifestyle as well as improve their language ability. While homestays can occur in any destination worldwide, some countries do more to encourage homestay than others as a means of developing their tourism industry. Hosting a homestay participant also allows the local family to earn some additional, needed income. Having low profitability, as it is, homestay can not be regarded as strictly commercial activity, but more of cross cultural exchange. Students generally arrange a homestay with their school or educational institution, but can also informally arrange to stay with a family through social connections, and through a variety of private agencies. There are a number of online homestay agencies that connect students with hosts all over the world (usually for a nominal fee).

Types of Homestays

Homestay scenarios can range from a completely immersive family experience, to a very basic room rental. In the immersive family experience a homestay student lives, eats, and shares the majoritiy of their time in the host country with the hosts and their family. Family events such as dining out, amusement parks, camping, travel, etc. usually involve the host student who may or may not be expected to pay a portion for the participation (tickets, parking, gas, travel expenses, et al.) The student is invited to participate in Holiday festivities (Thanksgiving, Christmas, etc.) and family events (weddings, birthdays, etc.)

At the other end of the spectrum, students may simply be renting a room within a private home with minimal supervision from a host or family.

Additionally, there are a working homestay agreements where a student is expected to perform duties such as yard work, farm work, babysitting, maid services - usually in exchange for accommodation fees or as part of. Besides homestays for students/ study abroad programmes they are an upcoming, unusual and interesting way of travel.

Most property owners do this as a hobby simply because they enjoy hosting people. Homestays can be a very rewarding experience and leave you with memories that you would cherish forever. People in several holiday destinations with large homes invite travellers to stay in their homes as their guests for the duration of their travel. What travellers can expect at a homestay is a comfortable homely stay, homemade food (definitely the best way to experience local cuisine), local culture (unlike typical hotel accommodations) while having your privacy as well.

Another added bonus would be the wonderful people you meet who are not only extremely warm and hospitable hosts but also the best source of local information. http://www.namastay.in/India/Travel-Blogs/Travel-Reviews-Articles-of-India/art_id/31/heading/homestays/date/2010-05-01/author/namastay.in

Typical Contracts and Agreements

A clash of cultures can sometimes result between a homestay student and the host family. To mitigate any issues, most homestay arrangements involve a contract or written agreement between the host and student. A contract will outline what is expected of the homestay student and may include items such as;

- Chores to perform (cleaning, laundering)
- Curfews

- Use of the Internet, television
- Use of the telephone
- Guest visits
- Smoking/drinking rules

as well as the details of what is being provided by the host in terms of:

- Accommodations
- Furniture/facilities
- Meal provisions
- Transportation
- Communications (Internet, telephone)
- Entertainment (TV, radio)

Generally, a host must provide a private room for sleep and study that has a lock and a washroom must be available that is convenient for the student to use. Most other items are negotiable in terms of availability and price.

Risks for the Host

Typically, hosting a homestay student is a rich and rewarding experience that allows the sharing of cultures, information, and experience. However, studying abroad is often the first time the homestay student is away from the parents and home country. This may result in adjustment issues for the student. The host must be able to deal with separation issues, anxiety, and the like. Scams on the internet are becoming fairly commonplace — when engaging in financial transactions that may require international payments, cheques, and money orders being sent there is always the possibility of making oneself vulnerable to scams and fraud.

The host family is best to educate themselves on the issues, and protect themselves adequately through the use of a good contract.

A recent and common example of a scam perpetrated on host families plays as follows:

- Parents of a student email the host family to request a room - usually claiming to be from Europe/Asia.
- The host replies with availability and costs etc.
- The parent agrees to the fees, and offers to pay the fees up front.
- Usually some sort of family crisis arises, and the transaction must be handled with urgency.
- The parent sends payment with an overage, and aks the host to refund the excess payment.
- The host family refunds the payment.
- The initial payment (cheque, money order, etc.) bounces or is fraudulent.
- The host family has lost the money it has sent as a refund.

This scam can happen in any situation any time payment is required in the form of cheque/money order/cashiers cheque, etc. In-depth discussion on frauds of this type is beyond the scope of this study, but the host family is encouraged to exercise caution when dealing with overseas payments and transactions.

Risks for the Student/Guest

There are two basic motivations for a family to engage in the operation of a homestay:

1. The family is looking to assist students, inject culture, and better understand the world and its people through a mutual exchange of traditions, knowledge and culture.
2. The family is looking to augment their income.

Usually, a family bears a healthy mix of these two reasons in opening their home to students and international visitors. Occasionally, however, there are instances where a family, or individual, is looking only to capitalize on the financial opportunity and has little or no concern for the interests of the student. A student is encouraged to look at the history of students and guests that the family has hosted, and to ask for a reference from a student who has recently attended their homestay. If a family refuses to give a reference, a student is advised to stay away. Also, look for a contract that not only protects the interests of the homestay host, but also the interests of the student. There should be a clear listing of the obligations of both the student and host family.

BED AND BREAKFAST

A bed and breakfast (or B&B) is a small lodging establishment that offers overnight accommodation and breakfast, but usually does not offer other meals. Typically, bed and breakfasts are private homes with fewer than 10 bedrooms available for commercial use.

Overview

Generally, guests are accommodated in private bedrooms with private bathrooms, or in a suite of rooms including an en suite bathroom. Some homes have private bedrooms with a bathroom which is shared with other guests. Breakfast is served in the bedroom, a dining room, or the host's kitchen. B&Bs and guest houses may be operated either as a secondary source of income or a primary occupation. Usually the owners themselves prepare the breakfast and clean the room etc., but some bed and breakfasts hire staff for cleaning or cooking. Although some bed and breakfast owners hire professional staff, a property which hires professional management is usually no longer considered a bed and breakfast, but enters the category of inn or hotel. Some B&Bs operate in a niche market. Floating bed and breakfasts for example are a concept originating in Seattle in which a boat or houseboat offers B&B accommodation.

Regional Differences

Australia

Despite the cultural similarities and a population more than twenty times greater, there are far fewer B&Bs in the whole of Australia than there are in just the South Island of New Zealand.

Since the 1960s the average per capita disposable income of Australians has been greater than that of New Zealanders and this has mitigated the powerful incentive to let out rooms in their homes to travellers. Another factor may be that Australia has, apart from City States such as Singapore, the greatest concentration of city dwellers anywhere on the globe and these cities are amply supplied with budget hotels and motels.

British Isles

B&Bs, and frequently guest houses, are a budget option where owners often take pride in the high service levels, local knowledge and personal touch that they are able to offer.

There tend to be concentrations of B&Bs in seaside towns where, historically, the working classes holidayed such as County Down, Northern Ireland, and Blackpool, England, and isolated rural areas such as the Highlands of Scotland and Connemara where there is not the year-round concentration of travellers that would sustain an hotel. They are present in most towns and cities, and their numbers vary on trade such as for business travellers and tourists: York and Edinburgh for example both have several hundred establishments known as either B&Bs or guest houses. In very busy areas, B&Bs may display a sign saying "VACANCIES" (rooms available) or "NO VACANCIES", to save both the hosts and potential guests the trouble of them having to enquire within.

Breakfast is usually cooked on demand for the guest

and is usually some kind of full breakfast, but some offer a continental breakfast.

In recent years B&Bs in the UK have struggled against budget hotel chains such as Premier Inn and Travelodge. Traditionally, business travellers used B&Bs but many of these clients now tend to stay in budget hotel chains. However, in holiday areas the B&B and guest house still prevail. Unlike the hotel chains, they provide a more comprehensive service and breakfast is included in the price, and some who stay regularly may simply like knowing their hosts.

B&Bs tend to place their bedrooms within three different categories:

Deluxe: This standard of B&B accommodation in Ireland is considered to be very high and deluxe rooms would be available in high end B&Bs and guesthouse accommodation. Deluxe rooms would often have additional furniture or Jacuzzis in the bathroom. Check the description.

En-Suite: There is a private bathroom within the bedroom. This will always contain a WC and washbasin, and a shower or bath or both.

Standard: There is not a bathroom within the bedroom. In this case there will be shared bathroom facilities in another room on the corridor. Usually there will be a washbasin within the room.

Cuba

In Cuba, which opened up to tourism in the 1990s after the financial support of the Soviet Union ended, a form of B&B called *casa particular* ("private home") became the main form of accommodation outside the tourist resorts.

Israel

The Israeli B&B is known as a *zimmer* (German for *room*). All over the country, but especially in the north of the country and the Galilee, *zimmers* have become an alternative to hotels for romantic weekends or family vacations.

Italy

In Italy, regional law regulates B&Bs.

India

In India, the government is promoting the concept of bed & breakfast. The government is doing this to increase tourism, especially keeping in view the expected demand for hotels during the 2010 Commonwealth Games in Delhi. They have classified B&B in 2 categories - Gold & Silver B&B. All B&B will be approved by the Ministry of Tourism who will then categorize it as Gold or Silver based upon the pre-defined criteria.

Kyrgyzstan

The tourism industry in Kyrgyzstan includes some B&Bs. One group, called CBT, organizes homestays with people who own homes and rent rooms by the night. They help tourists and travelers in Kyrgyzstan find places to stay.

Pakistan

The trend of B&Bs in Pakistan is quite widespread. Popular resorts like Murree, which attract many tourists from different parts of the country, have a number of such resthouses. The expenses can vary, depending on the quality of facilities. Most bed and breakfast facilities tend to expediently cater to families, given the high level of group tourism, and offer suitable overnight lodging.

New Zealand

As in the USA, bed and breakfasts in New Zealand tend to be more expensive than motels and often feature historic homes and furnished bedrooms at a commensurate price.

North America

Many B&Bs in North America try to create a historical ambiance, with old properties turned into guesthouses decorated with antique furniture. For example, the Holladay House in Orange, Virginia is an 1830s Federal-style brick building that has been converted into a bed and breakfast. In the last ten years, B&B and Inn owners have been launching upscale amenities to improve business and move "up-market." It is not uncommon now to find free wireless Internet access, free parking, spa services, or nightly wine and cheese hours. Due to the need to stay competitive with the rest of the lodging industry, larger bed and breakfast inns have expanded to offer wedding services, business conference facilities, and meeting spaces as well as many other services a large hotel might offer.

The custom of opening one's home to travellers dates back the earliest day of Colonial America. Lodging establishments were few and far between in the 18th century, and apart from a limited number of coaching inns (a few of which survive as inns today), wayfarers relied on the kindness of strangers to provide a bed for the night. Hotels became more common with the advent of the railroad, and later, the automobile, and most towns had at least one prominent hotel.

During the Great Depression, tourist homes provided an economic advantage to both the traveller and the host. Driving through town (no Interstates then), travellers stopped at houses with signs reading Tourists or Guests, indicating that travellers could rent a room for the night for about $2. The money generated needed income for the home owner and saved money for the traveller.

After World War II, middle-class Americans began travelling in Europe in large numbers, many experiencing the European-style B&Bs (Zimmer frei in Germany, chambres d'hotes in France) for the first time. Some were inspired to open B&Bs in the U.S.; tourist home owners updated their properties as B&Bs. The interest in B&Bs coincided with an increasing interest in historic preservation, spurred by the U.S. Bicentennial in 1976 and assisted by two crucial pieces of legislation: the National Historic Preservation Act of 1966, and the Tax Reform Act of 1976, which provided tax incentives for the restoration and reuse of historic structures.

Through the 1980s and 1990s, B&Bs increased rapidly in numbers and evolved from homestay B&Bs with shared baths and a simple furnishings to beautifully renovated historic mansions with luxurious décor and amenities. The next big change started in the mid 1990s when the Internet became a major marketing force, making it affordable for innkeepers to promote their properties worldwide. Email marketing, in particular, serves as a useful tool for the Bed & Breakfast industry, for it proactively builds relationships with the existing guests after their stay. In addition, online reservation software has helped bed and breakfasts to capture more reservations and stay in touch with a rapidly changing technological world. At present, travellers research and book B&Bs online, checking out detailed photos, videos, and reviews. B&Bs are found in all states, in major cities and remote rural areas, occupying everything from modest cottages to opulent mansions, and in restored structures from schools to cabooses to churches. According to Destination Nexus, the most comprehensive directory of exceptional lodging like bed and breakfasts, there are currently more than 18,000 bed and breakfast inns in North America.

Spain

In Spain, B&Bs are often run by people who place personal or family needs ahead of wealth and profit maximization. The business attracts numerous entrepreneurs with predominantly lifestyle motives, yet challenges them in specific ways. Spain does not have a B&B culture like Great Britain. As anything "modern" rules, locals usually shake their head at tourists visiting B&Bs when they could stay at a "proper hotel" for the same money or less.

A study of the years 1997–2000, using a sample of 1131 Spanish firms, suggests that marketing must be done over the medium to long term to be effective.

Regulations

Regulations and laws vary considerably between jurisdictions both in content and extent and in enforcement.

The most common regulations B&Bs must follow pertain to safety. They are usually required by local and national ordinances to have fire resistance, a sufficient fire escape plan in place, and smoke detectors in each guest room. Kitchens and equipment used to serve meals are also often required to be monitored for hygienic operation, but there are significant national and local differences.

In Hawaii, it is illegal to open a new bed & breakfast on Oahu as of 1989. The reason for the moratorium is to force home owners with extra room to rent out their extra space to low income residents who otherwise cannot afford housing on crowded Oahu.

Professional and Trade Associations

Many inns and bed and breakfasts are members of professional associations. There are international, national, regional, and local associations, all of which provide services to both their members and the travelling public. Many require their members to meet specific standards of quality, while others simply require a lodging establishment to pay dues. These associations also facilitate marketing of the individual B&Bs and provide a stamp of approval that the business in question is reputable.

While various local governments have regulations and inspect lodging establishments for health and safety issues, membership in a state/provincial/national bed and breakfast association can indicate a higher standard of hospitality. Associations sometimes review their members' properties and tend to have additional standards of care. In the US for example, each state has an innkeeping association (usually non-profit) that exists to promote the industry and tourism. Within those state associations, many city and regional bed and breakfast associations can be found. Many state, city and regional associations, have inspection criteria that often exceed government requirements for safety and cleanliness. One US association, Select Registry, is an association of 400 distinguished inns nation-wide that must pass an inspection criteria in order to be accepted. In Australia, the industry is represented by the Bed & Breakfast, Farmstay and Accommodation Australia Ltd (BBFAA).

In the British Isles the national approval boards set up by governments are far more stringent than others,while in Ireland there is an association that will only use the national tourist board's approved members (Almara Accommodations Dublin)

Studies

Tourism Queensland Study

In January 2003 Tourism Queensland conducted a review of current research to gain a better understanding of the Bed & Breakfast (B&B) market:

> "Key needs that must be met for people staying at bed and breakfast style accommodation include: pampering and personalized service in an attractive location in an attractive house, opposed to more 'standard' hotelrooms."

The following attributes are also appealing:

> Homely or wholesome atmosphere (older segments) or luxurious/heritage surrounds
>
> Home style meals
>
> Area for conversing with other guests

Ability to tap into local knowledge of attractions and activities in local area.

Guests at B&Bs were asked to identify the features and factors which motivated them to choose the establishment they were staying at. The friendliness of the host was the most important factor, followed by easy access to other places, the site being the most appealing place in the region. Usually B & B´s are privately owned, and therefor very different from standard commercial hotels.

Bed & Breakfasts provide mutual benefits for both the visitor and the operator. Visitors have the opportunity for a relaxing break in a homely environment. Operators have the opportunity to develop a profitable business, make new friends and contacts, understand the cultures andlifestyles of others, and to educate guests about their way of life.

Income and leisure time have changed so that shorter breaks with greater choice of leisure activities are sought. Changing work patterns have increased the popularity of shorter breaks that minimize the absence from work and the effect of absences on workflow and involvement. Bed & Breakfast holidays tend to be short break holidays and could benefit from the increased popularity of short breaks, sought by people who aim for authenticity and personal service.

Michigan State University Study

"The profile of B&B guests confirms widely held impressions that this is a middle-aged, well-educated, (moderately) high income, professional market. On the last reported B&B trip, couples comprised two thirds of the travel parties.

Eighty-two percent of those sampled are married, and about half (44 percent) have children living at home. Average age for a travel party (respondent and spouse/partner ages are merged) is 40 years, with 60 percent under this age. This indicates that many B&B guests are at a mid-point in the traditional family cycle, when raising children is a primary activity. Newlyweds and "empty nesters" account for a smaller proportion. In fact, only 9 percent of the market is attributed to adults over 59 years of age.

Education levels are high, with the largest response category being completion of a college degree (31 percent). In addition, another one third had some graduate school or an advanced degree. It follows that the occupational profile is dominated by professionals and managers. Note that several categories such as business, health, education, and science are large enough for B&B's to consider promotion aimed specifically at these segments.

The unique touches that distinguish a B&B are clearly a primary reason for selecting this lodging option. Words like "charm," ambience," "quaintness," and "atmosphere" were often used by respondents to describe this intangible appeal. The importance of the "getaway" aspect demonstrates that B&B's have been well positioned to take advantage of shorter, more frequent weekend trips preferred by many two-income families. The lure of B&B's as a more personal alternative to the standard hotel/motel experience was reconfirmed by the 10 percent who called this the single most important reason for staying at a B&B, the most frequent response to this open-ended question.

Customers were for the most part satisfied with their most recent B&B experience, with 80 percent giving the experience an .. excellent" rating and another 17 percent calling it "good." Over 90 percent would both consider a return visit and recommend the B&B to friends and family.

According to this study, many bed and breakfast visitors make use of evaluations, given by other guests. This system of independent reviews is one of the fastest growing consumer content oriented sites on the net.

ComScore Study

Another study suggests that people trust online reviews posted by previous guests:

> People are willing to pay up to 99 percent more for services after reading positive online reviews about them, according to new research.

The study, conducted in October by comScore and The Kelsey Group, found that online, consumer-created reviews have a big impact on prospective buyers. The researchers said 24 percent of those who eventually pay for local services — such as restaurants, bed & breakfasts and automotive shops — read online reviews before making a choice.

The study showed consumers were so trusting of online reviews, they were willing to pay at least 20 percent, and up to 99 percent, more if a company was rated excellent or five-star than if a business received a good, or four-star, rating. The study was based on 2,078 survey respondents, including 508 who used online consumer reviews.

Professional critics, and owners of companies that receive less-than-excellent online reviews by laypersons, might question the ability of regular people to adequately judge a service. However, the comScore/Kelsey Group study found that 90 percent of the people who trusted consumer-written reviews found the critiques to be accurate. In fact, noted the researchers, "reviews generated by fellow consumers had a greater influence than those generated by professionals."

The study included specific bed & breakfasts among others services. At least 75 percent of those using online reviews for nearly every category of business included in the study said the amateur field reports significantly impacted their decision. Eighty-seven percent of those in search of hotels said the reviews played a big part in their choice. The take-away message for service providers, according to a statement issued by The Kelsey Group's research director,

Journal of Travel Research Study

A study by the Journal of Travel Research stated:

"While the hedonic price model has been used to evaluate willingness to pay in a variety of markets, its use in the tourism industry is limited. This research note highlights the usefulness of the hedonic price technique in this industry by evaluating willingness to pay for specific characteristics of bed and breakfast accommodations.

Heterogeneity in price and amenities offered by bed and breakfast accommodations enables us to generate estimates of willingness to pay for specific characteristics. Using data on price and amenities collected from bed and breakfast accommodations, the findings show a willingness to pay for specific characteristics such as sunny balconies, a five star Champagne breakfast, and a room furnished with antique treasures...

Prince Edward Island study

A 2007 study on Prince Edward Island

"The vast majority of visitors to B & B are pleasure travellers. The most important reasons why travellers choose a B & B are personalized service and hospitality, price and value ratio, physical element, atmosphere, image and location."

TIME Magazine

According to TIME magazine:

"Americans have a wide array of lodgings to choose from when they take a vacation: high-rise hotels, rustic resorts, motels by the bay. Yet more and more people are flocking to bed-and-breakfast inns, the most old-fashioned homes away from home. Just 20 years ago, there were only 1,000 B and Bs, as they are nicknamed, scattered throughout the country. Today there are more than 28,000 serving more than 50 million guests each year.

What's the appeal? Bed-and-breakfasts, often situated in elegant, historic homes, tap into everyone's fantasy of living another life. Many have been lovingly renovated with period decorations, inviting visitors to step back in time. Take a look at this popular arty one in Spain for example: www.valenciamansion.com. Others carry a theme throughout the house. Since on average they have only seven or eight rooms, they offer peace and quiet, a rare commodity in the average home.

The hosts, who nearly always live on the premises, provide plenty of coddling. They will recommend local attractions, help with dinner reservations, often provide an afternoon tea or glass of sherry—and, yes, prepare a delicious homemade breakfast. Prices at bed-and-breakfasts, which average $104 to $133 a night, depending on the region, rival the rates of good hotels. While some 10,000 B and Bs are private homes in which the owners offer a room or two, most are serious businesses, complete with websites and toll-free numbers.

The clientele tends to be couples, most of them affluent and well educated. Most are tourists or people who are in town to visit family or to celebrate a special occasion. Bed-and-breakfasts are popular with many foreign travelers, mostly from Britain, Germany, Canada, France and Australia, who have grown up going to B and Bs in their own countries."

SINGLE ROOM OCCUPANCY

A single room occupancy (more commonly SRO, sometimes called single resident occupancy) is a multiple tenant building that houses one or two people in individual rooms (sometimes two rooms, or two rooms with a bathroom or half bathroom), or to the single room dwelling itself. SRO tenants typically share bathrooms and / or kitchens, while some SRO rooms may include kitchenettes, bathrooms, or half-baths. Although many are former hotels, SROs are primarily rented as a permanent residence.

History

The term originated in New York City, probably in the 1930s (the Oxford English Dictionary provides an earliest citation of 1941), but the institutions date back at least fifty years before the nickname was applied to them. SROs exist in many American cities, and are most common in larger cities. The terms single room occupancy and SRO are not used in British English. Related British terms include house in multiple occupation, hostel, bedsit or boarding house.

In many cases, the buildings themselves were formerly hotels in or near a city's central business district. Others are former single family homes. Many of these buildings were built in the late 19th and early 20th centuries, and reflect a high order of architectural style and craftsmanship.

Uses

SROs are a viable housing option for poor people, students, single tenants, seasonal or other traveling workers, empty nester widows / widowers, or others who do not desire or require large dwellings or private domestic appliances. The smaller size and limited amenities in SROs generally makes them a more affordable housing option, especially in gentrifying neighborhoods or urban areas with high land values.

The rents of many disadvantaged tenants may be paid in full or in part by charitable, state and federal programmes, giving incentive to landlords to accept such tenants. Some SRO buildings are renovated with the benefit of a tax abatement, with the condition that the rooms are rented to tenants with low incomes, and sometimes specific low income groups, such as homeless people, people with mental illness, people with AIDS, and so on.

Conditions

Depending on the sensibilities of the landlords and the quality of the properties, SRO conditions can range from squalor to something like an extended-stay hotel. Some have been run in dormitory fashion. Others have been "cage" hotels, in which a large room is split into many smaller ones with corrugated steel or sheetrock dividers, which do not reach the height of the original ceiling. To prevent tenants from climbing over the walls into each others' spaces, the tops of the rooms are covered in chicken wire, making the rooms look something like cages.

SROs Today

As the value of urban land has increased, it has become economical to renovate these properties and make them available once again to higher bidders. This would play a role in the displacement of people who once lived in them, and could be one reason for the visible increase in the population of homeless people in the streets of American cities since the early 1980s. Recognizing that there is significant incentive for landlords to forcibly evict SRO tenants in gentrifying neighborhoods, some cities regulate the conversion of SROs to other use. In particular, if tenants testify that they have been harassed in any way, conversion can be delayed. In San Francisco, the city may take over particularly squalid SROs, and renovate them for the disadvantaged. Landlords who intend to convert SROs may try to convince their tenants to sign releases, which may require relocation by the landlord and / or compensating the tenant.

San Francisco similarly passed an SRO Hotel Conversion Ordinance in 1980, which restricts the conversion of SRO hotels to tourist use. SROs are prominent in the Tenderloin, Mission District and Chinatown communities. In 2001, San Francisco Supervisor Chris Daly sponsored legislation making it illegal for SRO landlords to charge "visitor fees" — a practice long run in order for hotel managers to get a "cut" on drug-dealing or prostitution activities in the building. After a rash of fires destroyed many SRO's in San Francisco and left nearly one thousand tenants homeless, a new programme to reduce fire risk in SRO Hotels was initiated.

RESTAURANT MANAGEMENT

Restaurant management is the profession of managing a restaurant. Associate, bachelor, and graduate degree programmes are offered in restaurant management by community colleges, junior colleges, and some universities in the United States.

Responsibilities

Floor Management

'Floor management' includes managing staff who give services to customers and allocate the duties of opening and closing restaurant. The manager is responsible for making sure his or her staff is following the service standards and health and safety regulations. The manager is the most important person in the front-of-the-house environment, since it is up to him or her to motivate the staff and give them job satisfaction. The manager also looks after and guides the personal well-being of the staff, since it makes the work force stronger and more profitable.

Kitchen Management

'Kitchen management' includes the managing staff working in the kitchen, especially the head chef. The kitchen is the most important part of the business and the main reason customers patronize the restaurant. Managing the kitchen staff helps to control food quality. As most commercial kitchens are a closed environment, the staff may become bored or tired from the work. Without proper management, this often results in an inconsistent food product. Kitchen management involves most importantly, cost control and budgeting. Meeting KPI's are a must for a restaurant to survive. Head chefs must instill and teach money management to apprentices. This is as important as teaching the art and skills of cookery.

Administration

'Administration' includes stock controlling, scheduling

rotations, budgeting the labor costs, balancing cost and profit according to seasonality, surveying and hiring staff, and maintenance of the commercial kitchen equipment.

HOSPITALITY INDUSTRY

The hospitality industry consists of broad category of fields within the service industry that includes lodging, restaurants, event planning, theme parks, transportation, cruise line, and additional fields within the tourism industry. The hospitality industry is a several billion dollar industry that mostly depends on the availability of leisure time and disposable income. A hospitality unit such as a restaurant, hotel, or even an amusement park consists of multiple groups such as facility maintenance, direct operations (servers, housekeepers, porters, kitchen workers, bartenders, etc.), management, marketing, and human resources.

The hospitality industry covers a wide range of organizations offering food service and accommodation. The industry is divided into sectors according to the skill-sets required for the work involved. Sectors include accommodation, food and beverage, meeting and events, gaming, entertainment and recreation, tourism services, and visitor information.

Competition & Usage Rate

Usage rate is an important variable for the hospitality industry. Just as a factory owner would wish a productive asset to be in use as much as possible (as opposed to having to pay fixed costs while the factory isn't producing), so do restaurants, hotels, and theme parks seek to maximize the number of customers they "process" in all sectors. This led to formation of services with the aim to increase usage rate provided by hotel consolidators. Information about required or offered products are brokered on business networks used by vendors as well as purchasers.

In viewing various industries, "barriers to entry" by newcomers and competitive advantages between current players are very important. Among other things, hospitality industry players find advantage in old classics (location), initial and ongoing investment support (reflected in the material upkeep of facilities and the luxuries located therein), and particular themes adopted by the marketing arm of the organization in question (such as a restaurant called the 51st fighter group that has a WW2 theme in music and other environmental aspects). Very important is also the characteristics of the personnel working in direct contact with the customers. The authenticity, professionalism, and actual concern for the happiness and well-being of the customers that is communicated by successful organizations is a clear competitive advantage.

Accommodations
- Hostels
- Hotels
- Motels

Restaurants & Bars
- Cafes
- Nightclubs
- Public houses
- Restaurants

Travel and Tourism
- Airline Cabin Staff
- Travel agents

HOSPITALITY CLUB

The Hospitality Club is an international, Internet-based hospitality service of appr. 647,000 members in 226 countries Its members use the website HospitalityClub.org to coordinate accommodation and other services, such as guiding or regaling travelers. Hospitality Club is currently the second largest such hospitality network.

History

Hospitality Club was founded by Veit Kühne in 2000 with the help of friends and family as a general-purpose Internet-based hospitality exchange organization. The organization, open to anybody, followed from a similar network organized by Veit Kühne exclusively for members of the student exchange organization AFS. The concept for Hospitality Club was inspired by the SIGHT hospitality network of Mensa and it is the successor of Hospex, the first Internet based hospitality exchange network, established in 1992 and with which it joined forces in 2005. Membership has since increased dramatically.

Functioning

Membership in the organization is free and is obtained simply by registering on the website. The core activity of the organization is exchange of accommodation. Acting as a host, a member offers the possibility of accommodation at his leisure. As a guest, a traveler may find possible hosts and contact them through the website. No money is involved — guests and hosts do not pay each other.

The duration of the stay, whether food is provided for free, for a fee or not at all, and all other conditions are agreed on beforehand to the convenience of both parties. After meeting, the host and guest may comment about each other. This provides a means to establish reputation which is the main security measure. Users have to provide their real identity, which is screened by volunteers, and protected against changes.

Apart from accommodation, members exchange other forms of hospitality, such as guiding visitors or providing travel-related advice. There are also wiki-like *Travel Guide* sections and forums where members may seek partners for travels, hitchhiking etc.

Volunteers within the club often arrange meetings or camps which are events that last several days that bring people together.

Organization and Policies

The club is based on the work of hundreds of volunteers around the world. The motivation behind it is *the idea that bringing people together and fostering international friendships will increase inter cultural understanding and strengthen peace.* It is one of the largest hospitality networks, and there is *a mission to find 1,000,000 friendly people.*

The policy of the club explicitly forbids alternative uses, such as dating, job-seeking, commercial use, and website promotions. In order to protect members' mailboxes from spam and to keep trust in the network at high levels a volunteer team scans the messages being sent across the site. Members may also opt-out of this service and receive all messages directly.

Website Analysis

There is no registered company behind the website, and the domain name is directly registered to the founder of the site, Veit Kühne, who in 2006 was working full time on Hospitality Club.

The site contains advertising in the form of Google's AdSense.

The website includes a forum with certain rules - for example it is forbidden to post personal data of other members, and volunteers prefer not to discuss the organization's strategy on the forum, but encourage members to contact them directly.

REFERENCES

Clifford J. Routes (1999). *Travel and Translation in the Late Twentieth Century.* Cambridge, MA: Harvard University Press.

Getz, Donald; Carlsen, Jack (January 2001), *Annals of Tourism Research* (Elselvier) 32 (1): 237–258,

Immanuel Velikovsky (1982). *Mankind in Amnesia.* Garden City, New York: Doubleday.

Jack D. Ninemeier and David K. Hayes (2005). *Restaurant Operations Management: Principles and Practices.* Pearson/Prentice Hall.

Jacques Derrida (2000). *Of Hospitality*. Trans. Rachel Bowlby. Stanford: Stanford University Press.

John B. Switzer (2007). "Hospitality" in *Encyclopedia of Love in World Religions*. Santa Barbara, CA: ABC-CLIO.

Joseph Oliver Dahl (1944). *Restaurant Management, Principles and Practice*. Harper & brothers.

Karen Lieberman & Bruce Nissen (2006). *Ethics in the Hospitality And Tourism Industry*

Koth, Barbara A, Assistant Extension Specialist; William C. Norman, Ph.D. candidate (6 June 2002). *The Minnesota Bed and Breakfast Market: A Guest Profile (Research Summaries)*, University of Minnesota Minnesota Extension Service

Merrifield, Andy (2002). *Dialectical Urbanism: Social Struggles in the Capitalist City*. New York: Monthly Review Press.

Mireille Rosello (2001). Postcolonial Hospitality. The Immigrant as Guest. Standford, CA: Stanford University Press.

Monty, Ben (2003). "Hedonic Pricing and Willingness to Pay for Bed and Breakfast Amenities in Southeast Wisconsin", *Journal of Travel Research* (La Follette School of Public Affairs at the University of Wisconsin—Madison, University of Wisconsin—Whitewater) 42 (2): 195–199.

Rivers, William P. (1998). "Is Being There Enough? The Effects of Homestay Placements on Language Gain During Study Abroad". *Foreign Language Annals* 31 (4): 492–500.

Steve Reece (1993). *The Stranger's Welcome: Oral Theory and the Aesthetics of the Homeric Hospitality Scene*. Ann Arbor: The University of Michigan Press.

2

Focus on Mehmaan Khana, Haveli, Hotel, Motel, Hostel, Resort and Restaurant

MEHMAAN KHANA

A Mehmaan Khana, is a drawing room where guests are entertained in many houses in North India, Bangladesh and Pakistan. Alternative names that are used include Hujra and Baithak. These rooms were a typical feature of many Mughal era havelis palaces and mansions in the region. Many houses in the rural areas of Bangladesh, Pakistan and India still have *mehmaan khanas* for guests. In Bangladesh, it is more commonly known as *baithak ghar* or *bangla ghar*

Hujra

The term *hujra* is especially prevalent in the predominantly Pashtun areas of Pakistan. Pashtun *hujras* are used mainly to entertain male guests in a household, although sometimes community *hujras* are also maintained by tribal units. In individual houses, the size and trappings of a *hujra* are sometimes indicative of family status.

Etymology

The term *mehmân khânâ* is direct derivation from Persian and means *"guest house or room."* In Iran and adjoining areas, the term can refer to hotels. The term (also spelled *memonkhona* in Latin script) is also used to describe a guest room in other parts of Central Asia. The term *baithak* literally means sitting room in Hindi-Urdu and Bangla. *Hujra* is derived from Arabic and means *room* or *cell*. In non-Pashtun Muslim households or North India and Pakistan, the term *hujra* can also refer to a dedicated prayer room. In Bangladesh, *hujra* usually refers to the sitting room of Imam in a Mosque.

HAVELI

Haveli is the term used for a private mansion in India and Pakistan. The word *haveli* is derived from Persian meaning "an enclosed place". They share similar features with other mansions derived from Islamic Architecture such as the traditional mansions in Morocco called Riads

Mughal Havelis

Many of the havelis of India and Pakistan were influenced by both Islamic Persian, Central Asian and Indian architecture. They usually contain a courtyard often with a fountain in the centre. The old cities of in Agra, Lucknow and Delhi in India and Lahore, Multan, Peshawar, Hyderabad in Pakistan have many fine examples of Mughal-style havelis.

Rajasthani Havelis

The term *Haveli* was first applied in Rajasthan by the Vaishnava sect to refer to their temples in Gujarat. In the northern part of India havelis for Lord Krishna are prevalent with huge mansion like constructions. The havelis are noted for their frescoes depicting images of gods, goddesses, animals, scenes from the British colonization, and the life stories of Lords Rama and Krishna.

Later on these temple architectures and frescoes were imitated while building huge individual mansions and now the word is popularly recognized with the mansions themselves. Between 1830 and 1930, Marwari's erected buildings in their homeland, Shekhawati and Marwar.

These buildings were called havelis. The Marwaris commissioned artists to paint those buildings which were heavily influenced by the Mughal architecture.

The havelis were status symbols for the Marwaris as well as homes for their extended families, providing security and comfort in seclusion from the outside world. The havelis were to be closed from all sides with one large main gate.

The typical havelis in Shekhawati consisted of two courtyards — an outer one for the men which serves as an extended threshold, and the inner one, the domain of the women. The largest havelis could have up to three or four courtyards and were two to three stories high. Most of the havelis are empty nowadays or are maintained by a watchman (typically an old man). These havelis are major attraction for tourists in Rajasthan.

The towns and villages of Shekhawati are famous for the embellished frescoes on the walls of their grandiose havelis, to the point of becoming popular tourist attractions.

The havelis in and around Jaisalmer Fort(also known as the Golden Fort), situated in Jaisalmer, Rajasthan, of which the three most impressive are Patwon Ki Haveli, Salim Singh Ki Haveli, and Nathmal-Ki Haveli, deserve special mention. These were the elaborate homes of Jaisalmer's rich merchants. The ostentatious carvings etched out in sandstone with infinite detail and then painstakingly pieced together in different patterns each more lavish than the next were commissioned to put on show the owner's status and wealth. Around Jaisalmer, they are typically carved from yellow sandstone.They are often characterized by wall paintings, frescoes, *jharokhas* (balconies) and archways.

The Patwon Ji ki Haveli is the most important and the largest haveli, as it was the very first erected in Jaisalmer. It is not a single haveli but a cluster of 5 small havelis. The first one in the row is also the most popular one and is also known as Kothari's Patwa Haveli. The first among these was commissioned and constructed in the year 1805 by Guman Chand Patwa, then a rich trader of jewellery and fine brocades, and is the biggest and the most ostentatious. Patwa was a rich man and a renowned trader of his time and he could afford and thus order the construction of separate stories for each of his 5 sons. These were completed in the span of 50 years. All five houses were constructed in the first 60 years of the 19th century. Patwon Ji Ki is renowned for it's ornate wall paintings, intricate yellow sandstone-carved *jharokhas* (balconies), gateways and archways. Although the building itself is made from yellow sandstone, the main gateway is brown.

Famous Havelis of Udaipur

Among the several Havelis in Udaipur, some of them are:

- Amet-ki-Haveli,
- Badnor-ki-Haveli,
- Bagore-ki-Haveli,
- Banera-ki-Haveli,
- Bansi-ki-Haveli,
- Bara Purohit-ki-Haveli,
- Bohera-ki-Haveli,
- Delwara-ki-Haveli,
- Deogadh-ki-Haveli,
- Dhabai-ki-Haveli,
- Kanor-ki-Haveli,
- Karjali-ki-Haveli,
- Mamaji-ki-Haveli,
- Mataji-ki-Haveli,
- Salumbar-ki-Haveli,
- Sardargarh-ki-Haveli.

Famous Havelis of Pakistan

- *Mubarak Haveli* in Lahore
- *Haveli Asif Jah* in Lahore
- *Haveli Wajid Ali Shah* in Lahore
- *Choona Mandi Haveli* in Lahore
- *Haveli Nau Nihal Singh* in Lahore
- *Haveli Barood Khana* in Lahore
- *Lal Haveli* or *Chandu Di Haveli* in Lahore
- *Haveli Man Singh* in Jhelum
- *Lal Haveli* in Rawalpindi
- *Saad Manzil* in Kamalia
- *Khan Club* in Peshawar
- *Waziristan Haveli* in Abbottabad

Havelis in Popular Culture

Haveli the title is a young adult novel by Suzanne Fisher Staples and is a sequel to her Newbery Award-winning novel *Shabanu: Daughter of the Wind*. Most of the book takes place in an old-fashioned haveli in Lahore, Pakistan.

HOTEL

A hotel is an establishment that provides paid lodging on a short-term basis. The provision of basic accommodation, in times past, consisting only of a room with a bed, a cupboard, a small table and a washstand has largely been replaced by rooms with modern facilities, including en-suite bathrooms and air conditioning or climate control. Additional common features found in hotel rooms are a telephone, an alarm clock, a television, a safe, a mini-bar with snack foods and drinks, and facilities for making tea and coffee. Luxury features include bathrobes and slippers, a pillow menu, twin-sink vanities, and jacuzzi bathtubs. Larger hotels may provide additional guest facilities such as a restaurant, swimming pool, fitness center, business center, childcare, conference facilities and social function services.

Hotel rooms are usually numbered (or named in some smaller hotels and B&Bs) to allow guests to identify their room. Some hotels offer meals as part of a room and board arrangement. In the United Kingdom, a hotel is required by law to serve food and drinks to all guests within certain stated hours. In Japan, capsule hotels provide a minimized amount of room space and shared facilities.

Etymology

The word *hotel* is derived from the French *hôtel* (coming from *hôte* meaning *host*), which referred to a French version of a townhouse or any other building seeing frequent visitors, rather than a place offering accommodation. In contemporary French usage, *hôtel* now has the same meaning as the English term, and *hôtel particulier* is used for t. e old meaning. The French spelling, with the circumflex, w.. also used in English, but is now rare. The circumflex .eplaces the 's' found in the earlier *hostel* spelling, which ovei time took on a new, but closely related meaning. Grammatically, hotels usually take the definite article - hence "The Astoria Hotel" or simply "The Astoria."

Types

Hotel operations vary in size, function, and cost. Most hotels and major hospitality companies that operate hotels have set widely accepted industry standards to classify hotel types. General categories include the following;

- Upscale Luxury
  o *Examples include Conrad Hotels, Ritz-Carlton, Four Seasons Hotels and Resorts, and JW Marriott Hotels*
- Full Service
  o *Examples include Hilton, Marriott, Doubletree, and Hyatt*

- Select Service
  - o *Examples include Courtyard by Marriott and Hilton Garden Inn*
- Limited Service
  - o *Examples include Hampton Inn, Fairfield Inn, Days Inn, and La Quinta Inns & Suites*
- Extended Stay
  - o *Examples include Homewood Suites by Hilton, Residence Inn by Marriott, and Extended Stay Hotels*
- Timeshare
  - o *Examples include Marriott Vacation Club International, Westgate Resorts, and Disney Vacation Club*
- Destination Club

Management

The management of a hotel operation is considered a major business operation. Degree programmes such as hospitality management studies and certification programmes prepare hotel managers for industry practice.

Historic Hotels

Some hotels have gained their renown through tradition, by hosting significant events or persons, such as Schloss Cecilienhof in Potsdam, Germany, which derives its fame from the Potsdam Conference of the World War II allies Winston Churchill, Harry Truman and Joseph Stalin in 1945. The Taj Mahal Palace & Tower in Mumbai is one of India's most famous and historic hotels because of its association with the Indian independence movement. Some establishments have given name to a particular meal or beverage, as is the case with the Waldorf Astoria in New York City, United States where the Waldorf Salad was first created or the Hotel Sacher in Vienna, Austria, home of the Sachertorte. Others have achieved fame by association with dishes or cocktails created on their premises, such as the Hotel de Paris where the crêpe Suzette was invented or the Raffles Hotel in Singapore, where the Singapore Sling cocktail was devised.

A number of hotels have entered the public consciousness through popular culture, such as the Ritz Hotel in London, United Kingdom, through its association with Irving Berlin's song, 'Puttin' on the Ritz'. The Algonquin Hotel in New York City is famed as the meeting place of the literary group, the Algonquin Round Table, and Hotel Chelsea, also in New York City, has been the subject of a number of songs and the scene of the stabbing of Nancy Spungen (allegedly by her boyfriend Sid Vicious). The Waldorf Astoria and Statler hotels in New York City are also immortalized in the names of Muppets Statler and Waldorf.

Unusual Hotels

Many hotels can be considered destinations in themselves, by dint of unusual features of the lodging or its immediate environment:

Treehouse Hotels

Some hotels are built with living trees as structural elements, for example the Costa Rica Tree House in the Gandoca-Manzanillo Wildlife Refuge, Costa Rica; the Treetops Hotel in Aberdare National Park, Kenya; the Ariau Towers near Manaus, Brazil, on the Rio Negro in the Amazon; and Bayram's Tree Houses in Olympos, Turkey.

Bunker Hotels

The Null Stern Hotel in Teufen, Appenzellerland, Switzerland and the Concrete Mushrooms in Albania are former nuclear bunkers transformed into hotels.

Shoe Hotels

Shoe hotels are hotels built into a giant shoe. The idea was inspired by the "Old Woman who lived in a shoe" myth. The largest such hotel is currently in Hokkaido, Japan. The most popular shoe hotels are modelled after a woman's platform dancing shoe.

Cave Hotels

The Cuevas Pedro Antonio de Alarcón (named after the author) in Guadix, Spain, as well as several hotels in Cappadocia, Turkey, are notable for being built into natural cave formations, some with rooms underground. The Desert Cave Hotel in Coober Pedy, South Australia is built into the remains of an opal mine.

Capsule Hotels

Capsule hotels are a type of economical hotel that are found in Japan, where people sleep in stacks of rectangular containers.

Ice and Snow Hotels

The Ice Hotel in Jukkasjärvi, Sweden, and the Hotel de Glace in Duschenay, Canada, melt every spring and are rebuilt each winter; the Mammut Snow Hotel in Finland is located within the walls of the Kemi snow castle; and the Lainio Snow Hotel is part of a snow village near Ylläs, Finland.

Garden Hotels

Garden hotels, famous for their gardens before they became hotels, include Gravetye Manor, the home of garden designer William Robinson, and Cliveden, designed by Charles Barry with a rose garden by Geoffrey Jellicoe.

Underwater Hotels

Some hotels have accommodation underwater, such as Utter Inn in Lake Mälaren, Sweden. Hydropolis, project cancelled 2004 in Dubai, would have had suites on the bottom of the Persian Gulf, and Jules Undersea Lodge in Key Largo, Florida requires scuba diving to access its rooms.

Other Unusual Hotels

- The Library Hotel in New York City, is unique in that each of its ten floors is assigned one category from the Dewey Decimal System.

- The Burj al-Arab hotel in Dubai, United Arab Emirates, built on an artificial island, is structured in the shape of a boat's sail.

- The Jailhotel Löwengraben in Lucerne, Switzerland is a converted prison now used as a hotel.

- The Luxor, a hotel and casino on the Las Vegas Strip in Paradise, Nevada, United States due to its pyramidal structure.

- The Liberty Hotel in Boston, used to be the Charles Street Jail.

- Built in Scotland and completed in 1936, The former ocean liner RMS *Queen Mary* in Long Beach, California, United States uses its first-class staterooms as a hotel, after retiring in 1967 from Transatlantic service.

- There are several hotels throughout the world built into converted airliners.

Resort Hotels

Some hotels are built specifically to create a captive trade, example at casinos and holiday resorts. Though of course hotels have always been built in popular desinations, the defining characteristic of a resort hotel is that it exists purely to serve another attraction, the two having the same owners.

In Las Vegas there is a tradition of one-upmanship with luxurious and extravagant hotels in a concentrated area known as the Las Vegas Strip. This trend now has extended to other resorts worldwide, but the concentration in Las Vegas is still the world's highest: nineteen of the world's twenty-five largest hotels by room count are on the Strip, with a total of over 67,000 rooms.

In Europe Center Parcs might be considered a chain of resort hotels, since the sites are largely man-made (though set in natural surroundings such as country parks) with captive trade, whereas holiday camps such as Butlins and Pontin's are probably not considered as resort hotels, since they are set at traditional holiday destinations which existed before the camps.

Railway Hotels

Frequently, expanding railway companies built grand hotels at their termini, such as the Midland Hotel, Manchester next to the former Manchester Central Station and in London the ones above St Pancras railway station and Charing Cross railway station also in London is the Chiltern Court Hotel above Baker Street tube station and Canada's grand railway hotels. They are or were mostly, but not exclusively, used by those travelling by rail.

Motels

A motel (motor hotel) is a hotel which is for a short stay, usually for a night, for motorists on long journeys. It has direct access from the room to the vehicle (for example a central parking lot around which the buildings are set), and is built conveniently close to major roads and intersections.

World Record Setting Hotels

Largest

In 2006, Guinness World Records listed the First World Hotel in Genting Highlands, Malaysia as the world's largest hotel with a total of 6,118 rooms. Similarly, the Venetian Palazzo Complex, in Las Vegas, has the most number of rooms. It has 7,117 rooms followed by MGM Grand Hotel, which contains 6,852 rooms.

Oldest

According to the Guinness Book of World Records, the

oldest hotel still in operation is the Hoshi Ryokan, in the Awazu Onsen area of Komatsu, Japan which opened in 718.

Tallest

The Rose Tower in United Arab Emirates is the tallest building used exclusively as a hotel. Originally, the tower was to be 380 m (1,250 ft) high, but design modification reduced it to 333 m (1,093 ft).

Hotel Rooms as an Investment

Some hotels sell individual rooms to investors. Timeshare is an example of this kind of investment. The buyer is allowed to stay in the room without charge or at a reduced rate for a given number of days each year.

The investor is paid a share of the takings for the room. Rooms can be sold on a leasehold basis, sometimes on a 999 year lease. Room owners are free to sell at any time.

Living in Hotels

A number of public figures have notably chosen to take up semi-permanent or permanent residence in hotels.

- Actor Richard Harris lived at the Savoy Hotel while in London. Hotel archivist Susan Scott recounts an anecdote that when he was being taken out of the building on a stretcher shortly before his death he raised his hand and told the diners "it was the food."
- Inventor Nikola Tesla lived the last 10 years of his life at the New Yorker Hotel until 1943 when he died in the hotel room.
- Millionaire Howard Hughes lived his last few years in a Las Vegas hotel.
- Egyptian actor Ahmad Zaki lived his last 15 years in Ramses Hilton Hotel - Cairo.

- Larry Fine (of the Three Stooges) and his family lived in hotels, due to his extravagant spending habits and his wife's dislike for housekeeping. They first lived in the President Hotel in Atlantic City, New Jersey, where his daughter Phyllis was raised, then the Knickerbocker Hotel in Hollywood. Not until the late 1940s did Larry buy a home in the Los Feliz area of Los Angeles, California.

- General Douglas McArthur lived his last 14 years in the penthouse of the Waldorf Towers, a part of the Waldorf-Astoria Hotel.

- American actress Elaine Stritch lived in the Savoy Hotel in London for over a decade.

- Fashion designer Coco Chanel lived in the Hotel Ritz Paris on and off for more than 30 years.

- Vladimir Nabokov and his wife Vera lived in the Montreux Palace Hotel in Montreux, Switzerland from 1961 until his death in 1977.

- British entrepreneur Jack Lyons lived in the Hotel Mirador Kempinski in Switzerland for several years until his death in 2008.

Fictitious Hotels

Hotels have been used as the settings for television programmes such as the British situation comedies Fawlty Towers and I'm Alan Partridge, the British soap opera Crossroads, and in films such as the Bates Motel in Hitchcock's 1960 film Psycho and The Dolphin Hotel in 1408, a short story by Stephen King which was adapted into a 2007 film.

Another is Tipton Hotel, a fictitious hotel in Disney's "The Suite Life of Zack and Cody." When the show later became a spinof*f into "The Suite Life on Deck," the Tipton evolved into the SS Tipton, run by the same company.

DESTINATION HOTEL

A destination hotel is a hotel whose location and amenities make the hotel itself a destination for tourists, rather than merely a convenient place to stay while traveling through or visiting the area for other reasons. Destination hotels are also called destination lodgings and sometimes destination resorts. The market for destination hotels is the subject of academic and business analysis.

A destination hotel is often characterized by:

- Upscale lodging, dining, and activities
- Recreation and entertainment on the hotel's own property
- Distinctive characteristics of the building, gardens, and sometimes history

History

Since the 1800s, the traditional concept of a destination hotel has been based upon a venue which is typically remote and has a natural feature as its attraction. For example, the Kviknes Hotel in Norway is a difficult to reach remote location which provides visitors access to the scenic fjord at Balestrand.

Historically there were certain built-in amenities such as gourmet cuisine, music recitals and shoreline trails; however, the amenities of modern (post 1980) destination hotels dwarf the scale of these earlier models.

Many of the Las Vegas and Caribbean resort hotels have complete shopping malls, conference centers and large entertainment halls on site; thus, the contemporary version of a destination often features large on-site capital investment in activities, although the access to a local natural feature is still retained by many newer destination hotels (e.g. Hotel l'Anjajavy in Madagascar).

Historic Examples

There are numerous historic venues which were well known in the 19th century, some of which survive to the present. Examples of these properties include:

- Eastern & Oriental Hotel, George Town, Penang, Malaysia
- Kviknes Hotel, Balestrand, Norway
- Metropole Hotel, Avalon, California, USA, circa 1887 Victorian style hotel
- Gilroy Yamato Hot Springs, Gilroy, California, USA
- Ahwahnee Hotel, Yosemite National Park, California
- Hotel Metropole, Vienna, Austria
- Mohonk Mountain House, New Paltz, New York. Owned and operated by the Smiley family since 1869.
- Greenbrier Resort, White Sulphur Springs, W. Va., USA
- Grand Hotel-Mackinac, Mackinac Island, Mich.

Types of Destination Hotels

There are several distinct types of destination hotels including:

- Geographically remote locations often associated with a noteworthy natural feature such as a volcano or rainforest
- Urban settings
- Conference center oriented
- Specialized activity settings (e.g. Disneyland Hotel)
- Hotels of unusual construction by virtue of being built into a specialized environment (e.g. ice hotels, cave hotels or treehouse hotels)
- Boutique hotels

APARTMENT HOTEL

An Apartment Hotel (also Aparthotel and Apart-hotel) is a serviced apartment complex that uses a hotel-style booking system. It is similar to renting an apartment, but with no fixed contracts and occupants can 'check-out' whenever they wish.

The standard zoning definition, nationwide is:

"Apartment hotel means a building designed for or containing both apartments and individual guestrooms or rental units, under resident supervision, and which maintains an inner lobby through which all tenants must pass to gain access to apartments, rooms or units."

Apartment hotels are flexible types of accommodation; instead of the rigid format of a hotel room, an apartment hotel complex usually offers a complete fully fitted apartment. These complexes are usually custom built, and similar to a hotel complex containing a varied amount of apartments. The length of stay in these apartment hotels is varied with anywhere from a few days to months or even years. The people that stay in apartment hotels use them as a home away from home, therefore they are usually fitted with everything the average home would require.

Origins

Apartment hotels were first created in holiday destinations as accommodation for families that needed to 'live' in an apartment rather than 'stay' as they would in a hotel. The apartments would provide a 'holiday home' but generally be serviced. Later on these apartments evolved to be complete homes, allowing occupants to do everything they would at home, such as cleaning, washing and cooking.

Services and Facilities

Essentially the apartment hotel combines the flexibility of apartment living with the service of a hotel. Many of the apartments take advantage of prime locations with panoramic views of cities seen through wall to ceiling windows. Suites usually include high quality finishes, broadband connection & interactive TV, servicing and integrated kitchen and bathroom. High quality leather sofas in the living area and king size beds bring the hotel experience to a whole new level. Those are the luxuries, they also come with the basics: satellite or cable TV, washer, dryer, dishwasher, cooker, oven, fridge, freezer, sink, shower, bath, wardrobes, all the furnishings to be expected in a luxury home. Self contained apartments usually provide kitchen facilities that travel residents are able to cook foods at their convenience.

Extended Stay Hotels

Extended stay hotels are a type of lodging with features unavailable at standard hotels. These features are intended to provide more home-like amenities. There are currently 27 extended stay chains in North America with at least 7 hotels, representing over 2,000 properties. There is substantial variation among extended stay hotels with respect to quality and the amenities that are available. Some of the economy chains attract clientele who use the hotels as semi-permanent lodging. Extended-stay hotels typically have self-serve laundry facilities and offer discounts for extended stays, beginning at 5 or 7 days. They also have guestrooms (or "suites") with kitchens. The kitchens include at a minimum usually: a sink, a refrigerator (usually full size), a microwave oven, and a stovetop. Some kitchens also have dishwashers and conventional ovens.

Extended stay hotels are popular with business travelers on extended assignments, families in the midst of a relocation, and anyone else in need of temporary housing. Extended stay hotels are also used by travelers who appreciate the larger space a typical suite provides.

Residence Inn is credited with popularizing the "extended stay" concept. The chain was launched in 1975 in Wichita, Kansas by Jack DeBoer, and acquired by Marriott

Corporation in 1987. As of April 2005, there were over 450 Residence Inn hotels in the United States, Canada and Mexico. Jack DeBoer has jumped back in the Extended Stay market developing a concept called Value Place.

Other upscale brands of extended-stay hotels, such as Staybridge Suites which is part of the InterContinental Hotels Group, have made this segment of the lodging industry one of the fastest-growing.

One of today's most popular long term lodging brands came from the merger of Extended Stay America and Homestead Hotels. Both these chains were already well established when they combined in 2004 to become Extended Stay Hotels with over 670 owned and operated properties nationwide.

Another worldwide hotel chain, Choice Hotels International, franchisor for name brands such as Comfort Inn, Comfort Suites, Sleep Inn and Quality Inn, entered the extended stay market with their MainStay Suites brand. They proceeded to acquire the Suburban Extended Stay hotel chain in 2005, making them a sizeable extended stay system with over 150 hotels open and under development.

In the United States, a popular low-budget extended stay chain is Intown Suites. The chain, which was founded in 1988, now has nearly 140 locations in 21 states, and is distinguised for offering weekly rates much lower than many other chain lodging companies in North America.

Since 1999, Motel 6, the popular U.S. budget lodging chain (owned by Accor Hotels) operates Studio 6, a chain of extended stay hotels that offer weekly rates and more amenities than the standard Motel 6 properties. Studio 6 provides a kitchen area in all its rooms, and allows pets. Studio 6 locations are in 18 U.S. states and Canada.

The extended stay concept is steadily spreading throughout Europe due to the increase in the number of travelers and business people visiting every year. The concept was organized by Belgium Housing and the chain of hotels covers 42 countries of Europe including all the major cities of the continent.

SECONDARY SUITE

Secondary suite is an urban planning term for an additional separate dwelling unit on a property that would normally accommodate only one dwelling unit. A secondary suite is considered "secondary" or "accessory" to the primary residence on the parcel. It normally has its own entrance, kitchen, bathroom and living area. Such a suite often is one of the following types:

- A suite above a rear detached garage,
- A suite above the main floor of a single-detached dwelling,
- A suite below the main floor of a single-detached dwelling (a "basement suite").
- A suite attached to a single-detached dwelling at grade, or
- A suite detached from the principal dwelling (a "garden suite" or "guesthouse").

In many municipalities, secondary suites are illegal because they do not conform to the zoning or land use district the property is in, they have been developed without the proper permits, or they do not meet the local building code. However, some localities only prohibit the renting out of secondary suites, and allow occupation by a relative or guest, leading to the use of the term "mother-in-law" house or apartment. Local jurisdictions may have rules regarding allowing certain relatives to live there and rules about what, if any, rent may be charged. Secondary suites can also be called accessory suites. Dual occupancy is sometimes used to refer to the development of two dwellings on one allotment of land. They may be either attached (semi-detached) or detached. The term is common in Australia.

Mother-in-Law House

A mother-in-law house is a form of guest accommodation that may be either completely detached (a guesthouse) or attached to a primary residence. An attached mother-in-law house often involves some spaces shared in common with an attached primary dwelling. It may, for instance, have a separate bedroom, bathroom, and kitchen, while sharing a living room and laundry facilities. Mother-in-Law houses are sometimes abbreviated as MIL in internet or newspaper listings.

Mother-in-Law Apartment

A mother-in-law apartment is a small apartment accessory to a primary residence. Alternative names include "granny flat", "granny suite","in-law suite", and "accessory apartment", the first being used primarily in Australia and Britain, where it is the most familiar of these terms, but also in parts of the United States. Such apartments are frequently used to accommodate an elderly relative who is not capable of living on their own, but is not ready for a nursing home environment or other similar facility. The apartment may or may not have a communicating door to the main house, but virtually always has a separate entrance and is usually not part of the original design. Many are located above the garage of the main house or as a separate building in the rear yard.

Canada

Government Programmes

CMHC

The Canada Mortgage and Housing Corporation provides a financial assistance programme to help Canadians create affordable housing for low-income seniors and adults with a disability within a secondary suite. The programme is called the Residential Rehabilitation Assistance Programme (RRAP) — Secondary/Garden Suite. The maximum fully forgivable loan depends on the location of the property:

- Southern Areas of Canada: $24,000/unit
- Northern areas of Canada: $28,000/unit
- Far northern areas: $36,000/unit

A 25% supplement in assistance is available in remote areas.

British Columbia

The Housing Policy Branch of British Columbia's Ministry of Community, Aboriginal and Women's Services published a guide for local governments to implement secondary suite programmes called 'Secondary Suites: A Guide For Local Governments'. The current issue is dated September 2005. The intent of the guide is to "help local governments develop and implement secondary suite programmes". It also highlights good secondary suite practices as well as providing practical information to "elected officials, planners, community groups, homeowners, developers, and others interested in secondary suites".

It states its objectives as follows:

- Identify the benefits of secondary suites as a form of affordable housing, and encourage legalization of suites;
- Identify the challenges and issues associated with secondary suites;
- Highlight strategies local governments can use to design and implement secondary suite programmes.

Norway

In Norway, particularly in the bigger cities, it is quite common to build separate adjoined smaller flats for renting out. The owner of the main flat will rent out the smaller adjoined flats.

STUDIO APARTMENT

A studio apartment, also known as a studio flat (UK),

efficiency apartment or bachelor/bachelorette style apartment, is a self-contained, small apartment, which combines living room, bedroom and kitchenette into a single unit, barring a bathroom. "Bachelor" or "efficiency" apartments are sometimes smaller than studio apartments. In British usage, a studio flat has its own bathroom; a single room with cooking facilities and a shared bathroom is known as a bedsit. Studio, efficiency, and bachelor style apartments all tend to be the smallest apartments with the lowest rents in a given area, usually ranging around 300 to 450 square feet (25–45 square meters) in the United States, but considerably smaller in countries such as Japan, South Korea, and several European capitals. These kinds of apartments typically consist of one large room which serves as the living, dining, and bedroom. Kitchen facilities may be located in the central room, and the bathroom is often in its own smaller room.

United States

A variation common in New York City is the "L-shaped" or "alcove" studio, in which the central room branches off into a small alcove that can be used for sleeping or dining.

Singapore

Studio apartments, in the context of Singapore's public housing, are flats that are specifically built by the Housing and Development Board to cater to the growing senior citizen population. One must be at least 55 years old to purchase studio apartments. Many types of rooms are available in Singapore for rent. Common rooms and Master Rooms in Singapore.

Japan

Japan has an even smaller variation of the studio apartment known as the one room mansion.

New Zealand

Known as studio rooms in New Zealand, they frequently

feature a bedroom with study area and an en suite bathroom. Spaces such as kitchen, lounge and dining area are communal between other people staying in that apartment.

South Korea

Studio Apartment in Korea is called 'Officetel' or 'One Room'.

APARTMENT

An apartment (in American English) or flat (in British English) is a self-contained housing unit (a type of residential real estate) that occupies only part of a building. Such a building may be called an apartment building, apartment house (in American English), block of flats or, occasionally mansion block (in British English), especially if it consists of many apartments for rent. Apartments may be owned by an *owner/occupier* or rented by *tenants* (two types of housing tenure).

The term *apartment* is favoured in North America, whereas the term *flat* is commonly, but not exclusively, used in the United Kingdom, Singapore, Hong Kong and most Commonwealth countries.

In Malaysian English, *flat* often denotes a housing block of lesser quality meant for lower-income groups, while *apartment* is more generic and may also include luxury condominiums.

In Australian English, the two terms are independent: *apartment* has the US sense, while *flat* usually refers to any rental property, but especially one shared by students or another non-family group. Tenement law refers to the feudal basis of permanent property such as land or rents. May be found combined as in "Messuage or Tenement" to encompass all the land, buildings and other assets of a property. In the US and Canada, some apartment-dwellers own their own apartments, either as co-ops, in which the residents own shares of a corporation that owns the building or development; or in condominiums, whose residents own their apartments and share ownership of the public spaces. Most apartments are in buildings designed for the purpose, but large older houses are sometimes divided into apartments. The word *apartment* connotes a residential unit or section in a building. In some locations, particularly the United States, the word denotes a rental unit owned by the building owner, and is not typically used for a condominium.

In the UK, some flat owners own a share in the company that owns the freehold of the building. This is commonly known as a "share of freehold" flat. The freehold company has the right to collect annual ground rents from each of the flat owners in the building. The freeholder can also develop or sell the building, subject to the usual planning and restrictions that might apply.

In some countries the word unit is a more general term referring to both apartments and rental business suites. The word is generally used only in the context of a specific building; e.g., "This building has three units" or "I'm going to rent a unit in this building", but not "I'm going to rent a unit somewhere." In Australia, a unit refers to flats, apartments or even semi-detached houses. Some buildings can be characterized as *mixed use buildings*, meaning part of the building is for commercial, business, or office use, usually on the first floor or first couple floors, and there are one or more apartments in the rest of the building, usually on the upper floors.

When there is no tenant occupying an apartment, the apartment owner or landlord is said to have a *vacancy*. For apartment landlords, each vacancy represents a loss of income from rent-paying tenants for the time the apartment is vacant (i.e., unoccupied). Landlords' objectives are often to minimize the vacancy rate for their units. The owner of the apartment, typically when transferring possession to the occupant, gives him/her the key to the apartment entrance and any other keys needed, such as a common key to the building or any other common areas and a mailbox key. When the occupant(s) move out, these keys are typically returned to the owner.

Apartment Types and Characteristics

Apartments can be classified into several types. In North America the typical terms are a studio or bachelor apartment (efficiency or bedsit in the UK). These all tend to be the smallest apartments with the cheapest rents in a given area. These kinds of apartment usually consist mainly of a large room which is the living, dining, and bedroom combined. There are usually kitchen facilities as part of this central room, but the bathroom is its own smaller separate room.

Moving up from the bachelors/efficiencies are one-bedroom apartments, in which one bedroom is separate from the rest of the apartment. Then there are two-bedroom, three-bedroom, etc. apartments (Apartments with more than three bedrooms are rare). Small apartments often have only one entrance.

Large apartments often have two entrances, perhaps a door in the front and another in the back. Depending on the building design, the entrance doors may be directly to the outside or to a common area inside, such as a hallway. Depending on location, apartments may be available for rent furnished with furniture or unfurnished into which a tenant usually moves in with their own furniture.

A garden apartment complex consists of low-rise apartment buildings built with landscaped grounds surrounding them. The apartment buildings are often arranged around courtyards that are open at one end. A garden apartment has some characteristics of a townhouse: each apartment has its own building entrance, or just a few apartments share a small foyer or stairwell at each building entrance. Unlike a townhouse, each apartment occupies only one level. Modern garden apartment buildings are never more than three stories high, since they typically don't have elevators/lifts. However, the first "garden apartment" buildings in the United States, developed in the early 20th century, were five stories high. Some garden apartment buildings place a one-car garage under each apartment. The grounds are more landscaped than for other modestly scaled apartments.

Another definition of "garden apartment" is a unit built half below grade or at ground level. The implication is that there is a view or direct access to a garden from the apartment, but this is not necessarily the case.

Laundry facilities may be found in a common area accessible to all the tenants in the building, or each apartment may have its own facilities. Depending on when the building was built and the design of the building, utilities such as water, heating, and electricity may be common for all the apartments in the building or separate for each apartment and billed separately to each tenant (however, many areas in the US have ruled it illegal to split a water bill among all the tenants, especially if a pool is on the premises). Outlets for connection to telephones are typically included in apartments. Telephone service is optional and is practically always billed separately from the rent payments. Cable television and similar amenities are extra also. Parking space(s), air conditioner, and extra storage space may or may not be included with an apartment. Rental leases often limit the maximum number of people who can reside in each apartment. On or around the ground floor of the apartment building, a series of mailboxes are typically kept in a location accessible to the public and, thus, to the mail carrier too. Every unit typically gets its own mailbox with individual keys to it. Some very large apartment buildings with a full-time staff may take mail from the mailman and provide mail-sorting service. Near the mailboxes or some other location accessible by outsiders, there may be a buzzer (equivalent to a doorbell) for each individual unit. In smaller apartment buildings such as two- or three-flats, or even four-flats, rubbish is often disposed of in trash containers similar to those used at houses. In larger buildings, rubbish is often collected in a common trash bin or dumpster. For cleanliness or minimizing noise, many lessors will place restrictions on tenants regarding keeping pets in an apartment.

In some parts of the world, the word apartment refers to a new purpose-built self-contained residential unit in a building, whereas the word *flat* means a converted self-contained unit in an older building. An industrial, warehouse, or commercial space converted to an apartment is commonly called a loft, although some modern lofts are built by design. An apartment consisting of the top floor of a high apartment building can be called a *penthouse.*

When part of a house is converted for the ostensible use of a landlord's family member, the unit may be known as an *in-law* apartment or *granny flat*, though these (sometimes illegally) created units are often occupied by ordinary renters rather than family members. In Canada these suites are commonly located in the basements of houses and are therefore normally called *basement suites* or "mother-in-law suites."

A maisonette is an apartment with more than one floor.

In Milwaukee vernacular architecture, a Polish flat is an existing small house or cottage that has been lifted up to accommodate the creation of a new basement floor housing a separate apartment, then set down again; thus becoming a modest two-story flat.

In Russia, a communal apartment («êîììóíàëêà») is a room with a shared kitchen and bath. A typical arrangement is a cluster of five or so apartments with their common kitchen and bathroom and their own front door, occupying a floor in a pre-Revolutionary mansion. Traditionally a room is owned by the government and assigned to a family on a semi-permanent basis.

Property Classes

In every community there are several types of multi-family housing, properties are typically put into one of four property classes. Each "class" of properties has a letter grade. These grades are used to help investors and real estate brokers speak a common language so they can understand a property's characteristics and condition quickly. They are as follows:

Class A properties are luxury units. They are usually less than 10 years old and are often new, upscale apartment buildings. Average rents are high, and they are generally located in desirable geographic areas. White-collar workers live in them and are usually renters by choice.

Class B properties can be 10 to 25 years old. They are generally well maintained and have a middle class tenant base of both white and blue-collar workers. Some are renters by choice, and others by necessity.

Class C properties were built within the last 30 to 40 years. They generally have blue-collar and low- to moderate-income tenants, and the rents are below market. This is where you'll find many tenants that are renters "for life." On the other hand, some of their tenants are just starting out. And as they get better jobs, they work their way up the rental scale.

Class D properties are where you'll find many Section 8 in the US or government-subsidized housing tenants. They are generally positioned in lower socioeconomic areas.

History

Rome

In ancient Rome, the insulae (singular *insula*) were large apartment buildings where the lower and middle classes of Romans (the plebs) dwelled. The floor at ground level was used for tabernas, shops and businesses with living space on the higher floors. Ancient Roman insulae in Rome and other imperial cities reached up to 10 and more stories, some with more than 200 stairs. Several emperors, beginning with Augustus (r. 30 BC-14 AD), attempted to establish limits of 20–25 m for multi-storey buildings, but met with only limited success. The lower floors were typically occupied by either shops or wealthy families, while the upper stories were rented out to the lower classes. Surviving Oxyrhynchus Papyri indicate that seven-story buildings even existed in provincial towns, such as in 3rd century Hermopolis in Roman Egypt.

Egypt

During the medieval Arabic-Islamic period, the Egyptian capital of Fustat (Old Cairo) housed many high-rise residential buildings, some seven stories tall that could reportedly accommodate hundreds of people. In the 10th century, Al-Muqaddasi described them as resembling minarets, and stated that the majority of Fustat's population lived in these multi-storey apartment buildings, each one housing over 200 people. In the 11th century, Nasir Khusraw described some of these apartment buildings rising up to fourteen stories, with roof gardens on the top storey complete with ox-drawn water wheels for irrigating them.

By the 16th century, the current Cairo also had high-rise apartment buildings, where the two lower floors were for commercial and storage purposes and the multiple stories above them were rented out to tenants.

England

In the late 19th and early 20th century, the concept of the flat was slow to catch-on amongst the English middle-classes. Those who lived in these flats were assumed to be adaptable and 'different'. In London, everyone who could afford it occupied an entire house – even if a small one.

During the last quarter of the 19th Century, ideas began to change. Both urban growth and the increase in population meant that more imaginative housing concepts were going to be needed if the middle and upper classes were to maintain a Pied-à-terre in the capital. The traditional London town house was becoming increasingly expensive to maintain. Especially for male and female bachelors, the idea of renting a modern mansion flat came increasingly into vogue.

The first mansion flats in England were:

- Albert Mansions, who was developed by Philip Flower and designed by James Knowles (architect). These flats were constructed between 1867 and 1870, and were one of the earliest blocks of flats to fill the vacant spaces of the newly-laid out Victoria Street at the end of the 1860s. Today, only a sliver of the building remains, next to the Victoria Palace Theatre. Albert Mansions was really 19 separate 'houses', each with a staircase serving one flat per floor. Its tenants included Alfred, Lord Tennyson, whose connections with the developer's family were long-standing. Philip Flower's son was Cyril Flower, 1st Baron Battersea developed most of the mansion blocks on Prince of Wales Drive, London.

- Albert Hall Mansions, designed by Richard Norman Shaw in 1876. Because this was of a new type, risks were reduced as much as possible, each block was planned as a separate project with the building of each separate part contingent on the successful occupation of every flat in the previous block. The gamble paid off and the scheme was a success.

Scotland

In Scotland, the term 'tenement' lacks the pejorative connotations it carries elsewhere, and refers simply to any block of flats sharing a common central staircase and lacking an elevator, particularly those constructed prior to 1919. Tenements were, and continue to be, inhabited by a wide range of social classes and income groups.

During the 19th century tenements became the predominant type of new housing in Scotland's industrial cities, although they were very common in the Old Town in Edinburgh from the 15th century where they reached ten or eleven storeys high and in one case fourteen storeys. Built of sandstone or granite, Scottish tenements are usually three to five storeys in height, with two to four flats on each floor. (In contrast, industrial cities in England tended to favour "back-to-back" terraces of brick.) Scottish tenements are constructed in terraces of tenements, and each entrance within a block is referred to as a *close* or *stair* — both referring to the shared passageway to the individual flats. Flights of stairs and landings are generally designated common areas, and residents traditionally took turns to sweep clean the floors, and in Aberdeen in particular, took turns to make use of shared laundry facilities in the "back green" (garden or yard). It is now more common for cleaning of the common ways to be contracted out through a managing agent or "factor".

Tenements today are bought by a wide range of social types, including young professionals, older retiring people, and by absentee landlords, often for rental to students after they leave halls of residence managed by their institution. The National Trust for Scotland Tenement House Museum in Glasgow offers an insight into the lifestyle of tenement dwellers.

Many multi-storey tower blocks were built in the UK after the Second World War. A number of these are being demolished and replaced with low-rise buildings or housing estates known in Scotland as housing schemes, often modern interpretations of the tenement.

In Glasgow, where Scotland's highest concentration of tenement dwellings can be found, the urban renewal projects of the 1950s, 1960s and 1970s brought an end to the city's slums, which had primarily consisted of older tenements built in the early 19th century in which large extended families would live together in cramped conditions. They were replaced by high-rise blocks that, within a couple of decades, became notorious for crime and poverty. The Glasgow Corporation made many efforts to improve the situation, most successfully with the City Improvement Trust, which cleared the slums of the old town, replacing them with what they thought of as a traditional high street, which remains an imposing townscape. (The City Halls and the Cleland Testimonial were part of this scheme). National government help was given following World War I when Housing Acts sought to provide "homes fit for heroes". Garden suburb areas, based on English models, such as Knightswood were set up. These proved too expensive, so a modern tenement, three stories high, slate roofed and built of reconstituted stone, was re-introduced and a slum clearance programme initiated to clear areas such as the Calton and the Garngad.

Post Second World War, more ambitious plans, known as the Bruce Plan, were made for the complete evacuation of slums to modern mid-rise housing developments on the outskirts of the city. However, central government refused to fund the plans, preferring instead to depopulate the city to a series of New Towns Again, economic considerations meant that many of the planned "New Town" amenities were never built in these areas. These housing estates, known as "schemes", came therefore to be widely regarded as unsuccessful; many, such as Castlemilk, were just dormitories well away from the centre of the city with no amenities, such as shops and public houses ("deserts with windows", as Billy Connolly once put it). High rise living too started off with bright ambition - the Moss Heights are still desirable - (1950–1954) but fell prey to later economic pressure. Many of the later tower blocks were poorly designed and cheaply built and their anonymity caused some social problems.

In 1970 a team from Strathclyde University demonstrated that the old tenements had been basically sound, and could be given new life with replumbing with kitchens and bathroom. The Corporation acted on this principle for the first time in 1973 at the *Old Swan Corner*, Pollokshaws. Thereafter, *Housing Action Areas* were set up to renovate so-called slums. Later, privately owned tenements benefited from government help in "stone cleaning", revealing a honey-coloured sandstone behind the presumed "grey" tenemental facades. The policy of tenement demolition is now considered to have been short-sighted, wasteful and largely unsuccessful. Many of Glasgow's worst tenements were refurbished into desirable accommodation in the 1970s and 1980s and the policy of demolition is considered to have destroyed fine examples of a "universally admired architectural" style. The Glasgow Housing Association took ownership of the housing stock from the city council on 7 March 2003, and has begun a £96 million clearance and demolition programme to clear and demolish many of the high-rise flats.

Yemen

High-rise apartment buildings were built in the Yemeni city of Shibam in the 16th century. The houses of Shibam are all made out of mud bricks, but about 500 of them are tower houses, which rise 5 to 11 stories high, with each floor having one or two apartments. Shibam has been called "Manhattan of the desert". Some of them were over 100 feet (30 m) high, thus being the tallest mudbrick apartment buildings in the world to this day.

United States and Canada

In the 10th century, the Chacoan people constructed large, multi-room dwellings, some comprising more than 900 rooms, in the Chaco Canyon area of what is now northwest New Mexico.

In 1839, the first New York City tenement was built, housing mainly poor immigrants. The tenements were breeding grounds for outlaws, juvenile delinquents, and organized crime. Muckraker journalist Jacob Riis wrote in *How the Other Half Lives*:

> The New York tough may be ready to kill where his London brother would do little more than scowl; yet, as a general thing he is less repulsively brutal in looks. Here again the reason may be the same: the breed is not so old. A few generations more in the slums, and all that will be changed.

Tenements were also known for their price gouging rent. *How the Other Half Lives* notes one tenement district:

> Blind Man's Alley bear its name for a reason. Until little more than a year ago its dark burrows harbored a colony of blind beggars, tenants of a blind landlord, old Daniel Murphy, whom every child in the ward knows, if he never heard of the President of the United States. "Old Dan" made a big fortune—he told me once four hundred thousand dollars— out of his alley and the surrounding tenements, only to grow blind himself in extreme old age, sharing in the end the chief hardship of the wretched beings whose lot he had stubbornly refused to better that he might increase his wealth. Even when the Board of Health at last compelled him to repair and clean up the worst of the old buildings, under threat of driving out the tenants and locking the doors behind them, the work was accomplished against the old man's angry protests. He appeared in person before the Board to argue his case, and his argument was characteristic. "I have made my will," he said. "My monument stands waiting for me in Calvary. I stand on the very brink of the grave, blind and helpless, and now (here the pathos of the appeal was swept under in a burst of angry indignation) do you want me to build and get skinned, skinned? These people are not fit to live in a nice house. Let them go where they can, and let my house stand." In spite of the genuine anguish of the appeal, it was downright amusing to find that his anger was provoked less by the anticipated waste of luxury on his tenants than by distrust of his own kind, the builder. He knew intuitively

what to expect. The result showed that Mr. Murphy had gauged his tenants correctly.

The Dakota (1884) was one of the first luxury apartment buildings in New York City. The majority, however, remained tenements.

Many reformers, such as Upton Sinclair and Jacob Riis, pushed for reforms in tenement dwellings. As a result in 1901, New York state passed a law called the New York State Tenement House Act to improve the conditions in tenements.

More improvements followed. In 1949, President Harry S. Truman signed the Housing Act of 1949 to clean slums and reconstruct housing units for the poor.

Some significant developments in architectural design of apartment buildings came out of the 1950s and 60s. Among them were groundbreaking designs in the 860-880 Lake Shore Drive Apartments (1951), New Century Guild (1961), Marina City (1964) and Lake Point Tower (1968).

Apartment buildings are multi-story buildings where three or more residences are contained within one structure. In more urban areas, apartments close to the downtown area have the benefits of proximity to jobs and/or public transportation. However, prices per square foot are often much higher than in suburban areas.

The distinction between rental apartments and condominiums is that while rental buildings are owned by a single entity and rented out to many, condominiums are owned individually, while their owners still pay a monthly or yearly fee for building upkeep. Condominiums are often leased by their owner as rental apartments. A third alternative, the cooperative apartment building (or "co-op"), acts as a corporation with all of the tenants as shareholders of the building. Tenants in cooperative buildings do not own their apartment, but instead own a proportional number of shares of the entire cooperative.

As in condominiums, cooperators pay a monthly fee for building upkeep. Co-ops are common in cities such as New York, and have gained some popularity in other larger urban areas in the U.S.

In the United States, tenement is a label usually applied to the less expensive, more basic rental apartment buildings in older sections of large cities. Many of these apartment buildings are "walk-ups" without an elevator, and some have shared bathing facilities, though this is becoming less common.

Apartments were popular in Canada, particularly in urban centres like Vancouver, Toronto, Ottawa, and Montreal in the 1950s to 1970s. By the 1980s, many multi-unit buildings were being constructed as condominiums instead of apartments, and both are now very common. In Toronto and Vancouver, high-rise apartments and condominiums have been spread around the city, giving even the major suburbs a skyline.

The slang term dingbat has been coined to describe cheap urban apartment buildings from the 1950s and 1960s with unique and often wacky façades to differentiate themselves within a full block of apartments. They are often stilted, and with parking spots underneath.

Australia

In Australia, the term "flat" and "apartment" are largely used interchangeably. Newer high-rise buildings are more often marketed as "apartments", as the term "flats" can carry negative connotations of public housing. The term condominium or condo is rarely used in Australia despite attempts by developers to market it. A high-rise apartment building is commonly referred to as a *residential tower*, *apartment tower*, or *bloc of flats* in Australia.

Apartment buildings in Australia are typically managed by a body corporate or "owners corporation" in which owners pay a monthly fee to provide for common maintenance and help cover future repair. Many apartments are owned through strata title. Due to legislation, Australian banks will either apply loan to value ratios of over 70% for strata titles of less than 50 square metres, the big four Australian banks will not loan at all for strata titles of less than 30 square metres. These are usually classified as studio apartments or student accommodation. Australian legislation enforces a minimum 2.4m floor-ceiling height which differentiates apartment buildings from office buildings.

In Australia, apartment living is a popular lifestyle choice for DINKY, yuppies, university students and more recently empty nesters, however rising land values in the big cities in recent years has seen an increase in families living in apartments. In Melbourne and Sydney apartment living is sometimes not a matter of choice for the many socially disadvantaged people who often end up in public housing towers.

Australia has a relatively recent history in apartment buildings. Terrace houses were the early response to density development, though the majority of Australians lived in fully detached houses. Apartments of any kind were legislated against in the Parliament of Queensland as part of the Undue Subdivision of Land Prevention Act 1885.

The earliest apartment buildings were in the major cities of Sydney and Melbourne as the response to fast rising land values. Melbourne Mansions on Collins Street, Melbourne (now demolished), built in 1906 for mostly wealthy residents is believed by many to be the earliest. Today the oldest surviving self-contained apartment buildings are in the St Kilda area including the Fawkner Mansions (1910), Majestic Mansions (1912 as a boarding house) and the Canterbury (1914 - the oldest surviving buildings contained flats). Kingsclere, built in 1912 is believed to be the earliest apartment building in Sydney and still survives.

During the interwar years, apartment building continued in inner Melbourne (particularly in areas such as St Kilda and South Yarra), Sydney (particularly in areas such as Potts Point, Darlinghust and Kings Cross) and in Brisbane (in areas such as New Farm, Fortitude Valley and Spring Hill). Post World War II, with the Australian Dream apartment buildings went out of vogue and flats were seen as accommodation only for the poor. Walk-up "flats" (without a lift) of two to three storeys however were common in the middle suburbs of cities for lower income groups.

The main exceptions were Sydney and the Gold Coast, Queensland where apartment development continued for more than half a century. In Sydney a limited geography and highly sought after waterfront views (Sydney Harbour and beaches such as Bondi) made apartment living socially acceptable. While on the Gold Coast views of the ocean, proximity to the beach and a large tourist population made apartments a popular choice. Since the 1960s, these cities maintained much higher population densities than the rest of Australia through the acceptance of apartment buildings.

In other cities apartment building was almost solely restricted to public housing. Public housing in Australia was common in the larger cities, particularly in Melbourne (by the Housing Commission of Victoria) where a huge number of hi-rise housing commission flats were built between the 1950s and 1970s by successive governments as part of an urban renewal programme. Areas affected included Fitzroy, Flemington, Collingwood, Carlton, Richmond and Prahran. Similar projects were run in Sydney's lower socio economic areas like Redfern. In the 1980s, modern apartment buildings sprang up in riverside locations in Brisbane (along the Brisbane River) and Perth (along the Swan River). In Melbourne in the 1990s a trend began for apartment buildings without the requirement of spectacular views. As a continuation of the gentrification of the inner city, a fashion became New York "loft" style apartments and a large stock of old warehouses and old abandoned office buildings in and around the CBD became the target of developers. The trend of adaptive reuse extended to conversion of old churches and schools. Similar warehouse conversions and gentrification began in Brisbane suburbs such as Teneriffe, Queensland and Fortitude Valley and in Sydney in areas such as Ultimo. As supply of buildings for conversion ran out, reproduction and post modern style apartments followed. The popularity of these apartments also stimulated a boom in the construction of new hi-rise apartment buildings in inner cities. This was particularly the case in Melbourne which was fuelled by official planning policies (Postcode 3000), making the CBD the fastest growing, population wise in the country. Apartment building in the Melbourne metropolitan area has also escalated with the advent of the Melbourne 2030 planning policy. Urban renewal areas like Docklands, Southbank, St Kilda Road and Port Melbourne are now predominately apartments. There has also been a sharp increase in the amount of student apartment buildings in areas such as Carlton in Melbourne.

Despite their size, other smaller cities including Canberra, Darwin, Newcastle, Adelaide and Geelong have begun building apartments in the 2000s.

Today, residential buildings Eureka Tower and Q1 are the tallest in the country. In many cases, apartments in inner city areas of the major cities can cost much more than much larger houses in the outer suburbs.

There are Australian cities, such as Gold Coast, Queensland, which are inhabited predominately by apartment dwellers.

Advantages

High Security

Some apartment buildings have high levels of security.

For example, to enter a high-security building, a person must validate their smartcard at the door. In some apartments while at the lift the smartcard would be used again to be able to press the button for lift access. Finally, the person walks towards apartment and uses their key to unlock the entrance door. This 2 or 3-tier security will in most cases prevent home invasions and theft. Some buildings may have a doorman to guard the premises. Many middle and upper tier apartments have video phones, whereby residents can see and verify who is at the main entrance before allowing access to the building.

Apartments are also more convenient than owning a house as the general maintenance and landscaping is taken care of by the owner. This is particularly the case in regions with climate extremes, such as the long and snowy winters in the Nordic countries of northern Europe where there is much snow clearing work for house residents.

Real Estate Investment

The total cost for the construction of an apartment is much less than the cost invested in the construction of a single house. When the cost of a single unit in the apartment is compared to a single house of the same dimension, the difference in cost is very large. The cost of land is shared by all the owners of the apartment. But the price at which the flats are sold is not exactly proportional to the difference, but the real estator makes a big share of profits because the price at which the flats are sold are almost equal to the price of the houses in specific areas of the city. In this way apartment construction is an advantage to the real estator.

Disposable Income

In Scandinavian countries apartment dwelling and renting through non-profit housing co-operatives is common place. Apartment users are allowed to modify the interior of the apartment to suit their wishes. Often the extended families have a shared holiday house in the countryside.

The investment in real estate for a family is reduced leading to greater disposable income for quality of life.

Disadvantages

Energy Use

Buildings over 4 to 7 stories have a lower energy footprint / m2 than mid /high rise greater than 7 stories. There seems to be a tradeoff with many other variable in a life cycyle analysis which would suggest that 7 stories (around fifty dwelling units per hectare for optimum transport petroleum use (Kenworthy)) is the optimum density in T1 urban areas, the city of Paris being an example (Mehaffy). Buildings not requiring lifts (around 4 floors though it could be five with a final two storey apartment (maisonette)) are normally more energy efficient. Note this is dependant on the particular country's accessibility requirements.

Climate Factors

High rise buildings cast a significant shadow over nearby buildings reducing solar energy harvesting. They also cast shadows over public spaces, reducing their amenity value and which are a very valuable resource in mid-density cities. Wind turbulence can also be a significant problem at ground level if design provisions are not made. The prevailing cooling breezes in summer can be disrupted for nearby buildings also.

MOTEL

A motel is a hotel designed for motorists, and usually has a parking area for motor vehicles. In the United States, the term is considered somewhat outdated; few motel chains still exist (Motel 6 and Super8 are two of the most popular still in existence). Motels peaked in popularity in the 1960s with rising car travel. In the year 2000, the American Hotel-Motel Association removed 'motel' from its name after considerable market research, and is now the American

Hotel and Lodging Association. The association felt that the term 'lodging' more accurately reflects the large variety of different style hotels, including luxury and boutique hotels, suites, inns, budget, and extended stay hotels.

Entering dictionaries after World War II, the word motel, a portmanteau of *motor* and *hotel* or *motorists' hotel*, referred initially to a type of hotel consisting of a single building of connected rooms whose doors faced a parking lot and, in some circumstances, a common area; or a series of small cabins with common parking. As the United States highway system began to develop in the 1920s, long distance road journeys became more common and the need for inexpensive, easily accessible overnight accommodation sited close to the main routes, led to the growth of the motel concept.

History

Auto camps predated motels by a few years. Unlike motels, auto camps and tourist courts typically provided bed and breakfast or hotel-style service, usually with stand-alone cabins. After the introduction of the motel, auto camps continued in popularity through the Depression years and after World War II, their popularity finally starting to diminish with the construction of freeways and changes in consumer demands. Examples include the Rising Sun Auto Camp in Glacier National Park and Blue Bonnet Court in Texas. Such facilities were "mom-and-pop" facilities, on the outskirts of a town, that were as quirky as their owners. The 1935 City Directory for San Diego, CA lists "motel" type accommodations under Tourist Camps.

In contrast, though they remained "Mom and Pop" operations, motels quickly adopted a more homogenized appearance and were designed from the start to cater purely to motorists. The motel concept originated with the Motel Inn of San Luis Obispo, constructed in 1925 by Arthur Heineman. In conceiving of a name for his hotel Heineman abbreviated *motor hotel* to *mo-tel*. Motels are typically constructed in an 'I'- or 'L'- or 'U'-shaped layout that includes guest rooms, an attached manager's office, a small reception and, in some cases, a small diner. Post-war motels sought more visual distinction, often featuring eye-catching neon signs which employed themes from popular culture, ranging from Western imagery of cowboys and Indians to contemporary images of spaceships and atomic era iconography.

Motels differ from hotels in their location along highways, as opposed to the urban cores favoured by hotels, and their orientation to the outside (in contrast to hotels whose doors typically face an interior hallway). Motels almost by definition include a parking lot, while older hotels were not usually built with automobile parking in mind. With the 1952 introduction of Kemmons Wilson's Holiday Inn, the mom-and-pop motels of that era started to decline. The emergence of the interstate highway system, along with other factors, led to a blurring of the motel and the hotel, though family-owned motels with as few as five rooms may still be found, especially along older highways. In the late 20th century, a majority of motels in the United States came under the ownership of people of Indian descent, particularly Gujaratis.

Long-Term

Motels/hotels with low rates sometimes serve as housing for people who are not able to afford an apartment or have recently lost their home and need somewhere to stay until further arrangements are made. Motels catering to long-term stays often have kitchenettes. However, even though most of these establishments that were previously called motels may still look like motels, most are now called hotels, inns, lodges, etc.

Film, TV and Stage Depictions

The Bates Motel is an important part of *Psycho*, a 1959 novel by Robert Bloch and Alfred Hitchcock's 1960 film, *Psycho*. Film sequels, *Psycho II* and *Psycho III*, also feature the motel as does the 1987 television movie, *Bates Motel*. The motel makes appearances in *Psycho IV: The Beginning*, but is not featured as much as in previous films. The Bates Motel returned to prominence in the 1998 remake of the original film.

The scenario of an isolated motel being operated by a serial killer, whose guests subsequently become victims, has been exploited in a number of other horror films, notably *Motel Hell* (1980) and *Mountaintop Motel Massacre* (1986). More recently, the genre has been revived with such films as *Mayhem Motel* (2001), *Murder Inn* (2005), *Vacancy* (2007), and its direct-to-video prequel, *Vacancy 2: The First Cut* (2009).

Several of these horror films also incorporate the sub-theme of voyeurism, whereby the motel owner spies on (or even films) the sexual exploits of the guests. This plays on the long-established connotations of motels and illicit sexual activity, which has itself formed the basis for numerous other films, variously representing the thriller, comedy, teen film and sexploitation genres. Stephen C. Apostolof's *Motel Confidential* (1967) and the porn film *Motel for Lovers* (1970) were two notable early examples. More recent manifestations include *Paradise Motel* (1985), *Talking Walls* (1987), *Desire and Hell at Sunset Motel* (1991) and the Korean films *Motel Cactus* (1997) and *The Motel* (2005).

In countless other movies and TV series, the motel - invariably depicted as an isolated, rundown and seedy establishment - has served as the setting for sordid events often involving equally sordid characters. Examples include *Pink Motel* (1982), *Motel Blue 19* (1993), *Backroad Motel* (2001), *Stateline Motel* (2003), *Niagara Motel* (2006) and *Motel 5150* (2008). In the film *Sparkle Lite Motel* (2006) and the TV miniseries *The Lost Room* (2006), the motel made forays into the realms of science fiction.

In the theatre, the seedy motel room has been the

setting for two-hander plays, *Same Time, Next Year* (1975) and *Bug* (2006). Both were later adapted as films. Broadway musicals have also paid homage to the lowbrow reputation of motel culture, demonstrated by songs such as 'The No-Tel Motel' from *Prettybelle* and 'At the Bed-D-by Motel' from *Lolita, My Love*.

Legal Problems

Motels have also served as a haven for fugitives from the law. In the past, the anonymity and a simple registration process helped fugitives to remain ahead of the law. However, several changes have reduced the capacity of motels to serve this purpose. Credit card transactions, which in the past were more easily approved and took days to report, are now approved or declined on the spot and are instantly recorded in a database, thereby allowing law enforcement access to this information. This system was implemented in 1993 after the abduction and murder of Donna Martz, whose credit card was used by her killers following her death to purchase food, gasoline and to pay for overnight motel stays. The story of Martz's disappearance, leading to the development of this system, was described on *The FBI Files*. Laws in many places now require registering guests to present a government-issued photo ID, even when paying with cash. Local law enforcement agencies frequently check motels when they suspect a wanted fugitive is within their jurisdiction.

HOSTEL

Hostels provide budget oriented, sociable accommodation where guests can rent a bed, usually a bunk bed, in a dormitory and share a bathroom, lounge and sometimes a kitchen. Rooms can be mixed or single-sex, although private rooms may also be available. Hostels are generally cheaper for both the operator and the occupants; many hostels have long-term residents whom they employ as desk clerks or housekeeping staff in exchange for free accommodation.

In a few countries, such as the UK, Ireland, the Netherlands, India, and Australia, the word hostel sometimes also refers to establishments providing longer-term accommodation (often to specific classes of clientele such as nurses, students, drug addicts, court defendants on bail) where the hostels are sometimes run by Housing Associations and charities.

In the rest of the world, the word hostel refers only to properties offering shared accommodation to travellers or backpackers. Within the 'traveller' category, another distinction can be drawn between hostels which are members of Hostelling International (HI), a UK-based, non-profit organization encouraging outdoor activities and cultural exchange for the young (formerly the IYHA), and independently operated hostels. Hostels for travellers are sometimes called backpackers' hostels, particularly in Australia and New Zealand (often abbreviated to just "backpackers").

History

In 1912, in Altena Castle in Germany, Richard Schirrmann created the first permanent *Jugendherberge* or "Youth Hostel". These first Youth Hostels were an exponent of the ideology of the German Youth Movement to let poor city youngsters breathe fresh air outdoors. The youths were supposed to manage the hostel themselves as much as possible, doing chores to keep the costs down and build character as well as being physically active outdoors. Because of this, many Youth Hostels closed during the middle part of the day. Very few hostels still require chores beyond washing up after self-catered meals or have a "lockout".

Differences from Hotels

There are several differences between hostels and hotels, including:

1. Hostels tend to be budget-oriented; rates are

considerably lower, and many hostels have programmes to share books, DVDs and other items.

2. For those who prefer an informal environment, hostels do not usually have the same level of formality as hotels.

3. For those who prefer to socialize with their fellow guests, hostels usually have more common areas and opportunities to socialize. The dormitory aspect of hostels also increases the social factor

Hostels are Generally Self-Catering

Communal Accommodation

There is less privacy in a hostel than in a hotel. Sharing sleeping accommodation in a dormitory is very different from staying in a private room in a hotel or bed and breakfast, and might not be comfortable for those requiring more privacy. The lessened privacy is also an advantage in some ways, because it encourages more social interaction between guests. Theft can be a problem, since guests may share a common living space, but this can be avoided by securing guests' belongings.

Most hostels offer some sort of system for safely storing valuables, and an increasing number of hostels offer private lockers. Noise can make sleeping difficult on occasions, whether from snoring, sexual activity, someone either returning late or leaving early or the proximity of so many people. This can be mitigated by carrying earplugs.

Types of Hostels

The traditional hostel format involved dormitory style accommodation. Some newer hostels also include en-suite accommodation with single, double or quad occupancy rooms, though to be considered a hostel they must also provide dormitory accommodation. In recent years, the numbers of independent and backpackers' hostels have increased greatly to cater for the greater numbers of overland, multi-destination travellers (such as gap-year travellers, and rail-trippers).

The quality of such places has also improved dramatically. While a few hostels do still insist on a curfew, daytime lockouts, and/or require occupants to do chores, this is becoming a rare exception rather than the rule, as hostels adapt to meet the changing expectations of guests.

Hostelling International (HI)

Richard Schirrmann's idea of hostels rapidly spread overseas and eventually resulted in Hostelling International, an organization composed of more than 90 different Youth Hostel associations representing over 4500 Youth Hostels in over 80 countries.

Some HI Youth Hostels cater more to school-aged children (sometimes through school trips) and parents with their children, whereas others are more for travellers intent on learning new cultures. However, while the exploration of different cultures and places is emphasized in many hostels, particularly in cities or popular tourist destinations, there are still many hostels providing accommodation for outdoor pursuits such as hillwalking, climbing and bicycle touring; these are often small friendly hostels retaining much of the original vision and often provide valuable access to more remote regions. Despite their name, in most countries membership is not limited to youth.

Independent Hostels

Independent hostels are not necessarily affiliated with one of the national bodies of Hostelling International, Youth Hostel Association or any other licensing body. Often, the word *independent* is used to refer to non-HI hostels even when the hostels do belong to another hostelling organization.

The term "youth" is less often used with these properties. These non-HI hostels are often called "backpackers' hostels".

Unlike a hotel chain where everything is standardized, these hostels can be very diverse, typically not requiring a membership card.

As the hostel industry evolves, independent hostels and HI hostels are becoming more similar, with the word "backpackers" also now applying to many Hostelling International hostels.

Boutique Hostels

The general backpacking community is no longer exclusively typified by gap year student travelers and extreme shoe string budgets. In response to demand, as well as increasing competition between the rapidly growing number of hostels, the overall quality of hostels has improved across the industry. In addition to the increase in quality, new styles of hostels have developed that have a focus on a more trendy, design interior.

The phrase "boutique hostel" is an often-arbitrary marketing term typically used to describe intimate, luxurious or quirky hostel environments. The term has started to lose meaning because the facilities of many "boutique hostels" are often no different from hostels that aren't referred to with that label. Also, marketers and online booking websites sometimes include boutique hotels in lists of "boutique hostels," further diluting any specific meaning of the phrase.

Mobile Hostels

A mobile hostel is a hostel with no fixed location. It can exist in the form of a campsite, a temporary building, or a short term agreement in a permanent building. Mobile hostels most often sprout up at large festivals where there exists a shortage of budget accommodation. As with regular hostels, mobile hostels generally provide budget accommodation for backpackers or travelers on a shoe string budget. As long as there has been a hospitality industry there has been temporary or otherwise unconventional accommodation. Seasonal B&B's and opportunistic locals who offer their private dwellings during high season are examples of this. The first ever commercial example of a mobile hostel can be linked to Hostival. It has sprouted up at Oktoberfest, Carnival, San Fermin, Las Fallas, and the 2010 World Cup.

Industry Growth

The independent hostel industry is growing rapidly in many cities around the world, such as New York, Rome, Buenos Aires and Miami. This is reflected in the development and expansion of dozens of hostel chains worldwide. The recent eruption in independent hostels has been called "probably the single biggest news in the world of low-cost travel".

The development of independent backpackers hostels is a strong business model, with some cities reporting a higher average income per room for hostels than hotels. For example, in the city of Honolulu, Hawaii, upscale hotels are reportedly making $141 to $173 per room, while hostel rooms in the same city can bring in as much as $200 per night. Even during the 2008 economic crisis, many hostels are reporting increased occupancy numbers in a time when hotel bookings are down.

> Even as the city's hotel occupancy rate has fallen to 66 percent in February, from 81 percent in the same month last year, despite steep discounts, many youth hostels are reporting banner business.
>
> —*New York Times*

Though in the past, hostels have been seen as low-quality accommodation for less wealthy travellers, at least one Australian study has shown that backpackers (who typically stay at hostels) spend more than non-backpackers, due to their longer stays. Backpackers make up as much as 10% of international visitors in Australia. In New Zealand, backpackers hostels had a 13.5% share of accommodation guest/nights in 2007.

Hostels in Popular Culture

Motion pictures have portrayed hostels in two ways: as fun places for young people to stay (*for example*, The Journey of Jared Price and A Map for Saturday), or alternately, as dangerous places where unsuspecting Americans face potential horrors in Eastern Europe. There are some popular misconceptions that a hostel is a kind of a flophouse, homeless shelter, or halfway house, though this does not reflect the high quality and level of professionalism in many modern hostels.

Self Contained Facilities and Services

In attempts to attract more visitors hostels nowadays provide additional services not previously available, such as airport shuttle transfers, internet cafes, swimming pools and spas, tour booking. and Car rentals

RESORT

A resort is a place used for relaxation or recreation, attracting visitors for holidays or vacations. Resorts are places, towns or sometimes commercial establishment operated by a single company.

Towns which are resorts — or where tourism or vacationing is a major part of the local activity — are sometimes called resort towns. If they are by the sea they are called seaside resorts. Inland resorts include ski resorts, mountain resorts and spa towns. Towns such as Sochi in Russia, Sharm el Sheikh in Egypt, Barizo in Spain, Cortina d'Ampezzo in Italy, Druskininkai in Lithuania, Nice in France, Newport, Rhode Island, St. Moritz in Switzerland, and Blackpool in England are well-known resorts.

The term "resort" is now also used for a self-contained commercial establishment which attempts to provide for most of a vacationer's wants while remaining on the premises, such as food, drink, lodging, sports, entertainment, and shopping. The term may be used to identify a hotel property that provides an array of amenities and typically includes entertainment and recreational activities. A hotel is frequently a central feature of a resort, such as the Grand Hotel at Mackinac Island, Michigan. A resort is not merely a commercial establishment operated by a single company, although in the late twentieth century this sort of facility became more common.

The Walt Disney World Resort is a prominent example of a modern, self-contained commercial resort. Self-contained resorts are common in the United States, but exist throughout the world. Resorts are especially prevalent in Central America and the Caribbean. Closely related to resorts are convention and large meeting sites. Generally these occur in cities where special meeting halls, together with ample accommodations as well as varied dining and entertainment are provided.

Resort Towns

Seaside Resorts

Seaside resorts are located on a coast. Many seaside towns have turned to other entertainment industries, and some of them have a good deal of nightlife. The cinemas and theatres often remain to become host to a number of pubs, bars, restaurants and nightclubs. Most of their entertainment facilities cater to local people and the beaches still remain popular during the summer months. Although international tourism turned people away from British seaside towns, it also brought in foreign travel and as a result, many seaside towns offer foreign language schools, the students of which often return to vacation and sometimes to settle.

Ski Resorts

In Europe, ski resorts are towns and villages in ski areas, with support services for skiing such as hotels and chalets, equipment rental, ski schools and ski lifts to access the slopes.

Self-Contained Resorts

Destination Resort

A destination resort is a resort that contains, in and of itself, the necessary guest attraction capabilities—that is to say that a destination resort does not need to be near a destination (town, historic site, theme park, or other) to attract its public. A commercial establishment at a resort destination such as a recreational area, a scenic or historic site, a theme park, a gaming facility or other tourist attraction may compete with other businesses at a destination. Consequently, another characteristic of a destination resort is that it offers food, drink, lodging, sports, entertainment, and shopping within the facility so that guests have no need to leave the facility throughout their stay. Commonly these facilities are of higher quality than would be expected if one were to stay at a hotel or eat in a town's restaurants. Some examples are Atlantis in the Bahamas, Costa do Sauípe in the Northeastern Brazil, Laguna Phuket in Thailand and Sun City near Johannesburg in South Africa.

All-Inclusive Resort

An all-inclusive resort is a resort that, besides providing all of the common amenities of a resort, charges a fixed price that includes most or all items. At a minimum, most inclusive resorts include lodging, unlimited food, drink, sports activities, and entertainment for the fixed price. In recent years, the number of resorts offering "all-inclusive" amenities has decreased dramatically; in 1961, over half offered such plans and in 2007, less than ten percent do so.

All-inclusive resorts are found in the Caribbean, particularly Cuba, and elsewhere. Notable examples are Club Med and Sandals Resorts.

Spa Resorts

A spa resort is a short term residential/lodging facility with the primary purpose of providing individual services for spa-goers to develop healthy habits. Historically many such spas were developed at the location of natural hot springs or sources of mineral waters. Typically over a seven-day stay, such facilities provide a comprehensive programme that includes spa services, physical fitness activities, wellness education, healthy cuisine and special interest programming.

Golf Resorts

Golf resorts are resorts that cater specifically to the sport of golf, and include access to one or more golf course and or clubhouse. Golf resorts typically provide golf packages that provide visitors with all greens and cart fees, range balls, accommodations and meals.

Ski Resorts

In North America a ski resort is generally a destination resort in a ski area, and is less likely to refer to a town or village.

Luxury Resorts

A luxury resort is an expensive vacation facility which is fully staffed and has been rated with five stars. Luxury resorts often boast many visitor activities and attractions such as golf, watersports, spa and beauty facilities, skiing, natural ecology and tranquility. Because of the extent of amenities offered, a luxury resort is also considered a destination resort.

Megaresorts

A Megaresort is a type of destination resort which is of an exceptionally large size, sometimes featuring large-scale attractions (casino, golf course, theme park, multiple accommodations). The hotels and casinos along the Las Vegas Strip are often considered megaresorts due to their immense size and complexity.

Integrated Resorts

In Singapore an integrated resort is a euphemism for a casino-based destination resort.

Holiday Villages and Holiday Camps

A holiday village is a type of self-contained resort in Europe, where the accommodation is generally in villas. A holiday camp in the United Kingdom refers to a resort where the accommodation is in chalets. The term "holiday park" is used for a resort where the accommodation includes static caravans and chalets.

Historical Resorts

A famous resort of the ancient world was Baiae, Italy, popular over 2,000 years ago. Capri, an island near Naples, Italy, has attracted visitors since Roman times. Another famous historical resort was Monte Ne near Rogers, Arkansas, which was active in the early 20th century. At its peak more than 10,000 people a year visited its hotels. It closed in the 1930s, and was ultimately submerged under Beaver Lake in the 1960s.

RESTAURANT

A restaurant prepares and serves food, drink and dessert to customers in return for money. Meals are generally served and eaten on premises, but many restaurants also offer take-out and food delivery services. Restaurants vary greatly in appearance and offerings, including a wide variety of the main chef's cuisines and service models.

While inns and taverns were known from antiquity, these were establishments aimed at travelers, and in general locals would rarely eat there. Modern restaurants are dedicated to the serving of food, where specific dishes are ordered by guests and are prepared to their request. The modern restaurant originated in 18th century France, although precursors can be traced back to Roman times.

A restaurant owner is called a *restaurateur* both words derive from the French verb *restaurer*, meaning "to restore". Professional artisans of cooking are called chefs, while preparation staff and line cooks prepare food items in a more systematic and less artistic fashion.

History

In Ancient Rome, thermopolia (singular thermopolium) were small restaurant-bars which offered food and drinks to the customer. A typical thermopolia had L-shaped counters into which large storage vessels were sunk, which would contain either hot or cold food. They are linked to the absence of kitchens in many dwellings and the ease with which people could purchase prepared foods. Besides, eating out was also considered an important aspect of socialising.

In Pompeii, 158 thermopolia with a service counter have been identified across the whole town area. They were concentrated along the main axes of the town and the public spaces where they were frequented by the locals.

Food catering establishments which may be described as restaurants were known since the 11th century in Kaifeng, China's northern capital during the first half of the Song Dynasty (960–1279). With a population of over 1,000,000 people, a culture of hospitality and a paper currency, Kaifeng was ripe for the development of restaurants. Probably growing out of the tea houses and taverns that catered to travellers, Kaifeng's restaurants blossomed into an industry catering to locals as well as people from other regions of China. Stephen H. West argues that there is a direct correlation between the growth of the restaurant businesses and institutions of theatrical stage drama, gambling and prostitution which served the burgeoning merchant middle class during the Song Dynasty.

Restaurants catered to different styles of cuisine, price brackets, and religious requirements. Even within a single restaurant much choice was available, and people ordered the entree they wanted from written menus. An account from 1275 writes of Hangzhou, the capital city for the last half of the dynasty:

> *"The people of Hangzhou are very difficult to please. Hundreds of orders are given on all sides: this person wants something hot, another something cold, a third something tepid, a fourth something chilled; one wants cooked food, another raw, another chooses roast, another grill".*

The restaurants in Hangzhou also catered to many northern Chinese who had fled south from Kaifeng during the Jurchen invasion of the 1120s, while it is also known that many restaurants were run by families formerly from Kaifeng.

Types of Restaurants

Restaurants range from unpretentious lunching or dining places catering to people working nearby, with simple food served in simple settings at low prices, to expensive establishments serving refined food and wines in a formal setting. In the former case, customers usually wear casual clothing. In the latter case, depending on culture and local traditions, customers might wear semi-casual, semi-formal, or even in rare cases formal wear. Typically, customers sit at tables, their orders are taken by a waiter, who brings the food when it is ready, and the customers pay the bill before leaving. In finer restaurants there will be a host or hostess or even a maître d'hôtel to welcome customers and to seat them. Other staff waiting on customers include busboys and sommeliers.

Restaurants often specialize in certain types of food or present a certain unifying, and often entertaining, theme. For example, there are seafood restaurants, vegetarian restaurants or ethnic restaurants. Generally speaking, restaurants selling food characteristic of the local culture are simply called restaurants, while restaurants selling food of foreign cultural origin are called accordingly,

Restaurant Regulations

Depending on local customs and the establishment, restaurants may or may not serve alcohol. Restaurants are often prohibited from selling alcohol without a meal by alcohol sale laws; such sale is considered to be activity for bars, which are meant to have more severe restrictions. Some restaurants are licensed to serve alcohol ("fully licensed"), and/or permit customers to "bring your own" alcohol (BYO / BYOB). In some places restaurant licenses may restrict service to beer, or wine and beer.

Restaurant Guides

Restaurant guides review restaurants, often ranking them or providing information for consumer decisions (type of food, handicap accessibility, facilities, etc.). In 12th century Hangzhou (mentioned above as the location of the first restaurant), signs could often be found posted in the city square listing the restaurants in the area and local customer's opinions of the quality of their food. This was an occasion for bribery and even violence. One of the most famous contemporary guides, in Western Europe, is the Michelin series of guides which accord from 1 to 3 stars to restaurants they perceive to be of high culinary merit. Restaurants with stars in the Michelin guide are formal, expensive establishments; in general the more stars awarded, the higher the prices. The main competitor to the Michelin guide in Europe is the guidebook series published by Gault Millau. Unlike the Michelin guide which takes the restaurant décor and service into consideration with its rating, Gault Millau only judges the quality of the food. Its ratings are on a scale of 1 to 20, with 20 being the highest. In the United States, the Forbes Travel Guide (previously the Mobil travel guides) and the AAA rate restaurants on a similar 1 to 5 star (Forbes) or diamond (AAA) scale. Three, four, and five star/diamond ratings are roughly equivalent to the Michelin one, two, and three star ratings while one and two star ratings typically indicate more casual places to eat. In 2005, Michelin released a

New York City guide, its first for the United States. The popular Zagat Survey compiles individuals' comments about restaurants but does not pass an "official" critical assessment. In the United States Gault Millau is published as the *Gayot* guide, after founder Andre Gayot. Its restaurant ratings use the same 20 point system, and are all published online.

The Good Food Guide, published by the Fairfax Newspaper Group in Australia, is the Australian guide listing the best places to eat. Chefs Hats are awarded for outstanding restaurants and range from one hat through three hats. The Good Food Guide also incorporates guides to bars, cafes and providers. *The Good Restaurant Guide* is another Australian restaurant guide that has reviews on the restaurants as experienced by the public and provides information on locations and contact details. Any member of the public can submit a review.

Nearly all major American newspapers employ food critics and publish online dining guides for the cities they serve. A few papers maintain a reputation for thorough and thoughtful review of restaurants to the standard of the good published guides, but others provide more of a listings service.

More recently Internet sites have started up that publish both food critic reviews and popular reviews by the general public. Their major competition comes from bloggers, particularly publishers of food blogs, also called foodies. These writers and publishers represent the common dining aficionado rather than the gourmet, and thus do not provide "official" reviews, but nonetheless are capable of garnering large, loyal followings.

Economics

United States

As of 2006, there are approximately 215,000 full-service restaurants in the United States, accounting for $298 billion, and approximately 250,000 limited-service (fast food) restaurants, accounting for $260 billion. One study of new restaurants in Cleveland, Ohio found that 1 in 4 changed ownership or went out of business after one year, and 6 out of 10 did so after three years. (Not all changes in ownership are indicative of financial failure.) The three-year failure rate for franchises was nearly the same.

Canada

There are 86,915 commercial foodservice units in Canada, or 26.4 units per 10,000 Canadians. By segment, there are:

- 38,797 full-service restaurants
- 34,629 limited-service restaurants
- 741 contract and social caterers
- 6,749 drinking places

Fully 63% of restaurants in Canada are independent brands. Chain restaurants account for the remaining 37%, and many of these are locally owned and operated franchises.

REFERENCES

Allen Salkin (2009). In Hostel Basement, Newcomer Sets Sights Far Up the Ladder," *New York Times*, March 14.

Behrens-Abouseif, Doris (1992). *Islamic Architecture in Cairo*, Brill Publishers, p. 6,

Bryson, Bill (1996). *Made in America*, Harper Perennial, ISBN 978-0380713813

Ellis, Steven J. R. (2004). "The Distribution of Bars at Pompeii: Archaeological, Spatial and Viewshed Analyses", *Journal of Roman Archaeology*, Vol. 17, pp. 371–384 (374f.)

Gregory S. Aldrete (2004). "Daily Life in the Roman City: Rome, Pompeii and Ostia".

Helfritz, Hans (April 1937). "Land without shade", *Journal of The Royal Central Asian Society* 24 (2): 201–16

Hogan, Meghan (2006). Eden in the City *Preservation Magazine* online.

Jackson, Kristin (25 April 1993). "The World's First Motel Rests Upon Its Memories". Seattle Times.

Kerry Miller (2005). "The Restaurant Failure Myth", *Business Week*, April 16, 2007. Cites an article by H.G. Parsa in *Cornell Hotel & Restaurant Administration Quarterly*.

Laboy, Suzette (2009-07-27). "South Beach becoming backpacker hot spot" (in en). Associated Press.

Lindsay, James E. (2005). *Daily Life in the Medieval Islamic World*, Greenwood Publishing Group, p. 122.

McGrath, Ginny (2008-04-29). "Whatever happened to Youth Hostels?" (in en). London: Times Online.

Mortada, Hisham (2003). *Traditional Islamic principles of built environment*, Routledge, p. viii.

Pamela Jerome, Giacomo Chiari, Caterina Borelli (1999). "The Architecture of Mud: Construction and Repair Technology in the Hadhramaut Region of Yemen", *APT Bulletin* 30 (2-3): 39–48, 44

Peter J. Claus, Sarah Diamond, Margaret Ann Mills (2003). *South Asian folklore: an encyclopedia : Afghanistan, Bangladesh, India, Nepal, Pakistan, Sri Lanka*, Taylor & Francis.

Shipman, J. G. T. (June 1984). "The Hadhramaut", *Asian Affairs* 15 (2): 154–62.

Spang, Rebecca L. (2001). "The Invention of the Restaurant: Paris and Modern Gastronomic Culture", Harvard University Press.

3

Reflections on Hotel Amenities, Guest Rooms and Other Facilities

HOTEL AMENITY

A hotel amenity is something of a premium nature provided in addition to the room and its basics when renting a room at a hotel, motel, or other place of lodging. The amenities provided in each hotel vary. In some places of lodging, certain amenities may be standard with all rooms. In others, they may be optional for an additional cost.

In the Room

Kitchen Facilities

Some places of lodging offer kitchen facilities to enable guests to cook and/or store food. In some hotels, this may be in the form of a kitchenette. It may include a full-size or half-size refrigerator, an oven, a stove, and possibly some cabinets. This is common in extended stay hotels. Other places may include just a refrigerator (often half-sized) and/or a microwave oven. When both are included, it is often marketed as a "microfridge." Coffeemakers are also often found in rooms. Hotels that offer no kitchen facilities in guest rooms sometimes provide them in the lobby for all guests to use.

Television

A television set is a standard item in most hotel rooms. In the past, coin-operated pay TVs existed. Currently, standards TV channels are free to watch, but some lodging facilities charge extra for cable or satellite TV services that are offered.

Internet Access

Most places of lodging currently offer internet access in some form. Most common is wi-fi, which can be used by guests who bring their own computers in their rooms. In most hotels, this is free, though some charge a fee. Some hotels offer hard-wired internet service requiring the use of a cable for the hook-up. Some hotels also provide computers in the lobby for all guests to use, or more rarely, in each guest room.

Personal Items

Many personal items are provided complimentary for use by guests. These may include irons and ironing boards, hair dryers, soap, shampoo, mouthwash, or shower caps.

Hair Dryer

In some hotels, a hair dryer is offered for guests use.

Towels

Hotels generally provide towels to guests for their use. One concern with the provision of towels is theft. Towel theft has proven costly to hotels, though hotels have been reported to do little to combat the problem. In 2003, Holiday Inn offered amnesty to those who returned stolen towels.

Outside the Room

Dining

Various forms of dining are offered in various places of lodging. Some hotels offer a continental breakfast that is often complimentary to guests. Items often served include cereal, pastries, waffles, sausage, fruits, and beverages. Some hotels have on-site restaurants. In most cases, the meals must be paid for. In some hotels, room service is available to guests. Some resorts are all inclusive, allowing guests access to food at little or no charge at all times of day throughout their visits.

Vending

Vending machines are provided at many hotels and motels. These machines usually sell soft drinks, snacks, and other items commonly sold in vending machines. Ice dispensers are also standard. While in some hotels, the ice may be complimentary, there may be a fee to obtain ice in others.

Exercise

Some hotels have fitness centers allowing guests to work out during their visits.

Recreation

Many resorts offer various recreational activities, such as golf, tennis, and other popular sports.

Swimming Pools

Some hotels offer swimming pools to their guests. Outdoor pools may be open seasonally in temperate climates. Indoor pools can be open year round in any climate.

LOBBY

A lobby is a room in a building which is used for entry from the outside. Sometimes referred to as a foyer or an entrance hall. Many office buildings, hotels and skyscrapers go to great lengths to decorate their lobbies to create the right impression. Since the mid 1980s there has been a growing trend to think of lobbies as more than just ways to get from the door to the elevator, but instead as social spaces and places of commerce.

Some research has even been done to develop scales to measure lobby atmosphere in order to improve hotel lobby design. Many places that offer public services, such as a doctor's office, use their lobbies as more of a waiting room for the people waiting for a certain service.

In these types of lobbies it is common for there to be comfortable furniture, such as couches and lounge chairs, so that the customer will be able to wait in comfort. Also, there may be television sets, books, and/or magazines to help the customer pass time as they wait to be served.

WAITING ROOM

A waiting room is a building, or more commonly a part of a building where people sit or stand until the event they are waiting for occurs. There are generally two types of waiting room. One is where individuals leave one at a time, for instance at a doctor's office or a hospital, or outside a school headmaster's office. The other is where people leave en masse such as those at train stations, bus stations, and airports. These two examples also highlight the difference between waiting rooms where one is asked to wait (private waiting room) and waiting rooms one can just enter at will (public waiting rooms).

Most waiting rooms contain seats for people so they do not have to stand. Some have adjacent toilets. It is not uncommon to find vending machines in public waiting rooms or books and magazines in private waiting rooms. In some countries there are special waiting rooms especially for those who have paid for them, for example at airports and railway stations. These will generally be less crowded and will have superior seating and more facilities. The films *Brief Encounter* and *The Terminal* use waiting rooms as sets for a large part of their duration. They are used elsewhere in the arts to symbolise waiting in the general sense, to symbolise transition in life and for scenes of a romantic or sad nature.

FRONT OFFICE

Front office is a business term that refers to a company's

departments that come in contact with clients, including the marketing, sales, and service departments. In the hotel industry, the front office welcomes guests to the accommodation section: meeting and greeting them, taking and organizing reservations, allocating check in and out of rooms, organizing porter service, issuing keys and other security arrangements, passing on messages to customers and settling the accounts.

In American professional sports, the term refers to upper management of a club, especially player personnel decision-makers.

GIFT SHOP

A gift shop is a store primarily selling souvenirs relating to a particular topic or theme. The items sold often include coffee mugs, stuffed animals, t-shirts, postcards, handmade collections and other souvenirs. Gift shops are normally found in areas visited by many tourists. Hotels and Motels in Canada and the United States often feature a gift shop near their entrance. Venues such as zoos, aquariums, national parks, and museums have their own gift shops; in some cases these shops sell items of higher value than gift shops not associated with a venue, as well as trinkets. These stores are sometimes a source of financial support for educational institutions.

CAFETERIA

A cafeteria is a type of food service location in which there is little or no waiting staff table service, whether a restaurant or within an institution such as a large office building or school; a school dining location is also referred to as a dining hall or canteen (in UK English). Cafeterias are different from coffeehouses, although that is the Spanish meaning of the English word.

Instead of table service, there are food-serving counters/ stalls, either in a line or allowing arbitrary walking paths. Customers take the food they require as they walk along, placing it on a tray. In addition, there are often stations where customers order food and wait while it is prepared, particularly for items such as hamburgers or tacos which must be served hot and can be quickly prepared. Alternatively, the patron is given a number and the item is brought to their table. Sometimes, for some food items and drinks, customers collect an empty container, pay at the check-out, and fill the container after the check-out. Free second servings are often allowed under this system. For legal purposes (and the consumption patterns of customers), this system is rarely or never used for alcoholic beverages in the USA.

Customers are either charged a flat rate for admission (as in a buffet), or pay at the check-out for each item. Some self-service cafeterias charge by the weight of items on a patron's plate.

As cafeterias require few employees, they are often found within a larger institution, catering to the clientele of that institution. For example, schools, colleges and their residence halls, department stores, hospitals, museums, military bases, prisons, and office buildings often have cafeterias.

At one time, upscale cafeteria-style restaurants dominated the culture of the Southern United States, and to a lesser extent the Midwest. There were several prominent chains of them: Bickford's, Morrison's Cafeteria, Piccadilly Cafeteria, S&W Cafeteria, Apple House, K&W, Britling, Wyatt's Cafeteria, and Blue Boar among them. Currently two midwest chains still exist, Sloppy Jo's Lunchroom and Manny's, both located in Illinois. There were also a number of smaller chains, usually in and around a single city. These institutions, with the exception of K&W, went into a decline in the 1960s with the rise of fast food and were largely finished off in the 1980s by the rise of "casual dining". A few chains — notably Luby's and Piccadilly Cafeterias (which took over the Morrison's chain), continue to fill some of the gap left by the decline of the older chains. Many of the smaller Midwestern chains, such as MCL Cafeterias centered around Indianapolis, are still very much in business.

The world's largest non-military cafeteria is in the Brody Complex at Michigan State University.

History

Perhaps the first self-service restaurant (not necessarily cafeteria) in the United States was the Exchange Buffet in New York City, opened September 4, 1885, which catered to an exclusively male clientele. Food was purchased at a counter, and patrons ate standing up. This represents the predecessor of two formats: the cafeteria, described below, and the automat. During the 1893 World's Columbian Exposition in Chicago, an entrepreneur named John Kruger built an American version of the smörgåsbords he had seen while traveling in Sweden. Emphasizing the simplicity and light fare, he called it the "Cafeteria" - Spanish for "coffee shop". The exposition attracted over 27 million visitors (half the US population at the time) in six months, and it was initially through Kruger's operation that America first heard the term and experienced the self-service dining format.

Meanwhile, in everyday, hometown America, the chain of Childs Restaurants was quickly growing from about 10 locations in New York City (in 1890), to hundreds across the United States and Canada (by 1920). Childs is credited with the critical innovation of adding trays and a "tray line" to the self-service format, which they introduced in 1898 at their 130 Broadway location. Childs did not change its format of sit-down dining, however. This was soon the standard design for most Childs Restaurants - and many imitators - from coast-to-coast, and ultimately the dominant design for cafeterias.

It has also been said that the "cafeteria craze started in May 1905, when a woman named Helen Mosher opened a humble downtown L.A. restaurant where people chose their food at a long counter and carried their own trays to their tables." California does have a long and rich history in the cafeteria format - most notably the many Boos Brothers Cafeterias, and also Clifton's and Schaber's. However, the facts do not warrant the "wellspring" characterization that some have ascribed to the region. The earliest cafeterias in California were opened at least 12 years after Kruger's Cafeteria, and Childs already had several dozen locations scattered around the country. Finally, Horn & Hardart, an automat format chain (only slightly different from the cafeteria), was also well established in the mid-Atlantic region before 1900.

Between 1960 and 1980, the popularity of cafeteria format restaurants was gradually overcome by the emergence of the fast food restaurant and fast casual restaurant formats.

Other Names

A cafeteria in a U.S. military installation is known as a chow hall, a mess hall, a galley, mess decks or, more formally, a dining facility, whereas in common British Armed Forces parlance, it is known as a cookhouse or mess. Students in the USA often refer to cafeterias as lunchrooms, though breakfast as well as lunch is often eaten there. Cafeterias serving university dormitories are sometimes called dining halls or dining commons. A food court is a type of cafeteria found in many shopping malls and airports featuring multiple food vendors or concessions, although a food court could equally be styled as a type of restaurant as well, being more aligned with public, rather than institutionalised, dining.

Some monasteries, boarding schools and older universities refer to their cafeteria as a refectory. Modern-day British cathedrals and abbeys, notably in the Church of England, often use the phrase refectory to describe a cafeteria open to the public. Historically, the refectory was generally only used by monks and priests. For example, although the original 800-year-old refectory at Gloucester Cathedral (the stage setting for dining scenes in the Harry Potter movies) is now mostly used as a choir practice area, the relatively modern 300-year-old extension, now used as a cafeteria by staff and public alike, is today referred to as the refectory.

A cafeteria located in a television studio is often called a commissary. NBC's commissary, The Hungry Peacock, was often joked about by Johnny Carson on The Tonight Show.

College Cafeteria

A college cafeteria is a term in the United States that denotes a cafeteria that is designed to serve college students at the university. In the UK the word *refectory* is often used. Also see the different meanings of the word college around the Anglosphere. These cafeterias can be a part of a residence hall or in a separate building. Many of these colleges employ their own students to work in the cafeteria. The amount of meals served to students varies from school to school, but is normally around 20 meals per week. Like normal cafeterias, a person will have a tray to select the food that they want, but instead of paying money, they pay beforehand by purchasing a meal plan.

The method of payment for college cafeterias is commonly in the form of a meal plan, whereby the patron pays a certain amount at the start of the semester and the details of the plan are stored on a computer system. Student ID cards are then used to access the meal plan. A meal plan is not necessary to eat at a college cafeteria however. Meal plans can vary widely in their details to best fit the needs of the students.

Typically, the college tracks the student's usage of their plan by counting either the number of pre-defined meal servings, points, dollars, or number of buffet dinners. The plan may give the student a certain number of any of the above per week or semester and they may or may not roll over to the next week or semester.

Many schools offer several different options for using their meal plans. The main cafeteria is usually where most of the meal plan is used but smaller cafeterias, cafés, restaurants, bars, or even fast food chains located on campus may accept meal plans. A college cafeteria system often has a virtual monopoly on the students due to an isolated location or a requirement that residence contracts include a full meal plan. It is not uncommon for the entire food service operation to be outsourced to a managed services company such as Aramark, Sodexo and Compass Group (under the Scolarest name in the United Kingdom).

CAFÉ

A café also spelled cafe[a], may in the United States mean an informal restaurant, offering a range of hot meals and made-to-order sandwiches, while in most other countries it refers to an establishment which focuses on serving coffee, like an American coffeehouse. Origin of the term "café" is from French for coffee.

In Europe

In most European countries, such as Austria, France, Denmark, Germany, Norway, Sweden, Portugal, etc., the term café implies primarily serving coffee, typically accompanied by a slice of cake/tart/pie, a "danish pastry", a bun, or similar sweet pastry. Many (or most) cafés also serve light meals such as sandwiches. European cafés often have tables on the pavement as well as indoors. Some cafés also serve alcoholic beverages, particularly in Southern European countries.

In the United Kingdom and Republic of Ireland a café (with the acute accent) is similar to those in other European countries, while a cafe (without acute accent) is more likely to be a greasy spoon style eating place, serving mainly fried food, in particular breakfast dishes.

In the Netherlands and Belgium, a *café* is the equivalent of a bar, and also sells alcoholic beverages. A coffeeshop in the Netherlands sells soft drugs (cannabis and hashish) and is generally not allowed to sell alcoholic beverages.

In North America

A café or coffee shop is a restaurant with full-service tables and counters and broad menu offerings over extended periods of the day. In hotels, the coffee shop is a more popular-priced alternative to the formal dining room. Coffee shops often encourage families and provide special menus for children. To establish a family-friendly atmosphere, in many localities they do not serve wine or beer.

The most common English spelling, *café*, is the French, Portuguese and Spanish spelling, and was adopted by English-speaking countries in the late 19th century. As English generally makes little use of diacritical marks, anglicisation includes a tendency to omit them and to place the onus on the readers to remember how it's pronounced, without being given the accents. Thus the spelling *cafe* has become very common in English-language usage throughout the world, especially for the less formal, i.e. "greasy spoon" variety (although orthographic proscriptivists often disapprove of it). The Italian spelling, *caffè*, is also sometimes used in English. In southern England, especially around London in the 1950s, the French pronunciation was often facetiously altered to /Ềkæf/ and spelt *caff*.

The English words *coffee* and *café* both descend from the continental European translingual word root /kafe/, which appears in many European languages with various naturalized spellings, including Italian (*caffè*); Portuguese, Spanish, and French (*café*); German (*Kaffee*); Polish (*kawa*); and others.

European awareness of coffee (the plant, its seeds, the beverage made from the seeds, and the shops that sell the beverage) came through Europeans' contact with Turkey, and the Europeans borrowed both the beverage and the word root from the Turks, who got them from the Arabs. The Arabic name *qahwa* was transformed into *kaweh* (strength, vigor) in the Ottoman Empire, and it spread from there to Europe, probably first through the Mediterranean languages (Italian, Spanish, French, Catalan, etc.) and thence to German, English, and others, though there is another well-based theory that it first spread to Europe through Poland and Ukraine, through their contacts with the Ottoman Empire.

COFFEEHOUSE

A coffeehouse or coffee shop is an establishment which primarily serves prepared coffee or other hot beverages. It shares some of the characteristics of a bar, and some of the characteristics of a restaurant, but it is different from a cafeteria. As the name suggests, coffeehouses focus on providing coffee and tea as well as light snacks. Many coffee houses in the Middle East, and in West Asian immigrant districts in the Western world, offer *shisha* (*nargile* in Turkish and Greek), flavored tobacco smoked through a hookah. From a cultural standpoint, coffeehouses largely serve as centers of social interaction: the coffeehouse provides social members with a place to congregate, talk, write, read, entertain one another, or pass the time, whether individually or in small groups of 2 or 3.

In the United States, the French word for coffeehouse (café) means an informal restaurant, offering a range of hot meals.

History

The Ottoman chronicler Ibrahim Peçevi reports the opening of the first coffeehouse in Istanbul:

> Until the year 962 [1555], in the High, God-Guarded city of Constantinople, as well as in Ottoman lands generally, coffee and coffee-houses did not exist. About

that year, a fellow called Hakam from Aleppo and a wag called Shams from Damascus came to the city; they each opened a large shop in the district called Tahtakale, and began to purvey coffee.

Various legends involving the introduction of coffee to Istanbul at a "Kiva Han" in the late 15th century circulate in culinary tradition, but with no documentation.

Coffeehouses in Mecca soon became a concern as places for political gatherings to the imams who banned them, and the drink, for Muslims between 1512 and 1524. In 1530, the first coffee house was opened in Damascus, and not long after there were many coffee houses in Cairo.

The 17th Century French traveler Jean Chardin gave a lively description of the Persian coffeehouse scene:

> People engage in conversation, for it is there that news is communicated and where those interested in politics criticize the government in all freedom and without being fearful, since the government does not heed what the people say. Innocent games... resembling checkers, hopscotch, and chess, are played. In addition, mollas, dervishes, and poets take turns telling stories in verse or in prose. The narrations by the mollas and the dervishes are moral lessons, like our sermons, but it is not considered scandalous not to pay attention to them. No one is forced to give up his game or his conversation because of it. A molla will stand up in the middle, or at one end of the qahveh-khaneh, and begin to preach in a loud voice, or a dervish enters all of a sudden, and chastises the assembled on the vanity of the world and its material goods. It often happens that two or three people talk at the same time, one on one side, the other on the opposite, and sometimes one will be a preacher and the other a storyteller.

Coffee in Europe

In the 17th century, coffee appeared for the first time in Europe outside the Ottoman Empire, and coffeehouses were established and quickly became popular. The first coffeehouses reached Western Europe probably through the Kingdom of Hungary, (thus this was the mediator between the Holy Roman Empire and the Ottoman Empire) and appeared in Venice, due to the trafficks between La Serenissima and the Ottomans; the very first one is recorded in 1645. The first coffeehouse in England was set up in Oxford in 1652 by a Jewish man named Jacob at the Angel in the parish of St Peter in the East in a building now known as "The Grand Cafe". A plaque on the wall still commemorates this and the cafe is now a trendy cocktail bar. Oxford's Queen's Lane Coffee House, established in 1654, is also still in existence today. The first coffeehouse in London was opened in 1652 in St Michael's Alley, Cornhill. The proprietor was Pasqua Rosée, the Armenian servant of a trader in Turkish goods named Daniel Edwards, who imported the coffee and assisted Rosée in setting up the establishment in St Michael's Alley, Cornhill.

By 1675, there were more than 3,000 coffeehouses in England. Pasqua Rosée also established Paris' first coffeehouse in 1672 and held a city-wide coffee monopoly until Procopio Cutò opened the Café Procope in 1686. This coffeehouse still exists today and was a major meeting place of the French Enlightenment; Voltaire, Rousseau, and Denis Diderot frequented it, and it is arguably the birthplace of the *Encyclopédie*, the first modern encyclopedia. America had its first coffeehouse in Boston, in 1676.

A rebuted tale of Vienna's first cafeteria said that it was founded in 1683 by a Polish resident, Jerzy Franciszek Kulczycki. In general, the first Polish cafes where founded in Warsaw in 1724 by one of the courtiers of Polish King August II Sass. However the whole culture of drinking coffee was itself widespread in the country in the second half of XVIII century. The first registered coffee house in Vienna was founded by the Greek Johannes Theodat (also known as Johannes Diodato) in 1685. Fifteen years later, four Greek owned coffeehouses had the privilege to serve coffee.

Though Charles II later tried to suppress the London coffeehouses as "places where the disaffected met, and spread scandalous reports concerning the conduct of His Majesty and his Ministers", the public flocked to them. For several decades following the Restoration, the Wits gathered round John Dryden at Will's Coffee House, in Russell Street, Covent Garden. The coffee houses were great social levellers, open to all men and indifferent to social status, and as a result associated with equality and republicanism. More generally, coffee houses became meeting places where business could be carried on, news exchanged and the *London Gazette* (government announcements) read. Lloyd's of London had its origins in a coffeehouse run by Edward Lloyd, where underwriters of ship insurance met to do business. By 1739, there were 551 coffeehouses in London; each attracted a particular clientele divided by occupation or attitude, such as Tories and Whigs, wits and stockjobbers, merchants and lawyers, booksellers and authors, men of fashion or the "cits" of the old city center. According to one French visitor, Antoine François Prévost, coffeehouses, "where you have the right to read all the papers for and against the government," were the "seats of English liberty."

The banning of women from coffeehouses was not universal, but does appear to have been common in Europe. In Germany women frequented them, but in England and France they were banned. Émilie du Châtelet purportedly wore drag to gain entrance to a coffeehouse in Paris. In a well-known engraving of a Parisian coffeehouse of c. 1700, the gentlemen hang their hats on pegs and sit at long communal tables strewn with papers and writing implements. Coffeepots are ranged at an open fire, with a hanging cauldron of boiling water. The only woman present presides, separated in a canopied booth, from which she serves coffee in tall cups.

The traditional tale of the origins of the Viennese café begins with the mysterious sacks of green beans left behind when the Turks were defeated in the Battle of Vienna in

1683. All the sacks of coffee were granted to the victorious Polish king Jan III Sobieski, who in turn gave them to one of his officers, Jerzy Franciszek Kulczycki. Kulczycki began the first coffeehouse in Vienna with the hoard. However, it is now widely accepted that the first coffeehouse was actually opened by an Greek merchant named Johannes Diodato.

In London, coffeehouses preceded the club of the mid-18th century, which skimmed away some of the more aristocratic clientele. Jonathan's Coffee-House in 1698 saw the listing of stock and commodity prices that evolved into the London Stock Exchange. Auctions in salesrooms attached to coffeehouses provided the start for the great auction houses of Sotheby's and Christie's. In Victorian England, the temperance movement set up coffeehouses for the working classes, as a place of relaxation free of alcohol, an alternative to the public house (pub).

In the 19th and 20th century, coffeehouses were commonly meeting point for writers and artists, across Europe.

Coffee in the United States

Coffee shops in the United States arose from the espresso- and pastry-centered Italian coffeehouses of the Italian American immigrant communities in the major U.S. cities, notably New York City's Little Italy and Greenwich Village, Boston's North End, and San Francisco's North Beach. From the late 1950s onward, coffeehouses also served as a venue for entertainment, most commonly folk performers during the American folk music revival. This was likely due to the ease at accommodating in a small space a lone performer accompanying himself or herself only with a guitar. Both Greenwich Village and North Beach became major haunts of the Beats, who were highly identified with these coffeehouses.

As the youth culture of the 1960s evolved, non-Italians consciously copied these coffeehouses. The political nature of much of 1960s folk music made the music a natural tie-in with coffeehouses with their association with political action. A number of well known performers like Joan Baez and Bob Dylan began their careers performing in coffeehouses. Blues singer Lightnin' Hopkins bemoaned his woman's inattentiveness to her domestic situation due to her overindulgence in coffeehouse socializing in his 1969 song "Coffeehouse Blues". Starting in 1967 with the opening of the historic Last Exit on Brooklyn coffeehouse, Seattle became known for its thriving countercultural coffeehouse scene; the Starbucks chain later standardized and mainstreamed this espresso bar model.

From the 1960s through the mid-1980s, many churches and individuals in the United States used the coffeehouse concept for outreach. They were often storefronts and had names like *The Gathering Place* (Riverside, CA), *Catacomb Chapel* (New York City), and *Jesus For You* (Buffalo, NY). Christian music (guitar-based) was performed, coffee and food was provided, and Bible studies were convened as people of varying backgrounds gathered in a casual "unchurchy" setting. These coffeehouses usually had a rather short life, about three to five years or so on average. An out-of-print book, published by the ministry of David Wilkerson, titled, *A Coffeehouse Manual*, served as a guide for Christian coffeehouses, including a list of name suggestions for coffeehouses.

In general, prior to about 1990, true coffeehouses were little known in most American cities, apart from those located on or near college campuses, or in districts associated with writers, artists, or the counterculture. During this time the word "coffeeshop" usually denoted family-style restaurants that served full meals, and of whose revenue coffee represented only a small portion. More recently that usage of the word has waned and now "coffeeshop" often refers to a true coffeehouse.

Format

Cafes may have an outdoor section (terrace, *pavement*

or sidewalk cafe) with seats, tables and parasols. This is especially the case with European cafes. Cafes offer a more open public space compared to many of the traditional pubs they have replaced, which were more male dominated with a focus on drinking alcohol.

One of the original uses of the cafe, as a place for information exchange and communication, was reintroduced in the 1990s with the Internet café or Hotspot (Wi-Fi). The spread of modern style cafes to many places, urban and rural, went hand in hand with computers. Computers and Internet access in a contemporary-styled venue helps to create a youthful, modern, outward-looking place, compared to the traditional pubs or old-fashioned diners that they replaced. Coffee shops like The Coffee Bean & Tea Leaf and Peet's now offer free Wi-Fi in most stores.

International Variation

In the Middle East, the coffeehouse (āÞåìð *maqhan* in Arabic, Þåææå ÎÇäå *qahveh-khaneh* in Persian or *kahvehane* or *kýraathane* in Turkish) serves as an important social gathering place for men. Men assemble in coffeehouses to drink coffee (usually Arabic coffee) or tea, listen to music, read books, play chess and backgammon, and in many coffeehouses around the Middle East, hookah is traditionally served as well.

In Australia, coffee shops are generally called 'cafés'. Since the post-World War II influx of Italian immigrants introduced espresso coffee machines to Australia in the 1950s, there has been a steady rise in café culture. The past decade has seen a rapid rise in demand for locally (or on-site) roasted specialty coffee, particularly in Melbourne due in part to the hipster, student, or artist population, with the 'Flat-White' (an Auckland, New Zealand invention) a popular coffee drink.

In the United Kingdom, traditional coffeehouses as gathering places for youths fell out of favour after the

1960s, but the concept has been revived since the 1990s by chains such as Starbucks, Coffee Republic, Costa Coffee, Caffè Nero and Prêt as places for professional workers to meet and eat out or simply to buy beverages and snack foods on their way to and from the workplace.

In France, a café also serves alcoholic beverages. French cafés often serve simple snacks such as sandwiches. They may have a restaurant section. A *brasserie* is a café that serves meals, generally single dishes, in a more relaxed setting than a restaurant. A *bistro* is a café / restaurant, especially in Paris. After the enlightenment era however, coffee houses became increasingly difficult to distinguish from taverns as they ceased to be popular meeting places for scientists and philosophers and were replaced by a growing number of tea gardens which served a drastically different purpose.

In China, an abundance of recently-started domestic coffeehouse chains may be seen accommodating business people. These coffee houses are more for show and status than anything else, with coffee prices often even higher than in the West.

In Malaysia and Singapore, traditional breakfast and coffee shops are called kopi tiams. The word is a portmanteau of the Malay word for *coffee* (as borrowed and altered from the Portuguese) and the Hokkien dialect word for *shop* (— ^; POJ: tiàm). Menus typically feature simple offerings: a variety of foods based on egg, toast, and coconut jam, plus coffee, tea, and Milo, a malted chocolate drink which is extremely popular in Southeast Asia and Australasia, particularly Singapore and Malaysia.

In parts of the Netherlands where the sale of cannabis is decriminalized, many cannabis shops call themselves coffeeshops. Foreign visitors often find themselves quite at a loss when they find that the shop they entered to have a coffee actually has a very different *core business*.

Incidentally, most cannabis shops sell a wide range of (non-alcoholic) beverages.

In modern Turkey and the Arab World, coffeehouses attract many men and boys to watch TV or play chess and smoke *shisha*. Coffeehouses are called "'ahwah" in the Arab world and combine serving coffee as well as tea and herbal teas. Tea is called "shay", and coffee is also called "'ahwah". Finally, herbal teas, like hibiscus tea (called karkadeh, or Ennab) are also highly popular.

Espresso Bar

The espresso bar is a type of coffeehouse that specializes in coffee beverages made from espresso. Originating in Italy, the espresso bar has spread throughout the world in various forms. Prime examples that are internationally known are Starbucks Coffee, based in Seattle, Washington, U.S. and Costa Coffee, based in Dunstable, UK (the first and second largest coffeehouse chains respectively), although the espresso bar exists in some form throughout much of the world.

The espresso bar is typically centered around a long counter with a high-yield espresso machine (usually bean to cup machines, automatic or semiautomatic pump-type machine, although occasionally a manually-operated lever-and-piston system) and a display case containing pastries and occasionally savory items such as sandwiches. In the traditional Italian bar, customers either order at the bar and consume their beverages standing or, if they wish to sit down and be served, are usually charged a higher price. In some bars there is an additional charge for drinks served at an outside table. In other countries, especially the United States, seating areas for customers to relax and work are provided free of charge. Some espresso bars also sell coffee paraphernalia, candy, and even music.

North American espresso bars were also at the forefront of widespread adoption of public WiFi access points to provide Internet services to people doing work on laptop computers on the premises.

The offerings at the typical espresso bar are generally quite Italianate in inspiration; biscotti, cannoli and pizzelle are a common traditional accompaniment to a caffe latte or cappuccino. Some upscale espresso bars even offer alcoholic beverages such as grappa and sambuca. Nevertheless, typical pastries are not always strictly Italianate and common additions include scones, muffins, croissants, and even doughnuts. There is usually a large selection of teas as well, and the North American espresso bar culture is responsible for the popularization of the Indian spiced tea drink masala chai. Iced drinks are also popular in some countries, including both iced tea and iced coffee as well as blended drinks such as Starbucks' Frappucino.

A worker in an espresso bar is referred to as a barista. The barista is a skilled position that requires familiarity with the drinks being made (often very elaborate, especially in North American-style espresso bars), a reasonable facility with some rather esoteric equipment as well as the usual customer service skills.

The Expresso Bar in the United Kingdom

Haunts for teenagers in particular, Italian-run espresso bars and their formica-topped tables were a feature of 1950s Soho that provided a backdrop as well as a title for Cliff Richard's 1960 film *Expresso Bongo*. The first was The Moka in Frith Street, opened by Gina Lollobrigida in 1953. With their 'exotic Gaggia coffee machine[s],...Coke, Pepsi, weak frothy coffee and...Suncrush orange fountain[s]' they spread to other urban centres during the 1960s, providing cheap, warm places for young people to congregate and an ambience far removed from the global coffee bar standard which would be established in the final decades of the century by chains such as Starbucks and Pret A Manger.

BAR

A bar is a commercial establishment that serves alcoholic drinks — beer, wine, liquor, and cocktails — for consumption on the premises. Bars provide stools or chairs that are placed at tables or counters for their patrons. Some bars have entertainment on a stage, such as a live band, comedians, go-go dancers, or strippers. Types of bars range from dive bars to elegant places of entertainment for the elite. Many bars have a happy hour to encourage off-peak patronage. Bars that fill to capacity sometimes implement a cover charge during their peak hours. Such bars often feature entertainment, which may be a live band or a popular disk jockey. The term "bar" is derived from the specialized counter on which drinks are served. The "back bar" is a set of shelves of glasses and bottles behind that counter. In some establishments, the back bar is elaborately decorated with woodwork, etched glass, mirrors, and lights.

History

There have been many names throughout history for establishments where people gather to drink alcoholic beverages. Even when an establishment uses a different name, such as "tavern," the area of the establishment where the bartender serves alcoholic beverages is normally called "the bar." There were prohibitions of alcoholic beverages in the first half of the 20th century in several countries, including Finland, Iceland, Norway, and the United States.

In the United States, illegal bars during Prohibition were called speakeasies or blind pigs.

Legal Restrictions

Laws in many jurisdictions prohibit minors from entering a bar. Cities and towns usually have legal restrictions on where bars may be located and on the types of alcohol they may serve to their customers. Some Muslim countries, including Brunei, Iran, Libya, Saudi Arabia, and the UAE emirate of Sharjah, prohibit bars for religious reasons.

Some other Muslim countries, including Bahrain, Qatar, and the United Arab Emirates, do allow bars but only permit non-Muslims to drink in them.

Types of Bars

A bar's owners and managers will choose the bar's name, décor, drink menu, lighting, and other elements which they think will attract a certain kind of patron. However, they have only limited influence over who patronizes their establishment. Thus, a bar intended for one demographic can become popular with another. For example, a gay bar with a dance floor might, over time, attract an increasingly straight clientele. Or a blues bar may become a biker bar if most its patrons are bikers.

A cocktail lounge is an up scale bar that is typically located within a hotel, restaurant, or airport.

A wine bar is an elegant bar that serves only wine (no beer or liquor). Patrons of these bars may taste wines before deciding to buy them. Some wine bars also serve snacks.

A dive bar is a very informal bar.

Entertainment

Bars categorized by the kind of entertainment they offer include:

- Topless bars, where topless female employees dance or serve drinks
- Sports bars, where sports fans watch games on large-screen televisions
- Salsa bars, where patrons dance to Latin salsa music
- Dance bars, which have a dance floor where patrons dance to recorded music. But if a dance bar has a

large dance floor and hires well-known professional DJs, it is considered to be nightclub or discotheque.

Patrons

Bars categorized by the kind of patrons who frequent them include:

- Biker bars, which are bars frequented by motorcycle enthusiasts and (in some regions) motorcycle club members
- Gay bars, where gay men or women dance and socialize
- Cop bars, where off-duty law enforcement agents gather
- Singles bars where (mostly) unmarried people of both sexes can meet and socialize

Bar (Counter)

The counter at which drinks are served by a bartender is called "the bar". This term is applied, as a synecdoche, to drinking establishments called "bars". The bar typically stores a variety of beers, wines, liquors, and non-alcoholic ingredients, and is organized to facilitate the bartender's work.

The word "bar" in this context was already in use by 1592 at the latest, as the dramatist Robert Greene referred to one in his *A Noteable Discovery of Coosnage*. However, it has been suggested that the method of serving from a counter was invented by Isambard Kingdom Brunel, the great Victorian engineer, as a means of more quickly serving the sudden rush of customers caused by passenger trains arriving at the refreshment rooms at Swindon railway station while the Great Western Railway trains changed locomotives. It has also been claimed that the first bar to serve alcohol was installed at the Great Western Hotel on Paddington station, London.

Counters for serving other types of food and drink may

also be called bars. Examples include salad bars, sushi bars, and sundae bars.

Locations

Australia

In Australia the major form of licenced commercial alcohol outlet from the colonial period to the present was the pub, a local variant of the English original. Until the 1970s, Australian pubs were traditionally organized into gender-segregated d⸱ 'nking areas—the "public bar" was only open to men, while the 'lounge bar' or 'saloon bar' served both men and women (i.e. mixed drinking). This distinction was gradually eliminated as anti-discrimination legislation and women's rights activism broke down the concept of a public drinking area accessible to only men. Where two bars still exist in the one establishment, one (that derived from the 'public bar') will be more downmarket while the other (deriving from the 'lounge bar') will be more upmarket. Over time, with the introduction of gaming machines into hotels, many 'lounge bars' have or are being converted into gaming rooms.

Beginning in the mid-1950s, the formerly strict state liquor licencing laws were progressively relaxed and reformed, with the result that pub trading hours were extended. This was in part to eliminate the social problems associated with early closing times—notably the infamous "Six O'Clock Swill" — and the thriving trade in "sly grog" (illicit alcohol sales). More licenced liquor outlets began to appear, including retail "bottle shops" (over-the-counter bottle sales were previously only available at pubs and were strictly controlled). Particularly in Sydney, a new class of licenced premises, the wine bar, appeared; there alcohol could be served on the proviso that it was provided in tandem with a meal. These venues became very popular in the late 1960s and early 1970s and many offered free entertainment, becoming an important facet of the Sydney music scene in that period.

In the major Australian cities today there is a large and diverse bar scene with a range of ambiences, modes and styles catering for every echelon of cosmopolitan society.

Canada

Canada has absorbed many of the public house traditions common in the UK, such as the drinking of dark ales and stouts. Canada adopted the UK-style tavern (also adopted by the U.S), which was the most popular type of bar throughout the 1960s and 1970s, especially for working class people. Canadian taverns, which can still be found in remote regions of Northern Canada, have long tables with benches lining the sides. Patrons in these taverns often order beer in large quart bottles and drink inexpensive "bar brand" Canadian rye whisky. In some provinces, taverns used to have separate entrances for men and women.

Canada has adopted many of the newer U.S. bar traditions (such as the "biker bar", and the "sports bar") of the last decades. As a result the term "bar" has often come to be differentiated with the term "pub", in that bars are usually 'themed' and often have a dance floor (such as a dance bar), as opposed to establishments which call themselves pubs, which are often much more similar to a British tavern in style. Before the mid-1980s most "bar" like establishments that sold alcohol were simply referred to as taverns, regardless of what they looked like or what they sold. As with any major lifestyle trend that occurs in the U.S. the "bar" trend promptly spread to Canada. Canadian sports bars are usually decorated with merchandise and paraphernalia featuring the local hockey team, and patrons watch the games on large-screen televisions. Starting in the mid-1990s taverns started to take on the look, feel and even the names of the U.K type pubs. A simple example would be the name "The Fox and Fiddle" as a pub name, whereas names like these rarely existed before. There is huge proportion of bars compared to pubs.

Legal restrictions on bars are set by the Canadian provinces and territories, which has led to a great deal of variety. While some provinces have been very restrictive with their bar regulation, setting strict closing times and banning the removal of alcohol from the premises, other provinces have been more liberal. Closing times generally run from 2:00 to 4:00 a.m.

In Nova Scotia, particularly in Halifax, there was, until the 1980s, a very distinct system of gender-based laws were in effect for decades. Taverns, bars, halls, and other classifications differentiated whether it was exclusively for men or women, men with invited women, vice-versa, or mixed. After this fell by the wayside, the issue of water closets led many powder rooms in taverns being either constructed later, or in kitchens or upstairs halls where plumbing allowed, and the same in former sitting rooms for men's facilities.

India

Bars in India are mainly clustered in metro cities, like Delhi, Mumbai, Bangalore, Hyderabad, Goa Manipal etc. Bangalore is sometimes referred to as the city of pubs as there are over 200 bars and pubs located in the city. The state of Goa also has a large number of bars and pubs because of tourism. The rest of the country has very few bar formats. Mostly, drinks are served in establishments such as restaurants. Locally made liquor (fenny, toddy etc.) is also exclusively sold at establishments. They do not serve traditional liquor but usually serve several snacks and food. These establishments are usually run-down, and their clientele consists mainly of working-class people.

More recently, bars are showing up in smaller cities; but, these establishments cater to a mostly male clientele and are unlike the social hubs of the west. For example, in Chandigarh, one of the most modern city of India, administration has developed Taverns where people can buy liquor at market price and have it along with snacks being served in a decent sitting restaurant that accompanies the wine shop.

In Manipal, many bars serve patrons standing at the counter — no seating arrangements are provided. All the bars are crowded with students

In the last few years, many international brands have entered the market, like 'Hard Rock Cafe', 'TGI Friday's', Ruby Tuesday's', Pop Tate's, 'Ministry of Sound(MOS)', etc. Similar chains of bars are now starting to emerge from within the country. Shalom, Laidbackwaters, Geoffrey's Dhadkkan at Solan, Himachal Pradesh and All Sports Bar are among the few popular ones.

Italy

In Italy, a "bar" is a place more similar to a *café*, where people go during the morning or the afternoon, usually to take a coffee, a cappuccino, a hot chocolate and eat some kind of snack like pastries and sandwiches (*panini* or *tramezzini*). However, any kind of alcoholic beverages are served. Opening hours vary: some establishments are open very early in the morning and close relatively early in the evening; others, especially if next to a theater or a cinema, may be open until late at night. In larger cities like Milan, Rome, Turin or Genoa, many larger bars are also restaurants and disco clubs. Many Italian bars have introduced a so-called "aperitivo" time in the evening, in which everyone who purchases an alcoholic drink then has free access to a usually abundant buffet of cold dishes like pasta salads, vegetables and various types of appetizers.

Spain

Bars in Spain are very common and form an important part in Spanish culture. In Spain it is common for a town to have many bars and even to have several lined up in the same street. Most bars have a section of the street or plaza outside with tables and chairs with parasols if the weather allows it. Spanish bars are also known for serving a wide range of sandwiches (bocadillos), as well as snacks called tapas or pinchos.

Tapas and pinchos may be offered to customers in two ways, either complementary to order a drink or in some cases there are charged independently, either case this is usually clearly indicated to bar customers by display of wall information, on menus and price lists. The anti-smoking law has entered in effect January 1, 2011 and since that date it is prohibited to smoke in bars and restaurants as well as all other indoor areas, closed commercial and state owned facilities are now smoke free areas.

Spain is the country with the highest ratio of bars/population with almost 6 bars per thousand inhabitants, that's 3 times UK's ratio and 4 times Germany's, and it alone has double the number of bars than the oldest of the 15-members of the European Union. The meaning of the word 'bar' in Spain, however, does not have the negative connotation inherent in the same word in many other languages. For Spanish people a bar is essentially a meeting place, and not necessarily a place to engage in the consumption of alcoholic beverages. As a result, children are normally allowed into bars, and it's common to see families in bars during week-ends of the end of the day. In small towns, the 'bar' may constitute the very center of social life, and it's customary that, after social events, such as the Sunday catholic mass, people go to bars, including seniors and children alike.

United Kingdom

In the UK bars are either areas that serve alcoholic drinks within establishments such as hotels, restaurants, universities, or are a particular type of establishment which serves alcoholic drinks such as wine bars, "style bars", private membership only bars. However the main type of establishment selling alcohol for consumption on the premises is the public house or *pub*. Some bars are similar to nightclubs in that they feature loud music, subdued lighting, or operate a dress code and admissions policy, with inner city bars generally having door staff at the entrance.

'Bar' also designates a separate drinking area within a pub. Until recent years most pubs had two or more bars - very often the Public bar, and the Saloon Bar, where the decor was better and prices were sometimes higher. The designations of the bars varied regionally. In the last two decades many pub interiors have been opened up into single spaces, which some people regret as it loses the flexibility, intimacy and traditional feel of a multi-roomed public house.

One of the last dive bars in London was underneath the Kings Head pub in Gerrard Street, Soho.

United States

In the United States, legal distinctions often exist between restaurants and bars, and even between types of bars. These distinctions vary from state to state, and even among municipalities. *Beer bars* (sometimes called taverns or pubs) are legally restricted to selling only beer, and possibly wine or cider. *Liquor bars* also sell hard liquor.

Bars are sometimes exempt from smoking bans that restaurants are subject to, even if those restaurants have liquor licenses. The distinction between a restaurant that serves liquor and a bar is usually made by the percentage of revenue earned from selling liquor, although increasingly, smoking bans include bars too.

In most places, bars are prohibited from selling alcoholic beverages *to go* and this makes them clearly different from liquor stores. Some brewpubs and wineries can serve alcohol *to go*, but under the rules applied to a liquor store. In some areas, such as New Orleans and parts of Las Vegas and Savannah, Georgia, open containers of alcohol may be prepared *to go*. This kind of restriction is usually dependent on an open container law. In Pennsylvania and Ohio, bars may sell six packs of beer "to-go" in original (sealed) containers by obtaining a take-out license. New Jersey permits all forms of packaged goods to be sold at bars, and permits packaged beer and wine to be sold at any time on-premises sales of alcoholic beverages are allowed. Historically, the western United States featured saloons. Many saloons survive in the western United States, though their services and features have changed with the times. Newer establishments have been built in the saloon style to duplicate the feeling of the older establishments.

Many Irish or British-themed "pubs" exist throughout United States and Canada and in some continental European countries.

DESTINATION SPA

A destination spa is a short term residential/lodging facility with the primary purpose of providing individual services for spa-goers to develop healthy habits. Historically many such spas were developed at the location of natural hot springs or sources of mineral waters. Typically over a seven-day stay, such facilities provide a comprehensive programme that includes spa services, physical fitness activities, wellness education, healthy cuisine and special interest programming.

Some destination spas offer an all-inclusive programme that includes facilitated fitness classes, healthy cuisine, educational classes and seminars as well as similar services to a beauty salon or a day spa. Guests reside and participate in the programme at a destination spa instead of just visiting for a treatment or pure vacation. Some destination spas are in exotic locations or in spa towns.

Destination spas have been in use for a considerable time, and some are not used actively, but rather are historically preserved as elements of earlier history; for example, Gilroy Yamato Hot Springs in California is such a historically used spa whose peak patronage occurred in the late 19th and early 20th century.

Resort spas are generally located in resorts and offer similar services via rooms with services, meals, body treatments and fitness a la carte.

Types of Services

Typical services include:

- Balneotherapy
- Body treatments such as body wraps, aromatherapy
- Cooking lessons
- Facials — facial cleansing with a variety of products
- Fitness consultation
- Hair spa treatment
- Massage
- Medical treatment
- Nail care (manicure), pedicure
- Nutrition counseling
- Skin exfoliation — including chemical peels and microdermabrasion
- Waxing — the removal of body hair with hot wax
- Weight loss

4

Focus on Guest House Facilities, Amenities and Functionalities

HOUSE

A house is a home, building or structure that is a dwelling or place for habitation by human beings. The term house includes many kinds of dwellings ranging from rudimentary huts of nomadic tribes to free standing individual structures. In some contexts, "house" may mean the same as dwelling, residence, home, abode, lodging, accommodation, or housing, among other meanings. The social unit that lives in a house is known as a household.

Most commonly, a household is a family unit of some kind, though households can be other social groups, such as single persons, or groups of unrelated individuals. Settled agrarian and industrial societies are composed of household units living permanently in housing of various types, according to a variety of forms of land tenure. English-speaking people generally call any building they routinely occupy "home". Many people leave their houses during the day for work and recreation, and return to them to sleep and for other activities.

Etymology

House derives directly from Old English Hus meaning 'Dwelling, shelter, house," which in turn derives from Proto-Germanic Khusan (reconstructed by etymological analysis) which is of unknown origin.

Inside the House

Layout

Ideally, architects of houses design rooms to meet the needs of the people who will live in the house. Such designing, known as "interior design", has become a popular subject in universities. Feng shui, originally a Chinese method of moving houses according to such factors as rain and micro-climates, has recently expanded its scope to address the design of interior spaces with a view to promoting harmonious effects on the people living inside the house. Feng shui can also mean the "aura" in or around a dwelling. Compare the real-estate sales concept of "indoor-outdoor flow".

The square footage of a house in the United States reports the area of "living space", excluding the garage and other non-living spaces. The "square meters" figure of a house in Europe reports the area of the walls enclosing the home, and thus includes any attached garage and non-living spaces. How many floors, or levels, the home is will play a bug role in determining the square footage of a home.

Parts

Many houses have several large rooms with specialized functions and several very small rooms for other various reasons. These may include a living/eating area, a sleeping area, and (if suitable facilities and services exist) washing and lavatory areas. Additionally, spa room, indoor pool, indoor basketball goal, and so forth. In traditional agriculture-oriented societies, domestic animals such as chickens or larger livestock (like cattle) often share part of the house with human beings. Most conventional modern houses will at least contain a bedroom, bathroom, kitchen (or kitchen area), and a living room. A typical "foursquare house" (as pictured) occurred commonly in the early history of the United States of America where they were mainly built, with a staircase in the center of the house, surrounded by four rooms, and connected to other sections of the house (including in more recent eras a garage).

The names of parts of a house often echo the names of parts of other buildings, but could typically include:

- Atrium
- Attic
- Alcove
- Basement/cellar
- Bathroom (in various senses of the word)
- Bath/shower
- Toilet
- Bedroom (or nursery, for infants or small children)
- Box-room / storage room
- Conservatory
- Dining room
- Family room or den
- Fireplace (for warmth during winter; generally not found in warmer climates)
- Foyer
- Front room (in various senses of the phrase)
- Garage
- Hallway / passage / Vestibule
- Hearth – often an important symbolic focus of family togetherness
- Kitchen
- Larder
- Laundry room
- Library
- Living room
- Loft
- Nook

- Window
- Office or study
- Pantry
- Parlour
- Pew/porch
- Recreation room / rumpus room / television room
- Shrines to serve the religious functions associated with a family
- Stairwell
- Sunroom
- Workshop

Some houses have a pool in the background, or a trampoline, or a playground.

Construction

In the United States, modern house-construction techniques include light-frame construction (in areas with access to supplies of wood) and adobe or sometimes rammed-earth construction (in arid regions with scarce wood-resources). Some areas use brick almost exclusively, and quarried stone has long provided walling. To some extent, aluminum and steel have displaced some traditional building materials. Increasingly popular alternative construction materials include insulating concrete forms (foam forms filled with concrete), structural insulated panels (foam panels faced with oriented strand board or fiber cement), and light-gauge steel framing and heavy-gauge steel framing.

More generally, people often build houses out of the nearest available material, and often tradition and/or culture govern construction-materials, so whole towns, areas, counties or even states/countries may be built out of one main type of material. For example, a large fraction of American houses use wood, while most British and many European houses utilize stone or brick.

In the 1900s, some house designers started using prefabrication. Sears, Roebuck & Co. first marketed their Sears Catalog Homes to the general public in 1908. Prefab techniques became popular after World War II. First small inside rooms framing, then later, whole walls were prefabricated and carried to the construction site. The original impetus was to use the labor force inside a shelter during inclement weather. More recently builders have begun to collaborate with structural engineers who use computers and finite element analysis to design prefabricated steel-framed homes with known resistance to high wind-loads and seismic forces. These newer products provide labor savings, more consistent quality, and possibly accelerated construction processes.

Lesser-used construction methods have gained (or regained) popularity in recent years. Though not in wide use, these methods frequently appeal to homeowners who may become actively involved in the construction process. They include:

- Cannabrick construction
- Cordwood construction
- Geodesic domes
- Straw-bale construction
- Wattle and daub

Energy-Efficiency

In the developed world, energy-conservation has grown in importance in house-design. Housing produces a major proportion of carbon emissions (30% of the total in the UK, for example).

Development of a number of low-energy building types and techniques continues. They include the zero-energy house, the passive solar house, the autonomous buildings, the superinsulated and houses built to the *Passivhaus* standard.

Earthquake Protection

One tool of earthquake engineering is base isolation which is increasingly used for earthquake protection. Base isolation is a collection of structural elements of a building that should substantially decouple it from the shaking ground thus protecting the building's integrity and enhancing its seismic performance. This technology, which is a kind of seismic vibration control, can be applied both to a newly designed building and to seismic upgrading of existing structures.

Normally, excavations are made around the building and the building is separated from the foundations. Steel or reinforced concrete beams replace the connections to the foundations, while under these, the isolating pads, or *base isolators*, replace the material removed. While the *base isolation* tends to restrict transmission of the ground motion to the building, it also keeps the building positioned properly over the foundation. Careful attention to detail is required where the building interfaces with the ground, especially at entrances, stairways and ramps, to ensure sufficient relative motion of those structural elements.

Legal Issues

Buildings with historical importance have restrictions.

United Kingdom

New houses in the UK are not covered by the Sale of Goods Act. When purchasing a new house the buyer has less legal protection than when buying a new car. New houses in the UK may be covered by a NHBC guarantee but some people feel that it would be more useful to put new houses on the same legal footing as other products.

United States and Canada

In the US and Canada, many new houses are built in housing tracts, which provide homeowners a sense of "belonging" and the feeling they have "made the best use" of their money. However, these houses are sometimes built as cheaply and quickly as possible by large builders seeking to maximize profits. Many environmental health issues may be ignored or minimized in the construction of these structures. In one case in Benicia, California, a housing tract was built over an old landfill. Home buyers were never told, and only found out when some began having reactions to high levels of lead and chromium.

Identifying Houses

With the growth of dense settlement, humans designed ways of identifying houses and/or parcels of land. Individual houses sometimes acquire proper names; and those names may acquire in their turn considerable emotional connotations: see for example the house of *Howards End* or the castle of *Brideshead Revisited*. A more systematic and general approach to identifying houses may use various methods of house numbering.

Animal Houses

Humans often build "houses" for domestic or wild animals, often resembling smaller versions of human domiciles. Familiar animal houses built by humans include bird-houses, hen-houses/chicken-coops and doghouses (kennels); while housed agricultural animals more often live in barns and stables. However, human interest in building houses for animals does not stop at the domestic pet. People build bat-houses, nesting-sites for wild ducks and other birds, bee houses, giraffe houses, kangaroo houses, worm houses, hermit crab houses, as well as shelters for many other animals.

Shelter

Forms of (relatively) simple shelter may include:

1. Bus stop
2. Camper
3. Chalet

4. Cottage
5. Izba
6. Dugout (shelter)
7. Gazebo
8. Hangar
9. Houseboat
10. Hut
11. Lean-to
12. Log cabin
13. Nuclear bunker
14. Shack
15. Tent
16. Travel trailer
17. Umbrella
18. Yaodong

Houses and Symbolism

Houses may express the circumstances or opinions of their builders or their inhabitants. Thus a vast and elaborate house may serve as a sign of conspicuous wealth, whereas a low-profile house built of recycled materials may indicate support of energy conservation. Houses of particular historical significance (former residences of the famous, for example, or even just very old houses) may gain a protected status in town planning as examples of built heritage and/or of streetscape values.

Commemorative plaques may mark such structures. Home ownership provides a common measure of prosperity in economics. Contrast the importance of house-destruction, tent dwelling and house rebuilding in the wake of many natural disasters.

Peter Olshavsky's House for the Dance of Death provides a 'pataphysical variation on the house.

Heraldry

The house occurs as a rare charge in heraldry.

BASEMENT

A basement is one or more floors of a building that are either completely or partially below the ground floor. Basements are typically used as a utility space for a building where such items as the furnace, water heater, breaker panel or fuse box, car park, and air-conditioning system are located; so also are amenities such as the electrical distribution system, and cable television distribution point.

In British English the word "basement" is used for underground floors of, for example, department stores but is used for a space below the ground floor of a house only when it is habitable, with windows and (usually) its own access. The word cellar is used to apply to any such large underground room. Subcellar is a cellar that lies further underneath.

Purpose, Geography and History

A basement can be used in almost exactly the same manner as a additional above-ground floor of a house or other building. However, the use of basements depends largely on factors specific to a particular geographical area such as climate, soil, seismic activity, building technology, and real estate economics.

Basements in small buildings such as single-family detached houses are rare in very wet climates such as Great Britain and Ireland where flooding is a problem, though they may be used on larger structures. However basements are considered standard on all but the smallest new buildings in many places with temperate continental climates such as the American Midwest and the Canadian Prairies where a concrete foundation below the frost line is needed in any case, to prevent a building from shifting during the freeze-thaw cycle. Basements are much easier to construct in areas with relatively soft soils, and may be foregone in places where the soil is too compact for easy excavation. Their use may be restricted in earthquake zones, because of the possibility of the upper floors collapsing into the basement; on the other hand, they may be required in tornado-prone areas as a shelter against the violent winds. Adding a basement can also lower heating and cooling costs as it is a form of earth sheltering, and way to lower a building's surface area-to-volume ratio. The housing density of an area will also influence whether or not a basement is considered necessary.

Historically, basements have become much easier to build (in developed countries) since the industrialization of home building. Large internal-combustion-powered excavation machines such as backhoes and front-end loaders have reduced the time and manpower needed to dig a basement dramatically as compared to digging by hand with a spade, although this method made still be used in the developing world.

For most of its early history, the basement took one of two forms. It could be little more than a cellar, or it could be a section of a building containing rooms and spaces similar to those of the rest of the structure, as in the case of basement flats and basement offices.

However, beginning with the development of large, mid-priced suburban homes in the 1950s, the basement, as a space in its own right, gradually took hold. Initially, it was typically a large, concrete-floored space, accessed by indoor stairs, and with exposed columns and beams along the walls and ceilings, or sometimes, walls of poured concrete or concrete cinder block.

Types of Basement

Daylight Basement

A daylight basement or a "walk-out basement" is

contained in a house situated on a slope, so that part of the level is above ground, with a doorway to the outside. The part of the floor covered by the ground can be considered the true basement area. From the street, some daylight basement homes appear to be one story. Others appear to be a conventional two story home from the street (with the buried, or basement, portion in the back). Occupants can walk out at that point without having to use the stairs. For example, if the ground slopes downwards towards the back of the house, the basement is at or above grade (ground level) at the back of the house. It is a modern design because of the added complexity of uneven foundations; where the basement is above grade, the foundation is deeper at that point and must still be below the frostline.

Full-size windows can be installed in a daylight basement. These can provide exits for bedrooms (building bedrooms in basements is usually illegal without an outside escape). Ventilation is improved over fully-buried basement homes, with less dampness and mold problems.

Daylight basements can be used for several purposes - as a garage, as maintenance rooms, or as living space. The buried portion is often used for storage, laundry room, hot water tanks, and HVAC.

Daylight basement homes typically appraise higher than standard-basement homes, since they include more viable living spaces. In some parts of the U.S. however the appraisal for daylight basement space is half that of ground and above ground level square footage. Designs accommodated include split-foyer and split-level homes. Garages on both levels are sometimes possible. As with any multi-level home, there are savings on roofing and foundations.

Look-out Basement

In a "look-out" basement, the basement walls extend sufficiently above ground level that some of the basement windows are above ground level. Where the site slopes gently and is insufficient for a walk-out basement, a look-out basement tends to result. Sometimes, a look-out basement is deliberately constructed even on a flat site. The advantage is that the basement windows are all above grade. The disadvantage is that the main floor entry is above grade as well, necessitating steps to get up to the main floor. The raised bungalow design solves this by lowering the entry half-way between the main floor and basement to make a dramatic, high-ceiling foyer. It is a very economical design because the basement is shallower, and excavation costs are minimized.

Walk-up Basement

A "walk-up" basement is any basement that has an exterior entrance via a stairwell. Some designs cover the stairwell with angled "basement doors" or "bulkhead doors" to keep rain water from accumulating in the stairwell.

When initially built, the main floor joists are often exposed and the walls and floors concrete (with insulation, where appropriate). Unfinished basements allow for easy access to the main floor for renovation to the main floor. Finishing the basement can add significant floor space to a house (doubling it in the case of a bungalow) and is a major renovation project

Cellar

A cellar is a type of basement primarily used for the storage of food and drink (especially wine) for use throughout the year. A cellar is intended to remain at a constant cool (not freezing) temperature all year round and usually has either a small window/opening or some form of air ventilation (air/draught bricks, etc.) in order to help eliminate damp or stale air. Cellars are more common in the UK in older houses, with most terraced housing built during late 19th, and early 20th Century having cellars. These were important shelters from air raids during World War II. In parts of the U.S. that are prone to tornadoes, cellars still serve as shelter in the event of a direct hit on the house from a tornado or other storm damage caused by strong winds.

Except for Britain, Australia and New Zealand, cellars are popular in most western countries. In the UK, almost all new homes built since the 1960s have no cellar or basement due to the extra cost of digging down further into the sub-soil and a requirement for much deeper foundations and water-proof tanking. The obverse has recently become common, where the impact of smaller home-footprints has led to roof-space being utilised for further living space and now many new homes are built with third-floor living accommodation. For this reason people tend to store food and drink in a garage. The majority of continental European houses have cellars, although a large proportion of people live in apartments or flats rather than houses. In North America, cellars usually are found in rural or older homes on the coasts and in the South. However, full basements are commonplace in new houses in the US Midwest and other areas subject to tornado activity or requiring foundations below the frost line.

Crawl Space

A crawl space (as the name suggests) is a type of basement in which one cannot stand up — the height may be as little as a foot, and the surface is often soil. They offer a convenient access to pipes, substructures and a variety of other areas that may be difficult or expensive to access otherwise. While a crawlspace cannot be used as living space, it can be used as storage, often for infrequently used items. Care must be taken in doing so, however, as water from the damp ground, water vapor (entering from crawlspace vents), and moisture seeping through porous concrete can create a perfect environment for mold/mildew to form on any surface in the crawlspace, especially cardboard boxes, wood floors and surfaces, drywall and some types of insulation.

Health and safety issues must be considered when installing a crawl space. As air warms in a home, it rises and leaves through the upper regions of the house, much in the same way that air moves through a chimney. This phenomenon, called the "stack effect," causes the home to suck air up from the crawlspace into the main area of the home. Mold spores, decomposition odors, and fecal material from dust mites in the crawlspace can come up with the air, agitating breathing problems (such as asthma) and creating a variety of health-related problems.

It is usually desirable to finish a crawlspace with a plastic vapor barrier that will not support mold growth or allow humidity from the earth into the crawlspace. This helps insulate the crawlspace and discourages the habitation of insects and vermin by breaking the ecological chain in which insects feed off the mold and vermin feed on the insects, as well as creating a physical inorganic barrier that deters entrance into the space. Vapor barriers can end at the wall or be run up the wall and fastened to provide even more protection against moisture infiltration. Some pest control agencies recommend against covering the walls as it complicates their job of inspection and spraying. Almost unheard of as late as the 1990s, vapor barriers are becoming increasingly popular in recent years, in fact, the more general topic of conditioned vs. unconditioned crawlspaces has enjoyed much research over the last decade.

Design and Structural Considerations

Structurally, for houses, the basement walls typically form the foundation. In warmer climates, some houses do not have basements because they are not necessary (although many still prefer them). In colder climates, the foundation must be below the frost line. Unless constructed in very cold climates, the frost line is not so deep as to justify an entire level below the ground, although it is usually deep enough that a basement is the assumed standard. In places with oddly stratified soil substrata or high water tables, such as most of Texas, Oklahoma, Arkansas, and areas within 50 miles (80 km) of the Gulf of Mexico, basements are usually not financially feasible unless the building is a large apartment or commercial structure. In many earthquake-prone areas, such as Southern California, basements are not common because of the possibility of collapse during an earthquake.

Some designs elect to simply leave a crawl space under the house, rather than a full basement. Most other designs justify further excavations to create a full height basement, sufficient for another level of living space. Even so, basements in Canada and the northern United States were typically only 7 feet 10 inches (2.39 m) in height, rather than the standard full 8 feet (2.44 m) of the main floors. Older homes may have even lower basement heights as the basement walls were concrete block and thus, could be customized to any height. Modern builders offer higher basements as an option. The cost of the additional depth of excavation is usually quite expensive. Thus, houses almost certainly never have multi-story basements though 9' basements heights are a frequent choice among new home buyers. For large office or apartment buildings in prime locations, the cost of land may justify multi-story basement parking garages.

The concrete floor in most basements is structurally not part of the foundation; only the basement walls are. If there are posts supporting a main floor beam to form a post and beam system, these posts typically go right through the basement floor to a footing underneath the basement floor. It is the footing that supports the post and the footing is part of the house foundation. Load-bearing wood-stud walls rest directly on the concrete floor. Under the concrete floor is typically gravel or crushed stone to facilitate draining. The floor is typically four inches (100 mm) thick and it rests on top of the foundation footings. The floor is typically sloped towards a drain point, in case of leaks.

Since warm air rises, basements are typically cooler than the rest of the house. In summer, this makes basements damp, due to the higher relative humidity. Dehumidifiers are recommended. In winter, additional heating, such as a fireplace or baseboard heaters may be required. A well-defined central heating system may minimize this requirement. Heating ducts typically run in the ceiling of the basement (since there is not an empty floor below to run the ducts). Ducts extending from the ceiling down to the floor help heat the cold floors of the basement. Older or cheaper systems may simply have the heating vent in the ceiling of the basement.

The finished floor is typically raised off the concrete basement floor. In countries such as Canada, laminate flooring is an exception: It is typically separated from the concrete by only a thin foam underlay. Radiant heating systems may be embedded within the concrete floor. Even if unfinished and unoccupied, basements are heated in order to ensure relative warmth of the floor above, and to prevent water supply pipes, drains, etc. from freezing and bursting in winter. It is recommended that the basement walls be insulated to the frost line. In Canada, the walls of a finished basement are typically insulated to the floor with vapor barriers to prevent moisture transmission. However, a finished basement should avoid wood or wood-laminate flooring, and metal framing and other moisture resistant products should be used. Finished basements can be costly to maintain due to deterioration of waterproofing materials or lateral earth movement etc. Below-ground structures will never be as dry as one above ground, and measures must be taken to circulate air and dehumidify area.

Drainage Considerations

Basement floor drains need to be filled regularly to prevent the trap from drying out and sewer gas from escaping into the basement. The drain trap can be topped up automatically by the condensation from air conditioners or high-efficiency furnaces. A small tube from another downpipe is sometimes used to keep the trap from drying out. Some advocate the use of special radon gas traps. In areas where storm and sanitary sewers are combined, and there is the risk of sewage backing up, backflow prevention devices in all basement drains may be mandated by code and definitely are recommended even if not mandated.

The main water cut-off valve is usually in the basement. Basements often have "clean outs" for the sanitary and storm sewers, where these pipes can be accessed. The storm sewer access is only needed where the weeping tiles drain into the storm sewers. Other than with walk-out or look-out basements, windows in basements require a well and are below grade. Clear window well covers may be required to keep the window wells from accumulating rain water. There should be drains in the window well, connected to the foundation drains.

If the water table outside the basement is above the height of the basement floor, then the foundation drains or the weeping tiles outside the footings may be insufficient to keep the basement dry. A sump pump may be required. It can be located anywhere and is simply in a well that is deeper than the basement floor.

Even with functioning sump pumps or low water tables, basements may become wet after rainfall, due to improper drainage. The ground next to the basement must be graded such that water flows away from the basement wall. Downspouts from roof gutters should drain freely into the storm sewer or directed away from the house. Downspouts should not be connected to the foundation draintiles. If the draintiles become clogged by leaves or debris from the rain gutters, the roof water would cause basement flooding through the draintile. Damp-proofing or waterproofing materials are typically applied to outside of the basement wall. It is virtually impossible to make a concrete wall waterproof, over the long run, so drainage is the key.

There are draining membranes that can be applied to the outside of the basement that create channels for water against the basement wall to flow to the foundation drains.

Where drainage is inadequate, waterproofing may be needed. There are numerous ways to waterproof a basement, but most systems fall into one of three categories:

- Tanking – Systems that bond to the basement structure and physically hold back groundwater.

- Cavity Drainage – Dimpled plastic membranes are used to line the floors and walls of the basement, creating a "drained cavity." Any water entering this drained cavity is diverted to a sump pump and pumped away from the basement.

- Exterior Foundation Drain – Installing an exterior foundation drain that will drain away by gravity is the most effective means to waterproof a basement. An exterior system allows water to flow away from the basement without using pumps or electricity. An exterior drain also allows for the installation of a waterproof membrane to the foundation walls.

The waterproofing system can be applied to the inside or the outside walls of a basement. When waterproofing existing basements it is much cheaper to waterproof the basement on the inside. Waterproofing on the outside requires the expense of excavation, but does offer a number of advantages for a homeowner over the long term. Among them are:

- Gravity system
- No pumps or electrical wiring required
- Membrane applied to exterior walls to prevent dampness, mold, moisture, and soil gases from entering the home
- Permanent solution

Basement Culture/Finishings

Unfinished Basement

This first unfinished design, found principally in spaces larger than the traditional cellar, is common in residences throughout America and Canada. One usually finds within it a water heater, various pipes running along the ceiling and downwards to the floor, and sometimes a workbench, a freezer or refrigerator, or a washer/dryer set. Boxes of various materials, and objects unneeded in the rest of the house, are also often stored there; in this regard, the unfinished basement takes the place both of the cellar and of the attic. Home workshops are often located in the basement, since sawdust, metal chips, and other mess or noise are less of a nuisance there. The basement can contain all of these objects and still be considered to be "unfinished," as they are either mostly or entirely functional in purpose.

Finished Basement

In this case the space has been designed, either during construction or at a later point by the owners, to function as a fully habitable addition to the house. Frequently most or all of the basement is used as a recreation room or living room, but it is not uncommon as well to find there (either instead of or alongside the living/recreation room) a guest bedroom or teenager's room, a bathroom, a home office, a home gym, a home theater, a basement bar, a sauna, and one or more closets. Occasionally a part of the basement is unfurnished and is used for storage, a workshop, and/or a laundry room; when this is the case the water heater and furnace will also often be located there, although in some cases the entire basement is finished, and the water heater and furnace are boxed off into a closet.

Partially-finished Basement

The main point of distinction between this type of basement and the two others lies in its being either entirely unmodified (unlike the finished basement) beyond the addition of furniture, recreational objects and appliances, and/or exercise equipment on the bare floor, or slightly modified through the installation (besides any or all of the aforementioned items) of loose carpet and perhaps simple light fixtures. In both cases, the objects found there— many of which could be found in a finished basement as well—might include the following: weight sets and other exercise equipment; the boom boxes or entertainment systems used during exercise; musical instruments (which are not in storage, as they would technically be in an unfinished basement; an assembled drum set would be the most easily identified of these); football tables, chairs, couches and entertainment appliances of lesser quality than those in the rest of the house; refrigerators, stand-alone freezers, and microwaves (the first and the second being also sometimes used as supplementary storage units in an unfinished basement); and sports pennants and/or other types of posters which are attached to the walls.

As the description suggests, this type of basement, which also might be called "half-finished," is likely used by teenagers and children. The entire family might utilize a work-out area. It is also common to have a secondary (or primary) home office in a partially-finished basement, as well as a workbench and/or a space for laundry appliances.

Toilets and showers sometimes exist in this variety of basement, as many North American basements are designed to allow for their installation.

Fully Finished Basement - Retro Fit

In London UK the construction of finished retrofit basements is big business with a large number of project in the 100-200 square meter bracket. There are a smaller number of project in the 200-500 square meter bracket under construction. It is also not unusual to see multi level retro-fit basements. These are considerable works of civil engineering and require some skill and intuitive understanding as well as good engineering. Given the scale of the civil engineering problems are rare but it is notable that the long established companies have a significantly better track record than the more recent start ups.

Retro Fit - Reasons for it

Given high property values digging a basement actually creates capital value at between 2-5 times cost in most areas of central London. In a lot of central London homes there simply isn't the space to extend sideways or up so down is the only option for a lot families hard pressed for space and squeezed out of the moving market by high stamp duty.

Real Estate Floorspace Measures

In Canada, historically the basement area was excluded from advertised square footage of a house as it was not part of the living space. For example, a "2,000-square-foot bungalow" would, in reality, have 4,000 square feet (370 m) of floor space. More recently, finished space has become increasingly acceptable as a measure which includes the developed basement areas of a home. Due to fire code requirements, most jurisdictions require an emergency egress (through either egress-style windows, or, in the case of a walk-out basement, a door) to include the basement square footage as living space.

ROOM

A room, in architecture, is Any distinguishable space within a structure. Usually, a room is separated from other spaces or passageways by interior walls; moreover, it is separated from outdoor areas by an exterior wall, sometimes with a door. Historically the use of rooms dates at least to early Minoan cultures about 2200 BC, where excavations on Santorini, Greece at Akrotiri reveal clearly defined rooms within certain structures.

Historical Room Types

In early structures, diverse room types could be identified

to include bedrooms, kitchens, bathing rooms, reception rooms, and other specialized uses. The aforementioned Akrotiri excavations reveal rooms sometimes built above other rooms connected by staircases, bathrooms with alabaster appliances such as washbasins, bathing tubs, and toilets, all connected to an elaborate twin plumbing systems of ceramic pipes for cold and hot water separately. Ancient Rome manifested very complex building forms with a variety of room types, including some of the earliest examples of rooms for indoor bathing. The Anasazi civilization also had an early complex development of room structures, probably the oldest in North America, while the Maya of Central America had very advanced room configurations as early as several hundred CE. By at least the early Han Dynasty in China (e.g. approximately 200 BCE), complex multi-level building forms emerged, particularly for religious and public purposes; these designs featured many roomed structures and included vertical connections of rooms.

Box-Room

Many houses are built to contain a box-room (box room or boxroom) that is easily identifiable, being smaller than the others. The small size of these rooms limits their use, and they tend to be used as a small single bedroom, small child's bedroom, or as a storage room.

Traditionally, and often seen in country houses and larger suburban houses up until the 1930s in Britain, the box room was literally for the storage of boxes, trunks, portmanteaux, and the like, rather than for bedroom use.

STUDY ROOM

A study is a room in a house which is used for paperwork, computer work, or reading. Historically, the study of a house was reserved for use as the private office and reading room of a family father as the formal head of a household, but today studies are generally either used to operate a home business or else open to the whole family. Unused cellar space is often converted into a study.

A typical study might contain a desk, chair, computer, a desk lamp or two, and bookshelves. A spare bedroom is often utilized as a study, but many modern homes have a room specifically designated as a study. Such rooms are usually located in a convenient area on the main floor of the house and may be referred to as a den, home office, or library.

The study developed from the closet or cabinet of the Renaissance onwards. The advent of electronic communication and computer technology has widened the appeal of dedicated home working areas, with nearly 20% of all working adults in the United States reporting that they undertake at least some work from home as part of their primary employment.

BEDROOM

A bedroom is a private room where people usually sleep for the night or relax during the day. Many houses in North America, Australia and Europe have at least two bedrooms—usually a master bedroom (dedicated to the heads of the household, such as a husband and wife) and one or more bedrooms for either the children or guests.

In some jurisdictions there are basic features (such as a closet and a "means of egress") which a room must have in order to be qualify as a bedroom. In many states, such as Alaska, bedrooms are not required to have closets and must instead meet minimum size requirements.

In buildings with multiple self-contained housing units (e.g., apartments), the number of bedrooms varies widely. While many such units have at least one bedroom—frequently, these units have at least two—some of these units may not have a specific room dedicated for use as a bedroom. (These units may be known by various names, including *studio, efficiency, bedsit,* and others.)

Furniture and other items in bedrooms vary greatly, depending on taste and local tradition. For instance, a master bedroom may include a bed of a specific size (double, king or queen-sized); one or more dressers (or perhaps, a wardrobe armoire); a nightstand; one or more closets; and carpeting. Built-in closets are less common in Europe than in North America; thus there is greater use of freestanding wardrobes or armoires in Europe.

Bedding used in northern Europe (especially in Scandinavia) is significantly different from that used in North America and other parts of Europe. In Japan futons are common. Some bedrooms also include such items as a make-up desk, television, personal computer, air conditioning and various accessories (such as lamps, telephone and an alarm clock). Sometimes, a master bedroom is connected to a dedicated bathroom, often called an ensuite.

Children's Bedrooms

In addition to a bed (or, if shared by two or more children, a bunk bed), a child's bedroom may include a small closet or dressers, a toy box or computer game console, bookcase or other items.

DRAWING ROOM

A drawing room is a room in a house where visitors may be entertained. The name is derived from the sixteenth-century terms "withdrawing room" and "withdrawing chamber," which remained in use through the seventeenth century, and made its first written appearance in 1642 (*OED*). In a large sixteenth- to early eighteenth-century English house, a withdrawing room was a room to which the owner of the house, his wife, or a distinguished guest who was occupying one of the main apartments in the house could "withdraw" for more privacy. It was often off the great chamber (or the great chamber's descendant, the state room or salon) and usually led to a formal, or "state" bedroom.

In eighteenth-century London, the royal' morning

receptions that the French called *levées* were called "drawing rooms", with the sense originally that the privileged members of court would gather in the drawing room outside the king's bedroom, where he would make his first formal public appearance of the day.

During the American Civil War, in the White House of the Confederacy in Richmond, Virginia, the drawing room was just off of the parlor where C.S.A. President Jefferson Davis would greet his guests. At the conclusion of these greetings, the men would remain in the parlor to talk politics and the women would withdraw to the drawing room for their own conversation. This was common practice in the affluent circles of the Southern United States.

Until the mid-twentieth century, after a dinner the ladies of a dinner party would withdraw to the drawing room, leaving the gentlemen at table, where the cloth was removed. After an interval of conversation, the gentlemen would rejoin the ladies in the drawing room.

The term *drawing room* is not used as widely as it once was, and tends to be used in Britain only by those who also have other reception rooms, such as a morning room, a nineteenth-century designation for a sitting-room, often with east-facing exposure, suited for daytime calls, or the middle-class lounge, a late nineteenth-century designation for a room in which to relax; hence the drawing room is the smartest room in the house, usually used by the adults of the family when entertaining. Though this term is still widely used in India and Pakistan, probably since the colonial days, in the larger urban houses of the cities where there are many rooms.

The American equivalent was the parlor, or as many would later call it, living room. In French usage the room and the social gathering it contained are equally the *salon*.

Railroad Usage

The term has also been applied to passenger trains,

supplanting *parlor car*, to designate some of the most spacious and expensive private accommodations available on board a sleeping car or private railroad car. In North America, it meant a room that slept three or more, with a private washroom. While Amtrak has retired cars built with drawing rooms, they are currently still used by Via Rail Canada, although the traditional nomenclature is seen as archaic and are officially sold as "triple bedrooms".

Drawing-Room Plays

The drawing room, being a room in the house to entertain visitors, gave its name to drawing-room comedy, a genre of theatrical productions and motion pictures. Beginning with the early forms of drama, the drawing room play has evolved to encompass comedy as well as to include the forms of the dramatic monologue. The play format itself has also grown out of the traditional drawing room performance and back into main street theater and film. While the drawing room itself has fallen out of favour, the play format has continued to provide a source of entertainment.

Drawing room comedy typically features wit and verbal banter among wealthy, leisured, genteel, upper class characters. Drawing room comedy is also sometimes called the "comedy of manners." Oscar Wilde's *The Importance of Being Earnest* and several of the plays of Noel Coward are typical works of the genre. George Bernard Shaw's *Heartbreak House* adds an undercurrent of social criticism to the genre. Cary Grant appeared in a number of filmed drawing-room comedies. Ernst Lubitsch was especially known as a director of drawing-room comedies.

BATHTUB

A bath is a plumbing fixture used for bathing. Most modern bathtubs are made of acrylic or fiberglass, but alternatives are available in enamel over steel or cast iron, and occasionally waterproof finished wood. A bathtub is usually placed in a bathroom either as a stand-alone fixture or in conjunction with a shower.

Modern bathtubs have overflow and waste drains and may have taps mounted on them. They may be built-in or free standing or sometimes sunken. Until recently, most bathtubs were roughly rectangular in shape but with the advent of acrylic thermoformed baths, more shapes are becoming available. Bathtubs are commonly white in colour although many other colours can be found. The process for enamelling cast iron bathtubs was invented by the Scottish born American David Dunbar Buick.

Two main styles of bathtub are common:

- Western-style bathtubs in which the bather lies down. These baths are typically shallow and long.
- Eastern style bathtubs in which the bather stands up. These are known as ofuro in Japan and are typically short and deep.

Clawfoot Tub

The clawfoot tub or claw-foot tub was considered a luxury item in the late 19th century, originally made from cast iron and lined with porcelain. Modern technology has contributed to a drop in the price of clawfoot tubs, which may now be made of fiberglass, acrylic or other modern materials. Clawfoot tubs usually require more water than a standard bathtub. While true antique clawfoot tubs are still considered collectible items, new reproduction clawfoot tubs are chosen by remodellers and new home builders and much like the Western-style bathtubs clawfoot tubs can also sometimes include showers.

Clawfoot tubs come in 5 major styles:

- Classic Roll Rim, Roll Top, or Flat Rim tubs as seen in the picture above.
- Slipper tubs - where one end is raised and sloped creating a more comfortable lounging position.

- Double Slipper Tubs - where both ends are raised and sloped.

- Double Ended Tubs - where both ends of the tub are rounded. Notice how one end of the classic tub is rounded and one is fairly flat.

- Pedestal Tub - Pedestal tubs, unlike all the styles listed above, do not have claw feet. The tub rests on a pedestal in what most would term an art deco style. Evidence of pedestal tubs dates back to the Isle of Crete in 1000 BC.

Baby Bathtub

A baby bathtub is one used for bathing infants, especially those not yet old enough to sit up on their own. These can be either a small, stand-alone bath that is filled with water from another source, or a device for supporting the baby that is placed in a standard bathtub. Both types are designed to allow the baby to recline while keeping its head out of the water.

Hot Tubs

Hot tubs are common heated pools used for relaxation and sometimes for therapy. The "hippie" era (1950–1970) popularized them in America in songs and movies.

Whirlpool Tubs

Whirlpool tubs first became popular in America during the 1960s and 70s. A spa or hot tub is also called a "jacuzzi" since the word became a generic after plumbing component manufacturer Jacuzzi introduced the "Spa Whirlpool" in 1968. Air bubbles may be introduced into the nozzles via an air-bleed venturi pump.

History of Bathing

Documented early plumbing systems for bathing go back as far as around 3300 BC with the discovery of copper water pipes beneath a palace in the Indus Valley Civilization of ancient India; see sanitation of the Indus Valley Civilization. Evidence of the earliest surviving personal sized bath tub was found on the Isle of Crete where a 5-foot (1.5 m) long pedestal tub was found built from hardened pottery. This tub is the most likely forefather of the classic 19th century clawfoot tub.

The Roman Empire is most widely known as the early champions of bathing. Around 500 BC Roman citizens were encouraged to bathe daily in one of the many public baths. Private bathing rooms were far more ornate and typically would resemble shallow swimming pools that encompassed the entire room. The Romans used marble for the tubs, lead and bronze for pipes, and created a complex sewage system for sanitation purposes. The Roman empire set the early bar for modern personal hygiene.

Contrary to popular belief, bathing and sanitation were not a lost practice with the collapse of the Roman Empire. Soapmaking first became an established trade during the Early Middle Ages. Also, contrary to myth, chamberpots were not disposed of out the window and into streets in the Middle Ages - this was instead a Roman practice. Bathing in fact did not fall out of fashion until shortly after the Renaissance, replaced with the heavy use of sweat-bathing and perfume, as it was thought that water could carry disease into the body through the skin. Modern sanitation was not widely adopted until the 19th and 20th centuries.

The bathtub's modern spouse, the toilet, had problems gaining acceptance. Sir John Harington invented the first flushing toilet for himself and for his godmother, Queen Elizabeth I, in 1596. When Harington published a book describing his invention, he was roundly chided by peers, embarrassing him to the point of retirement from plumbing. His two toilets were the only ones he ever produced. The next water closet would not be seen for 200 years when it was introduced by Alexander Cummings in 1775. This event would mark the very beginnings of the modern bathroom.

It was now time for the piping to catch up with the fixtures. Until the 19th century, most water pipes in the US were made from hollow trees. In the early 19th century, cast-iron production began reducing American reliance on England for this material. Finally, in 1848, The National Public Health Act was passed in the US, creating a plumbing code for the first time.

In 1883, Standard Sanitary Manufacturing Company and Kohler Company began producing cast-iron bathtubs. Far from the ornate feet and luxury most associated with clawfoot tubs, an early Kohler example was advertised as a "horse trough/hog scalder, when furnished with four legs will serve as a bathtub." The item's use as hog scalder was considered a more important marketing point than its ability to function as a bathtub. Everyone knew what a hog scalder or horse trough was, but many people at that time had never bathed in a tub. The tubs eventually caught on because of the sanitary and easy-to-clean surfaces that prevent the spread of disease.

A few years later, Thomas Twyford created the first valveless toilet constructed from ceramic. Before this time, toilets were normally made from metal and wood. Thomas Crapper would gain fame as the inventor of the modern toilet when he bought the rights to a patent for a "Silent Valveless Water Waste Preventer", but he did not invent the toilet.

The end of World War I resulted in a housing construction boom in the United States and a new conception of the purpose-built modern bathroom. Bathrooms prior to World War I were typically converted bedrooms or spare rooms, not rooms built originally to contain bathroom fixtures. Complete with toilet, sink, and tub, the modern bathroom was a feature of 100% of new homes by the end of the 20th century, whereas only 1% of homes had had bathrooms in 1921.

In the latter half of the 20th century, the once popular

clawfoot tub morphed into a built-in tub with a small apron front. This enclosed style afforded easier maintenance and, with the emergence of colored sanitary ware, more design options for the homeowner. The Crane Company introduced colored bathroom fixtures to the US market in 1928, and slowly this influx of design options and easier cleaning and care led to the near demise of clawfoot-style tubs.

Firestopping a Bathtub Drain

If the bathtub is located in a building with multiple stories, where the floors are required to have a fire-resistance rating, the drain from the bathtub causes a service penetration firestop to be required, which must be built in accordance with the provisions of the local building code. Originally, the drain pipe is made of copper, which is non-combustible. Since the pipe itself will not give way in the event of a fire, the firestop can be made of conventional means, such as firestop mortar or silicone sealant, each topping off a packing material. If the pipe were made of plastic, however, the firestop would likely involve intumescent materials, which would expand in the event of a fire, in order to choke off and seal the melting and disappearing plastic pipe.

COMFORTER

A comforter (American English) is a type of blanket. Comforters are intended to keep the user warm, especially during sleep, although they can also be used as mattress pads. Comforters are generally large and rectangular in shape, filled with natural or synthetic insulative material and encased in a shell/covering. Like quilts, comforters are generally used with a set of bed sheets.

Comforter sizes correspond with bed sizes: twin, full, queen, king, and cal-king. Comforter sizes run slightly larger than actual bed sizes to allow for draping over the sides of the bed. Typical sizes in the United States for comforters are:

- Twin = 64" Width x 87" Length
- Queen / Full = 87" Width x 87" Length
- King = 101" Width x 90" Length.

A comforter is sometimes covered with a duvet (comforter) cover for protection and prolonged use. Duvet is French for "Down". Comforter covers are similar in principle to pillowcases, usually closed with zippers or buttons. In the United Kingdom, they are only known as special types of padding Duvets. Also common is the term bed in a bag. This usually denotes an entire set of bedding including either a comforter or duvet with the duvet cover. Sometimes the duvet cover is meant to cover the comforter or the duvet. Other times the comforter is one stand alone piece that matches the set. The duvet will need to be covered by the duvet cover and both will come in a bed in a bag set.

Comforters are sometimes packaged in a set that also includes a bed skirt, pillow shams, and sometimes pillows.

Construction

Filling - Comforters are filled with layers of material such as polyester batting, down feathers, wool, or silk. Comforters also can be made out of fur, usually with a backing of satin or silk. The loft of the filling determines the weight as well as the level of insulation. The comforter is stitched or quilted to secure the filling and keep it evenly distributed.

Shell / Covering - The outer shells of comforters are typically constructed using cotton, silk, or polyester fabrics or blends, of varying thread counts. Comforter shells vary in design and color, often designed to coordinate with other bedding.

QUILT

A quilt is a type of bed cover, traditionally composed of three layers of fiber: a woven cloth top, a layer of batting or wadding and a woven back, combined using the technique of quilting. "Quilting" refers to the technique of joining at least two fabric layers by stitches or ties. In most cases, two fabric layers surround a middle layer of batting (cotton, polyester, silk, wool or combinations of fibers) which is a lighter, insulating layer. Batting is often referred to as "wadding" in Britain. Some modern quilts are made with an upper fabric layer, quilted to a layer of microfleece, perhaps without a fabric backing. The most decorative fabric surface is called the "top", and is the design focus. A single piece of fabric (a "wholecloth quilt") may be used as the top, or the top may be "pieced" from smaller fabric pieces.

Sewing together smaller pieces of fabric into a larger patchwork "block" of fabric creates the basic unit. The "patchwork" of the top is typically made of a series of blocks (all identical, or of diverse design), which are made sequentially and then assembled. The blocks may be separated by plain fabric strips, called "sashing". The central design space may be small (a "medallion") or dominate the top of the quilt. Many tops have decorative "borders", of plainer design, surrounding the central panel of the top and enlarging the quilt. The "binding" is the final edge of fabric, that covers the entire edge, and seals the batting.

Most modern quilts are made of 100% cotton fabric, in a light weight, often called "calico". "Muslin" is a similar fabric (the name derived from Mosul, where quality cotton fabrics were produced in the Middle Ages), of lower quality on average. Silk and lightweight wool are also used, but less commonly than in the past. There are many traditions regarding the design and characteristics of quilts, and they may be made or given to mark important life events such as marriage, the birth of a child, a family member leaving home, or graduations. Modern quilts are not always intended for use as bedding, and may be used as wall hangings, table runners, or tablecloth. Quilting techniques are often incorporated into garment design. Quilt shows and competitions are held locally, regionally and in national shows. There are international competitions as well, particularly in the United States, Japan and Europe.

Uses of Quilts

- Bedding
- Decoration
- Armoury
- Commemoration (e.g., the "Twentieth Century Women of Faith" quilt on the Patchwork page)
- Education (e.g., a "Science" quilt)
- Campaigning
- Documenting events / social history etc.
- Artistic expression
- Traditional gift

Traditions

Quilting traditions are particularly prominent in the United States, where the necessity of creating warm bedding met the paucity of local fabrics in the early days of the colonies. Imported fabric was very expensive, and local "homespun" fabric was labor intensive to create and tended to wear out sooner than commercial fabric. It was essential for most families to use and preserve textiles efficiently. Saving or salvaging small scraps of fabric was a part of life for all households. Small pieces of fabric were joined together, to make larger pieces, in units called "blocks". Creativity could be expressed in the block designs, or simple "utility quilts", with minimal decorative value, could be produced. "Crib quilts" for infants were needed in the cold of winter, but even early examples of beautiful baby quilts indicate the efforts that women made to welcome a new baby. Quilting was often a communal activity, invovling women and girls in a family, or in a larger community. The tops were prepared in advance, and a "quilting bee" was arranged, during which the actual quilting was completed by multiple people. "Quilting frames" were often used to stretch the quilt layers, and maintain event tension to produce high quality quilting stitches, and to allow many individual quilters to work on a single quilt at one time. Quilting bees were important social events in many communities, and were typically held between periods of high demand for farm labor.

Quilts were frequently made to commemorate major life events, such as marriages. There are many traditions of the number of quilts a young woman (and her family) were expected to have made prior to her wedding, for the establishment of her new home. Given the demands on a new wife, and the learning curve in her new role, it was prudent to provide her some reserve time with quilts already completed. Specific wedding quilts continue to be made today. "Wedding ring" quilts have been made since the 1930s, and represent two interlocked rings in the patchwork design. White, wholecloth quilts with high quality, elaborate quilting and often trapunto decorations, are also traditional for weddings.

Interestingly, it was considered bad luck to incorporate heart motifs in a wedding quilt (the couples' hearts might be broken if such a design were included), so tulip motifs were often used to symbolize love in wedding quilts. Quilts were often made for other events, such as graduations, or when individuals left their homes for other communities. Farewell gifts for pastors were made, and some were "subscription" quilts. Community members would pay to have their names embroidered on the quilt top, and the proceeds were given to the departing minister.

Sometimes the quilts were auctioned, for further money, and the quilt might be donated back to the minister by the winner. It was a logical application of this tradition to raising money for other community projects, such as recovery from a flood or natural disaster, and later, for fundraising for war. Subscription quilts were made for all of America's wars. In a new tradition, quilt makers across the United States have been making quilts for wounded veterans of the Afghanistan and Iraq conflicts. These quilts symbolize the respect the community feels toward the veterans, who put themselves at risk, serving their country.

Techniques

Applique

Applique is a sewing technique where an upper layer of fabric is sewn onto a ground fabric, with the raw edges of the "applied" fabric tucked beneath the design to minimize raveling or damage. The upper, applied fabric shape can be of any shape or contour. The edge of the upper fabric is folded under as it is sewn down in the "needle turn" method, and small hand stitches are made to secure down the design. The stitches are made with a hem stitch, so that the thread securing the fabric is minimally visible from the front of the work. There are other methods to secure the raw edge of the applied fabric, and some people use basting stitches, fabric-safe glue, freezer paper, paper forms, or starching techniques to prepare the fabric that will be applied, prior to initiating sewing. Supporting paper or other materials are typically removed after the sewing is complete.

The ground fabric is often cut away from behind, after completion of the sewing of whatever method, in order to minimize the bulk of the fabric in that region. A special form of applique is "broderie perse", which invovles applique of specific motifs that have been selected from a printed fabric. For example, a series of flower designs might be cut out of one fabric with a vine design, rearranged and sewn down on a new fabric, to create the image of a rose bush.

Reverse Applique

Reverse applique is a sewing technique where a ground fabric is cut, and another piece of fabric is placed under the ground fabric, and the raw edges of the ground fabric are tucked under and the newly folded edge is sewn down to the lower fabric. Stitches are made as inconspicuous as possible. Reverse applique techniques are often used in combination with traditional applique techniques, to give a variety of visual effects.

Trapunto

Trapunto is a sewing technique where two layers of fabric surrounding a layer of batting are quilted together, and then additional material is added to a portion of the design to increase the profile of relief as compared to the rest of the work. The effect of the elevation of one portion is often heightened by closely quilting the surrounding region, to compress the batting layer in that part of the quilt, thus receding the background even further. "Cording" techniques may also be used, where a channel is created by quilting, and a cord or yarn is pulled through the batting layer, causing a sharp change in the texture of the quilt. For example, several pockets may be quilted in the pattern of a flower, and then extra batting pushed through a slit in the backing fabric (and this slit later sewn shut).

The stem of the rose might be corded, creating a dimensional effect. The background could be quilted densely in a stipple pattern, causing the space around the rose bush to become less prominent. These techniques are typically executed with whole cloth quilts, and with batting and thread that matches the top fabric. Some artists have used contrasting colored thread, to create an "outline" effect. Colored batting behind the surface layer can create a shadowed effect. Brightly colored yarn cording behind white cloth can give a pastel effect on the surface.

Embellishment

Additional elements may be added to the surface of a quilt. The most common objects sewn on are beads or buttons. Decorative trim, sequins, found objects, or other items can be secured to the surface.

English Paper Piecing

English paper piecing is a hand sewing technique, used to maximize accuracy when piecing complex angles together. A paper shape is cut the exact dimensions of the desired piece. Fabric is then basted to the paper shape. Adjacent units are then placed, face to face, and the seam is whip stitched together. When a given piece is completely surrounded by all the adjacent shapes, the basting thread is cut, and the basting and the paper shape are removed.

Foundation Piecing

Foundation piecing is a sewing technique that allows maximum stability of the work as the piecing is created, minimizing the distorting effect of working with slender pieces or bias cut pieces. In the most basic form, a piece of paper is cut the size of the desired block. For utility quilts, a sheet of newspaper was used. In modern foundation piecing, an elaborate design featuring pointed shapes, is used. A strip of fabric or a fabric scrap is sewn by machine to the foundation. The fabric is flipped back, and pressed. The next piece of fabric is sewn through the initial piece and paper. Subsequent pieces are added sequentially. The block may be trimmed, flush with the border of the foundation. After the blocks are sewn together, the paper is removed, unless the foundation is an acid-free material.

Quilting Styles

United States

Amish

Amish quilts are reflections of the Amish way of life. As a part of their religious commitment, Amish people have chosen to reject "worldly" elements in their dress and lifestyle, their quilts reflect this. Traditionally, they use only solid colors in their clothing and the quilts they intend for their own use, in colors that were approved by their local religious leaders. Early Amish quilts were typically made of light weight wool fabric, off the same bolts of fabric used for family clothing items. Black is a dominant color, in the oldest Amish quilt styles, particularly in quilts made in Eastern Pennsylvania. Although classic Amish quilts appear austere from a distance, the craftsmanship is often of the highest quality and the lush quilting patterns, that contrast with the plain background. Antique Amish quilts are among the most highly prized among collectors and quilting enthusiasts. The quilts created by Amish people in the early period reflect their strong, internal cultural influences, that were to some degree separate from the non-Amish culture around them. The color combinations can help experts determine the community in which the quilt was produced. Many consider these quilts the "art" of the Amish.

Baltimore Album

Baltimore album quilts originated in the region around Baltimore, Maryland in the 1840s, where a unique and highly developed applique style of quilt briefly flourished. The quilts are created as album quilts, which are collections of appliqued blocks, each with a different design. The designs are often feature floral patterns, but many other motifs are also used. Baskets of flowers, wreaths, buildings, books and birds were common motifs. Designs were often highly detailed, and displayed the maker's skill. New dying techniques were available, allowing new, bold colors which the quilters avidly used. New techniques with printing on the fabrics also allowed shaded portions of fabric to heighten the three dimensional effect of the designs. The background fabric is typically white, allowing maximal contrast to the delicate designs. India ink allowed handwritten accents, and allowed the blocks to be signed. Some of these quilts were created by professional quilters, and patrons could commission quilts made of new blocks, or select blocks that were already available for sale. There has been a resurgence of quilts in the Baltimore style, with many of the modern quilts experimenting with bending some of the old rules.

Crazy Quilts

Crazy quilts were named because their pieces are not regular, and are scattered across the top of the quilt like "crazed" (cracked or crackled) pottery glazing. They were very refined, luxury items, not made randomly. Geometric pieces of rich fabrics were sewn together, and highly decorative embroidery was added. Such quilts were often effectively samplers of embroidery stitches and techniques, displaying the development of needle skills of those in the well-to-do late nineteenth century home. They were show pieces, not used for warmth, but for late Victorian display. They often took years to complete. Fabrics used included silks, wools, linen and cotton. Mixtures of fabric textures, such as a smooth silk next to a textured brocade or velvet, were embraced. Designs were applied to the surface, and other elements such as ribbons, lace, and decorative cording were used exuberantly. Names and dates were often part of the design, and commemorated important events or associations of the maker. Politics were included in some, with printed campaign handkerchiefs and other pre-printed textiles (such as advertising silks) were often included to declare the maker's sentiments.

Hawaiian

Hawaiian quilts are whole-cloth (not pieced) quilts, featuring large-scale symmetrical appliqué in solid colors on a solid color (usually white) ground fabric. Traditionally, the quilter would fold a square piece of fabric into quarters or eighths and then cut out a border design, followed by a center design. The cutouts would then be appliquéd onto a contrasting background fabric. The center and border designs were typically inspired by local flora, and often had rich personal associations for the creator, with deep cultural resonances. The most common color for the appliquéd design was red, due to the wide availability of Turkey-red fabric. Some of these textiles were not in fact quilted, ultimately, but were used as decorative coverings without the heavier batting that was not needed in a tropical climate. Multiple colors were added over time, as the tradition developed. So called "echo quilting", where a quilted outline of the applique pattern is repeated like ripples to the edge of the quilt, is the most common quilting pattern employed on Hawaiian-style quilts. Beautiful examples are held in the collection of the Bernice Pauahi Bishop Museum, Honolulu, Hawai'i. Link to the Bishop Museum:

Native American Star Quilts

Star Quilts are a Native American form of quilting arising among Native women in the late 19th Century as communities adjusted to the difficulties of Reservation life and cultural disruption. They are made by many tribes, but came to be especially associated with Plains tribes, including the Lakota. While star patterns existed in earlier European-American forms of quilting, they came to take on special significance for many Native artisans. Star quilts are more than an art form but express important cultural and spiritual values of the Native women who make them, and continuing to have uses in ceremonies and for marking important points in a person's life- from curing or yuwipi ceremonies to memorials.

Anthropologists, such as Bea Medicine have documented important social and cultural connections between quilting and earlier important pre-reservation crafting traditions such as women's quill-working societies, and other crafts that were difficult to sustain after hunting and movement became restricted by the US government. Star quilts have also become a form of income for many Native women, but retain their spiritual and cultural importance to their makers.

Seminole

Seminole patchwork is a specific Native American tradition, and is seen in quilts and traditional clothing. Seminole patchwork is created by joining a series of horizontal strips, each designed with repetative, geometric designs.

Block Designs

There are many traditional block designs, and techniques that have been named. Log cabin quilts are pieced quilts featuring blocks made of strips of fabric typically encircling a small centered square (traditionally a red square, symbolizing the hearth of the home), with light strips forming half the square and dark strips on the other side. Dramatic contrast effects with light and dark fabrics are created by various layouts of the blocks when forming a quilt top. There are named variations, based on the placement of log cabin blocks. These include: Sunshine and Shadow, Straight Furrows, Streak of Lightening, Open Windows. Nine Patch blocks are often the first blocks a child is taught to make. The block consists of three rows of three squares. A checkerbaord effect with alternating dark and light squares is most commonly used.

The Double Wedding Ring pattern first came to prominence during the Great Depression. The design consists of interlocking circles, pieced with small arcs of fabrics. The finished quilts are often given to commemorate marriages. Cathedral Windows is a block that uses reverse applique, and large amounts of folded muslin, to form an interlocking circular design. The volume of fabric is high, and the tops are heavy. Because of the weight and the insulating value of all the fabric involved, these tops are often not quilted onto any batting or backing.

European Quilts

The History of quilting in Europe goes back at least to Medieval times. Quilting was done not only for traditional bedding but for warm clothing. Clothing quilted with fancy fabrics and threads was often a sign of nobility.

British Quilts

Henry VIII of England's household inventories record dozens of "quyltes" and "coverpointes" among the bed linen, including a green silk one for his first wedding to Catherine of Aragon quilted with metal threads, linen-backed, and worked with roses and pomegranates.

Otherwise known as Durham quilts, North Country quilts have a long history in north-east England, dating back to the Industrial Revolution and beyond. North Country quilts are often "whole-cloth" quilts, that emphasize the quilting. Some are made of sateen fabrics, which further heighten the effect of the quilting. From the late 18th to the early 20th century the Lancashire cotton industry produced quilts using a mechanised technique of weaving double cloth with an enclosed heavy cording weft, imitating the corded Provençal quilts made in Marseilles.

Italian Quilts

Quilting was particularly common in Italy during the Renaissance. One particularly famous surviving example, now in two parts, is the 1360-1400 Tristan Quilt, a Sicilian quilted linen textile representing scenes from the story of *Tristan and Isolde* and housed in the Victoria and Albert Museum and in the Bargello in Florence.

Provençal Quilts

Provençal quilts, now often referred to as "boutis", are wholecloth quilts traditionally made in the South of France from the 17th century onwards. Boutis is a Provençal word meaning 'stuffing', describing how two layers of fabric are quilted together with stuffing sandwiched between sections of the design, creating a raised effect. The three main forms of the Provençal quilt are *matelassage* (a double-layered wholecloth quilt with wadding sandwiched between), corded quilting or *piqure de Marseille* (also known as Marseilles work or *piqué marseillais*), and *boutis*. These terms are often debated and confused, but are all forms of stuffed quilting associated with the region.

Other Nations

Mola

Mola textiles are a distinct tradition, created by the

Kuna people of Panama and Colombia. They are famous for bright colors, and reverse applique techniques, creating designs with strong cultural and spiritual importance within the indigenous culture. Forms of animals, humans or mythological figures are featured, with strong geometric designs in the voids around the main image. These textiles are not traditionally used as bedding, but use techniques common to the larger international quilting tradition. Molas have been very influential on modern quilting design.

Sashiko

. Sashiko (:RW0P[, literally "little stabs") is a Japanese tradition, that evolved over time from a simple technique for re-enforcing fabric made for heavy use in fishing villages. A tradition of decorative stitches, with no overlap of any two stitches. Piecing is not part of the tradition, but the focus is on heavy cotton thread work with large, even stitches, on the base fabric. Deep blue indigo-dyed fabric, with white stitches is the most traditional form, but inverse work with blue on white are seen. Traditional medallion designs, tessellated and geometric designs are most often used.

Bangladeshi Quilts

Bangladeshi quilts, known as *Kantha*, are not pieced together. Rather, they are two to three pieces of cloth. They are made out of worn out clothes (saris) and are mainly used for bedding, as a blanket. They may be used as a decorative piece as well. They are made by women mainly in the Monsoon season before winter.

Tivaevae Cook Island Quilts

Tivaevae are also quilts made by Cook Island women for ceremonial occasions. Quilting is thought to have been imported to the Islands by missionaries. The quilts are highly prized and are given as gifts with other finely made works on important occasions such as weddings and christenings.

Ralli Quilts

Ralli quilts are traditional quilts made in Pakistan and India. *Ralli* quilts are also called rilli quilts. Handmade ralli quilts are used as blankets and bedspreads. They combine patchwork, appliqué and embroidery. Parents present rallis to their daughters on their weddings as a dowry. The another kind of ralli quilt is *sami ralli*, used by the samis, jogis and gypsies. This type of rall quilt is popular due to many colors and extensive hand stitching.

Other Terms

Quillow

A quillow is a quilt with an attached pocket into which the whole blanket can be folded, thus making a pillow. Once folded into the pocket, it can be used as a cushion during the day and unfolded into a blanket at night.

Quilting Technique

As an example, the quilt image above has 24 blocks arranged in a 4x6 pattern, set with dark sashing strips, corner stones in a contrasting color, an outside sashing strip but no border, and a multicolored binding. Click on the image to see these details in a larger view.

Quilts on Display

In 2010, the world renowned Victoria and Albert Museum put on a comprehensive display of quilts from 1700-2010. Amongst famous quilts in history is the AIDS Memorial Quilt, which was begun in San Francisco in 1987, and is cared for by The NAMES Project Foundation. Portions of it are periodically displayed in various arranged locations. Panels are made to memorialize a person lost to HIV, and each block is 3 feet by 6 feet. Many of the blocks are not made by traditional quilters, and amateur creators may lack technical skill, but their blocks speak directly to the love and loss they have experienced.

The blocks are not in fact "quilted," in that there is no

stitching holding together batting and backing layers. Exuberant designs, with personal objects applied, are seen, next to restrained and elegant designs. Each block is very personal, and they form a deeply moving sight when combined by the dozens and the hundreds. The "quilt" as a whole is still under construction, although the entire quilt is so large now that it cannot be assembled in complete form in any one location. The Museum of the American Quilter's Society (also known as the National Quilt Museum) is located in Paducah, Kentucky.

The museum houses a large collection of quilts, most of which are winning entries from the annual American Quilter's Society festival and quilt competition held in April. The Museum also houses other exhibits of quilt collections, both historic and modern.

Many historic quilts can be seen in Bath at the American Museum in Britain, and Beamish Museum preserves examples of the North East England quiltmaking tradition.

The largest known public collection of quilts is housed at the International Quilt Study Center at the University of Nebraska–Lincoln in Lincoln, Nebraska.

Examples of Tivaevae and other quilts can be found in the collection of the Museum of New Zealand Te Papa Tongarewa.

The San Jose Museum of Quilts and Textiles in California also display traditional and modern quilts. There is free admission to the museum on the first Friday of every month, as part of the San Jose Art Walk.

The New England Quilt Museum is located in Lowell, Massachusetts. Bernice Pauahi Bishop Museum, Honolulu, Hawai'i.

In Literature

- Ismat Chughtai wrote an Urdu-language story entitled "Lihaf" ("The Quilt", 1941) that lead to scandal and an unsuccessful attempt at legal prosecution of the author because it was about a lesbian relationship.

- *The Quilter's Apprentice* and many others by Jennifer Chiaverini
- *The Quiltmaker's Gift* and *The Quiltmaker's Journey* by Jeff Brumbeau, illustrated by Gail de Marcken
- *Alias Grace* by Margaret Atwood
- *Wild Goose Chase* by Terri Thayer
- *Old Maid's Puzzle* by Terri Thayer
- *How to Make an American Quilt* by Whitney Otto
- A Fine Balance by Rohinton Mistry
- *Everyday Use* by Alice Walker

Periodicals
- Quilters Newsletter Magazine
- Patchwork- und Quiltjournal
- European Quilt Art
- Celia Eddy, *Quilted Planet: A Sourcebook of Quilts from Around the World* ISBN 1400054575
- Carolyn Ducey, "Quilt History Timeline, Pre-History – 1800", International Quilt Study Center & Museum, University of Nebraska, Lincoln.
- Patricia Stoddard, *Ralli Quilts: The Traditional Textiles from Pakistan and India*

Quilting

Quilting is a sewing method done to join two or more layers of material together to make a thicker padded material. A quilter is the name given to someone who works at quilting. Quilting can be done by hand, by sewing machine, or by a specialist longarm quilting system.

The process of quilting uses a needle and thread to join two or more layers of material to make a quilt. Typical quilting is done with three layers: the top fabric or quilt top, batting or insulating material and backing material. The quilter's hand or sewing machine passes the needle and thread through all layers and then brings the needle back up. The process is repeated across the entire piece where quilting is wanted. A rocking, straight or running stitch is commonly used and these stitches can be purely functional or decorative and elaborate. Quilting is done to create bed spreads, art quilt wall hangings, clothing, and a variety of textile products. Quilting can make a project thick, or with dense quilting, can raise one area so that another stands out.

Quilt stores often sell fabric, thread, patterns and other goods that are used for quilting. They often have group sewing and quilting classes, where one can learn how to sew or quilt and work with others to exchange skills. Quilt stores often have quilting machines that can be rented out for use, or customers can drop off their quilts and have them professionally quilted.

History

Early Functional Quilting

The word quilt is derived from the Latin *culcita*, meaning a padded and tied mattress. Quilting originated for its utility, as the technique produced a thicker padded fabric either for warmth or for protection. The first evidence of quilting is found in Asia sometime before the 1st century CE. A quilted linen carpet dating from that time was found in a Siberian cave tomb. The central motifs (primarily animals, with abstract spirals on the borders) are worked in the backstitch, while the background is diamond quilted in a coarse running stitch.

Ancient Egyptian sculptures show figures which appear to be wearing quilted clothing, possibly for warmth in the chilly desert evenings. Quilting has been part of the needlework tradition in Europe from about the 5th century

CE. Early objects contain Egyptian cotton, which may indicate that Egyptian and Mediterranean trade provided a conduit for the technique.

Quilted objects were relatively rare in Europe until approximately the 12th century, when quilted bedding and other items appeared after the return of the Crusaders from the Middle East. The medieval quilted gambeson, aketon and arming doublet were garments worn under, or instead of, armor of maille or plate armor. These developed into the later quilted doublet worn as part of fashionable European male clothing from the 14th to 17th century. Quilting clothing began to be generally used in the 14th century, with quilted doublets and armor worn in France, Germany, and England and quilted tunics in Italy.

American Quilts

In American Colonial times, most women were busy spinning, weaving, and making clothing. Meanwhile, women of the wealthier classes prided themselves on their fine quilting of wholecloth quilts with fine needlework. Quilts made during the early 19th century were not constructed of pieced blocks but were instead whole cloth quilts. Broderie perse quilts and medallion quilts were made. Some antique quilts made in North America have worn-out blankets or older quilts as the internal batting layer, quilted between new layers of fabric and thereby extending the usefulness of old material.

During American pioneer days, "paper" quilting became popular. Paper was used as a pattern and each individual piece of cut fabric was basted around the paper pattern. Paper was a scarce commodity in the early American west, and women would save letters from home, newspaper clippings, and catalogs to use as patterns. The paper not only served as a pattern but as an insulator. The paper found between the old quilts has become a primary source of information about pioneer life.

Quilts made without any insulation or batting were referred to as summer quilts. They were not made for warmth, only to keep the chill off during cooler summer evenings.

African-American Quilts

African-American women developed a distinctive style of quilting, notably different from the style most strongly associated with the Amish. Harriet Powers, a slave-born African American woman, made two famous story quilts. She was just one of the many African American quilters who contributed to the evolution of quilting. The Gee's Bend quilting community was celebrated in an exhibition that travelled to museums including the Smithsonian. The contributions made by her and other quilters of Gee's Bend, Alabama has been recognized by the US Postal Service with a series of stamps. The *communal* nature of the quilting process (and how it can bring together women of varied races and backgrounds) was honored in the movie How to Make an American Quilt.

Art Quilting

During the late 20th century, art quilts became popular for their aesthetic and artistic qualities rather than for functionality (they are displayed on a wall or table rather than spread on a bed).

Types and Equipment

Many types of quilting exist today. The two most widely used are hand-quilting and machine quilting. Hand quilting is the process of using a needle and thread to sew a running stitch by hand across the entire area to be quilted. This binds the layers together. A quilting frame or hoop is often used to assist in holding the piece being quilted off the quilter's lap. A quilter can make one running stitch at a time; this is called a stab stitch.

Another option is called a rocking stitch, where the

quilter has one hand, usually with a finger wearing a thimble, on top of the quilt, while the other hand is located beneath the piece to push the needle back up. The third option is called "loading the needle" and involves doing four or more stitches before pulling the needle through the cloth. Hand quilting is still practiced by the Amish within the United States, and is enjoying a resurgence worldwide.

Machine quilting is the process of using a home sewing machine or a longarm machine to sew the layers together. With the home sewing machine, the layers are tacked together before quilting. This involves laying the top, batting, and backing out on a flat surface and either pinning (using large safety pins) or tacking the layers together. Longarm Quilting involves placing the layers to be quilted on a special frame. The frame has bars on which the layers are rolled, keeping these together without the need for basting or pinning. These frames are used with a professional sewing machine mounted on a platform. The platform rides along tracks so that the machine can be moved across the layers on the frame. A Longarm machine is moved across the fabric. In contrast, the fabric is moved through a home sewing machine.

Tying is another technique of fastening the three layers together (and is not a form of quilting at all). This is done primarily on quilts that are made to be used and are needed quickly. The process of tying the quilt is done with yarns or multiple strands of thread. Square knots are used to finish off the ties so that the quilt may be washed and used without fear of the knots coming undone. This technique is commonly called "tacking." In the Midwest, tacked bed covers are referred to as comforters.

Quilting is now taught in some American schools. It is also taught at senior centers around the U.S., but quilters of all ages attend classes. These forms of workshop or classes are also available in other countries in guilds and community colleges.

Contemporary quilters use a wide range of quilting designs and styles, from ancient and ethnic to post-modern futuristic patterns. There is no one single school or style that dominates the quilt-making world.

Processes and Definitions
Traditional

Traditional quilting is a six-step process that includes: 1) selecting a pattern, fabrics and batting; 2) measuring and cutting fabrics to the correct size to make blocks from the pattern; 3) piecing (sewing cut pieces of fabric together using a sewing machine or by hand to make blocks) blocks together to make a finished "top"; 4) layering the quilt top with batting and backing, to make a "quilt sandwich"; 5) quilting by hand or machine through all layers of the quilt sandwich; and 6) squaring up and trimming excess batting from the edges, machine sewing the binding to the front edges of the quilt and then hand-stitching the binding to the quilt backing. Note: If the quilt will be hung on the wall, there is an additional step: making and attaching the hanging sleeve.

Definitions

- Piecing: Sewing small pieces of cloth into patterns, called blocks, that are then sewn together to make a finished quilt top. These blocks may be sewn together, edge to edge, or separated by strips of cloth called sashing. Note: Whole cloth quilts typically are not pieced, but are made using a single piece of cloth for the quilt top.

- Layering: Placing the quilt top over the batting and the backing.

- Borders: Typically strips of fabric of various widths added to the perimeter of the pieced blocks to complete the quilt top. Note: borders may also be made up of simple or patterned blocks that are stitched together into a row, before being added to the quilt top.

- Binding: Long fabric strips cut on the bias that are attached to the borders of the quilt. Binding is typically machine sewn to the front side of the edge of the quilt, folded over twice, and hand sewn to the back side of the quilt.
- Quilting: Stitching through all three layers of the quilt (the quilt top, the batting, and the quilt back), typically in decorative patterns, which serves three purposes.

Quilting is usually completed by starting from the middle, and moving outward toward the edges of the quilt.

Quilting can be elaborately decorative, comprising stitching fashioned into complex designs and patterns, simple or complex geometric grids, "motifs" traced from published quilting patterns or traced pictures, freehand, or complex repeated designs called tessellations. The quilter may choose to emphasize these designs by using threads that are multicolored or metallic, or that contrast highly to the fabric. Conversely, the quilter may choose to make the quilting disappear, using "invisible" nylon or polyester thread,thread that matches the quilt top, or stitching within the patchwork seams themselves (commonly known as "stitch in the ditch"). Some quilters draw the quilting design on the quilt top before stitching, while others prefer to stitch "freehand."

Quilting is often combined with embroidery, patchwork, applique, and other forms of needlework.

Specialty Styles

- Foundation piecing - also known as paper-piecing - sewing pieces of fabric onto a temporary or permanent foundation
- Shadow or Echo Quilting - Hawaiian Quilting, where quilting is done around an appliquéd piece on the quilt top, then the quilting is echoed again and again around the previous quilting line.

- Ralli Quilting - Indian quilting, often associated with the Gujarat region.
- Sashiko quilting - Basic running stitch worked in heavy, white cotton thread usually on dark indigo colored fabric. It was originally used by the working classes to stitch layers together for warmth.
- Trapunto quilting - stuffed quilting, often associated with Italy.
- Machine Trapunto quilting - a process of using water soluble thread and an extra layer of batting to achieve trapunto design and then sandwiching the quilt and re-sewing the design with regular cotton thread.
- Shadow trapunto- This involves quilting a design in fine Lawn and filling some of the spaces in the pattern with small lengths of colored wool.
- Tivaevae or tifaifai - A distinct art from the Cook Islands.
- Watercolor Quilting - A sophisticated form of scrap quilting whereby uniform sizes of various prints are arranged and sewn to create a picture or design. See also Colorwash.
- Thread Art - A custom style of sewing where thread is layered to create the picture on the quilt. See this picture for an example (http://www.agww.net/html/agww_merchandise_2.html).

Quilting Software
- Quilted Photo Deluxe
- EQ6
- PC Quilt
- Quiltsoft
- QuiltPro
- Quilting Studio
- SewPrecise

LAUNDRY ROOM

A laundry room (also called a utility room) is a room where clothes are washed. In a modern home, a laundry room would be equipped with an automatic washing machine and clothes dryer,and often a large basin, called a laundry tub, for hand-washing delicate articles of clothing such as sweaters, and an ironing board. A typical laundry room is located in the basement of older homes, but in many modern homes, the laundry room might be found on the main floor near the kitchen or upstairs near the bedrooms.

Another typical location is adjacent to the garage and the laundry room serves as a mudroom for the entrance from the garage. As the garage is often at a different elevation (or grade) than the rest of the house, the laundry room that serves as an entrance from the garage that may be sunken from the rest of the house. This avoids or minimizes the need for stairs between the garage and the house.

Laundry rooms may also include storage cabinets, countertops for folding clothes, and, space permitting, a small sewing machine.

REFERENCES

Bernard Lewis (1989). *Istanbul and the Civilization of the Ottoman Empire*, University of Oklahoma Press, p. 132.

Charles Perry, "The cafeteria: an L.A. original", *The Los Angeles Times*, November 5, 2003

Colby, Averil. *Quilting*. New York: Charles Scribner's Sons, 1971.

John F. Mariani, *America Eats Out*, William Morrow & Co (October 1991), ISBN 978-0688099961

Lyn Perry, 'Cabbages and Cuppas', in *Adventures in the Mediatheque: Personal Selections of Films*, (London: BFI Southbank / University of the Third Age, 2008), pp 26–27.

Prévost, Abbé (1930) *Adventures of a man of quality* (translation of *Séjour en Angleterre*, v. 5 of *Mémoires et avantures d'un homme de qualité qui s'est retiré du monde*) G. Routledge & Sons, London, OCLC 396693

Rowe, Jeff. "Hotels Throw In Towel On Towel Theft". *Chicago Tribune.*

Sharon Pederson (2005). Sensational Sashiko, Japanese Applique and Quilting by Machine. p.5, Martingale & Co., Woodinville,WA

Teply, Karl (1980). Die Einführung des Kaffees in Wien. Verein für Geschichte der Stadt Wien, Wien, Vol. 6. p. 104.

Weinberg, Bennett Alan; Bonnie K. Bealer (2002). *The World of Caffeine: The Science and Culture of the World's Most Popular Drug.* Routledge. p. page 154. ISBN 0-415-92722-6.

Wild, Anthony (2005). *Coffee A Dark History.* W. W. Norton & Company. p. page 90. ISBN 0393060713.

Woodson, R. Dodge (1985). Build Your Dream Home for Less. Cincinnati: Betterway Books, pp 60-61.

Zeller, Dirk (2006). Success as a Real Estate Agent for Dummies. Wiley, p. 209

5

Related Elements of Tourism, Tourist Attraction, Destination and Holidays

TOURISM

Tourism is travel for recreational, leisure or business purposes. The World Tourism Organization defines tourists as people who "travel to and stay in places outside their usual environment for more than twenty-four (24) hours and not more than one consecutive year for leisure, business and other purposes not related to the exercise of an activity remunerated from within the place visited."

Tourism has become a popular global leisure activity. In 2008, there were over 922 million international tourist arrivals, with a growth of 1.9% as compared to 2007. International tourism receipts grew to US$944 billion (euro 642 billion) in 2008, corresponding to an increase in real terms of 1.8%. As a result of the late-2000s recession, international travel demand suffered a strong slowdown beginning in June 2008, with growth in international tourism arrivals worldwide falling to 2% during the boreal summer months. This negative trend intensified during 2009, exacerbated in some countries due to the outbreak of the H1N1 influenza virus, resulting in a worldwide decline of 4% in 2009 to 880 million international tourists arrivals, and an estimated 6% decline in international tourism receipts.

Tourism is vital for many countries, such as France,

Egypt, Greece, United States, Spain, Italy and Thailand, and many island nations, such as The Bahamas, Fiji, Maldives, Philippines and the Seychelles, due to the large intake of money for businesses with their goods and services and the opportunity for employment in the service industries associated with tourism. These service industries include transportation services, such as airlines, cruise ships and taxicabs, hospitality services, such as accommodations, including hotels and resorts, and entertainment venues, such as amusement parks, casinos, shopping malls, music venues and theatres.

Etymology

Theobald (1994) suggested that "etymologically, the word *tour* is derived from the Latin, 'tornare' and the Greek, 'tornos', meaning 'a lathe or circle; the movement around a central point or axis'. This meaning changed in modern English to represent 'one's turn'. The suffix –*ism* is defined as 'an action or process; typical behaviour or quality', while the suffix, –*ist* denotes 'one that performs a given action'. When the word *tour* and the suffixes –*ism* and –*ist* are combined, they suggest the action of movement around a circle. One can argue that a circle represents a starting point, which ultimately returns back to its beginning. Therefore, like a circle, a tour represents a journey in that it is a round-trip, i.e., the act of leaving and then returning to the original starting point, and therefore, one who takes such a journey can be called a tourist."

In 1941, Hunziker and Krapf defined tourism as people who travel "the sum of the phenomena and relationships arising from the travel and stay of non-residents, insofar as they do not lead to permanent residence and are not connected with any earning activity." In 1976, the Tourism Society of England's definition was: "Tourism is the temporary, short-term movement of people to destination outside the places where they normally live and work and their activities during the stay at each destination. It includes movements for all purposes." In 1981, the

International Association of Scientific Experts in Tourism defined tourism in terms of particular activities selected by choice and undertaken outside the home.

In 1994, the United Nations classified three forms of tourism in its *Recommendations on Tourism Statistics*:

- Domestic tourism, involving residents of the given country traveling only within this country.
- Inbound tourism, involving non-residents traveling in the given country.
- Outbound tourism, involving residents traveling in another country.

World Tourism Statistics and Rankings

Most Visited Countries by International Tourist Arrivals

In 2008, there were over 922 million international tourist arrivals, with a growth of 1.9% as compared to 2007. In 2009, international tourists arrivals fell to 880 million, representing a worldwide decline of 4% as compared to 2008. The region most affected was Europe with a 6% decline.

The World Tourism Organization reports the following ten countries as the most visited from 2006 to 2009 by the number of international travellers. When compared to 2006, Ukraine entered the top ten list, surpassing Russia, Austria and Mexico, and in 2008, surpassed Germany. In 2008, the United States displaced Spain from the second place. Most of the top visited countries continue to be on the European continent, followed by a growing number of Asian countries.

In 2009, Malaysia made it into the top 10 most visited countries' list. Malaysia secured the ninth position, just below Turkey and Germany. In 2008, Malaysia was in 11th position. Both Turkey and Germany climbed one rank in arrivals, occupying seventh and eighth positions respectively, while France continued to lead the ranks in terms of tourist arrivals.

International Tourism Receipts

International tourism receipts grew to US$944 billion (€642 billion) in 2008, corresponding to an increase in real terms of 1.8% from 2007. When the export value of international passenger transport receipts is accounted for, total receipts in 2008 reached a record of US$1.1 trillion, or over US$3 billion a day.

The World Tourism Organization reports the following countries as the top ten tourism earners for the year 2009. It is noticeable that most of them are on the European continent, but the United States continues to be the top earner.

International Tourism Expenditures

The World Tourism Organization reports the following countries as the top ten biggest spenders on international tourism for the year 2009. For the fifth year in a row, German tourists continue as the top spenders.

History

Wealthy people have always traveled to distant parts of the world, to see great buildings, works of art, learn new languages, experience new cultures and to taste different cuisines. Long ago, at the time of the Roman Republic, places such as Baiae were popular coastal resorts for the rich. The word *tourism* was used by 1811 and *tourist* by 1840. In 1936, the League of Nations defined *foreign tourist* as "someone traveling abroad for at least twenty-four hours". Its successor, the United Nations, amended this definition in 1945, by including a maximum stay of six months.

Leisure Travel

Leisure travel was associated with the Industrial Revolution in the United Kingdom – the first European country to promote leisure time to the increasing industrial population. Initially, this applied to the owners of the machinery of production, the economic oligarchy, the factory owners and the traders. These comprised the new middle class. Cox & Kings was the first official travel company to be formed in 1758.

The British origin of this new industry is reflected in many place names. In Nice, France, one of the first and best-established holiday resorts on the French Riviera, the long esplanade along the seafront is known to this day as the *Promenade des Anglais*; in many other historic resorts in continental Europe, old, well-established palace hotels have names like the *Hotel Bristol*, the *Hotel Carlton* or the *Hotel Majestic* – reflecting the dominance of English customers.

Many leisure-oriented tourists travel to the tropics, both in the summer and winter. Places of such nature often visited are: Bali in Indonesia, Brazil, Cuba, the Dominican Republic, Malaysia, Mexico the various Polynesian tropical islands, Queensland in Australia, Thailand, Saint-Tropez and Cannes in France, Florida, Hawaii and Puerto Rico in the United States, Barbados, Sint Maarten, Saint Kitts and Nevis, The Bahamas, Anguilla, Antigua, Aruba, Turks and Caicos Islands and Bermuda.

Winter Tourism

Although it is acknowledged that the Swiss were not the inventors of skiing it is well documented that St. Moritz, Graubünden, became the cradle of the developing winter tourism: Since that year of 1865 in St. Moritz, many daring hotel managers choose to risk opening their hotels in winter but it was only in the seventies of the 20th century when winter tourism took over the lead from summer tourism in many of the Swiss ski resorts. Even in Winter, portions of up to one third of all guests (depending on the location) consist of non-skiers.

Major ski resorts are located mostly in the various European countries (e.g. Andorra, Austria, Bulgaria, Czech Republic, France, Germany, Iceland, Italy, Norway, Poland, Serbia, Sweden, Slovenia, Spain, Switzerland), Canada, the United States (e.g. Colorado, California, Utah, New York, New Jersey, Michigan, Montana, Vermont, New England) New Zealand, Japan, South Korea, Chile, Argentina, Kenya and Tanzania.

Mass Tourism

Mass tourism could only have developed with the improvements in technology, allowing the transport of large numbers of people in a short space of time to places of leisure interest, so that greater numbers of people could begin to enjoy the benefits of leisure time.

In the United States, the first seaside resorts in the European style were at Atlantic City, New Jersey and Long Island, New York.

In Continental Europe, early resorts included: Ostend, popularised by the people of Brussels; Boulogne-sur-Mer (Pas-de-Calais) and Deauville (Calvados) for the Parisians; and Heiligendamm, founded in 1793, as the first seaside resort on the Baltic Sea.

Adjectival Tourism

Adjectival tourism refers to the numerous niche or specialty travel forms of tourism that have emerged over the years, each with its own adjective. Many of these have come into common use by the tourism industry and academics. Others are emerging concepts that may or may not gain popular usage. Examples of the more common niche tourism markets include:

- Agritourism
- Culinary tourism
- Cultural tourism

- Ecotourism
- Extreme tourism
- Geotourism
- Heritage tourism
- LGBT tourism
- Medical tourism
- Nautical tourism
- Pop-culture tourism
- Religious tourism
- Slum tourism
- Space tourism
- War tourism
- Wildlife tourism

Recent Developments

There has been an upmarket trend in the tourism over the last few decades, especially in Europe, where international travel for short breaks is common. Tourists have high levels of disposable income, considerable leisure time, are well educated, and have sophisticated tastes. There is now a demand for a better quality products, which has resulted in a fragmenting of the mass market for beach vacations; people want more specialised versions, quieter resorts, family-oriented holidays or niche market-targeted destination hotels.

The developments in technology and transport infrastructure, such as jumbo jets, low-cost airlines and more accessible airports have made many types of tourism more affordable. As of April 28, 2009 *The Guardian* article notes that, "the WHO estimates that up to 500,000 people are on planes at any time." There have also been changes in lifestyle, such as retiree-age people who sustain year round tourism. This is facilitated by internet sales of tourism products. Some sites have now started to offer dynamic packaging, in which an inclusive price is quoted for a tailor-made package requested by the customer upon impulse.

There have been a few setbacks in tourism, such as the September 11 attacks and terrorist threats to tourist destinations, such as in Bali and several European cities. Also, on December 26, 2004, a tsunami, caused by the 2004 Indian Ocean earthquake, hit the Asian countries on the Indian Ocean, including the Maldives. Thousands of lives were lost and many tourists died. This, together with the vast clean-up operation in place, has stopped or severely hampered tourism to the area.

The terms *tourism* and *travel* are sometimes used interchangeably. In this context, travel has a similar definition to tourism, but implies a more purposeful journey. The terms *tourism* and *tourist* are sometimes used pejoratively, to imply a shallow interest in the cultures or locations visited by tourists.

Sustainable Tourism

"Sustainable tourism is envisaged as leading to management of all resources in such a way that economic, social and aesthetic needs can be fulfilled while maintaining cultural integrity, essential ecological processes, biological diversity and life support systems." (World Tourism Organization)

Sustainable development implies "meeting the needs of the present without compromising the ability of future generations to meet their own needs" (World Commission on Environment and Development, 1987)

Sustainable tourism can be seen as having regard to ecological and socio-cultural carrying capacities and includes involving the community of the destination in tourism development planning. It also involves integrating tourism to match current economic and growth policies so as to mitigate some of the negative economic and social impacts of 'mass tourism'. Murphy (1985) advocates the use of an 'ecological approach', to consider both 'plants' and 'people' when implementing the sustainable tourism development process. This is in contrast to the 'boosterism' and 'economic' approaches to tourism planning, neither of which consider the detrimental ecological or sociological impacts of tourism development to a destination.

However, Butler (2006) questions the exposition of the term 'sustainable' in the context of tourism, citing its ambiguity and stating that "the emerging sustainable development philosophy of the 1990s can be viewed as an extension of the broader realization that a preoccupation with economic growth without regard to it social and environmental consequences is self-defeating in the long term." Thus 'sustainable tourism development' is seldom considered as an autonomous function of economic regeneration as separate from general economic growth.

Ecotourism

Ecotourism, also known as ecological tourism, is responsible travel to fragile, pristine, and usually protected areas that strives to be low impact and (often) small scale. It helps educate the traveler; provides funds for conservation; directly benefits the economic development and political empowerment of local communities; and fosters respect for different cultures and for human rights.

Pro-Poor Tourism

The pro poor tourism has to help the very poorest in developing countries has been receiving increasing attention by those involved in development and the issue has been addressed either through small scale projects in local communities and by Ministries of Tourism attempting to attract huge numbers of tourists. Research by the Overseas Development Institute suggests that neither is the best way to encourage tourists' money to reach the poorest as only 25% or less (far less in some cases) ever reaches the poor; successful examples of money reaching the poor include mountain climbing in Tanzania or cultural tourism in Luang Prabang, Laos.

Recession Tourism

Recession tourism is a travel trend, which evolved by way of the world economic crisis. Identified by American entrepreneur Matt Landau (2007), recession tourism is defined by low-cost, high-value experiences taking place of once-popular generic retreats. Various recession tourism hotspots have seen business boom during the recession thanks to comparatively low costs of living and a slow world job market suggesting travelers are elongating trips where their money travels further.

Medical Tourism

When there is a significant price difference between countries for a given medical procedure, particularly in Southeast Asia, India, Eastern Europe and where there are different regulatory regimes, in relation to particular medical procedures (e.g. dentistry), traveling to take advantage of the price or regulatory differences is often referred to as "medical tourism".

Educational Tourism

Educational tourism developed, because of the growing popularity of teaching and learning of knowledge and the enhancing of technical competency outside of the classroom environment. In educational tourism, the main focus of the tour or leisure activity includes visiting another country to learn about the culture, such as in Student Exchange Programmes and Study Tours, or to work and apply skills learned inside the classroom in a different environment, such as in the International Practicum Training Programme.

Creative Tourism

Creative tourism has existed as a form of cultural tourism, since the early beginnings of tourism itself. Its European roots date back to the time of the Grand Tour, which saw the sons of aristocratic families traveling for the purpose of mostly interactive, educational experiences. More recently, creative tourism has been given its own name by Crispin Raymond and Greg Richards, who as members of the Association for Tourism and Leisure Education (ATLAS), have directed a number of projects for the European Commission, including cultural and crafts tourism, known as sustainable tourism. They have defined "creative tourism" as tourism related to the active participation of travellers in the culture of the host community, through interactive workshops and informal learning experiences.

Meanwhile, the concept of creative tourism has been picked up by high-profile organizations such as UNESCO, who through the Creative Cities Network, have endorsed creative tourism as an engaged, authentic experience that promotes an active understanding of the specific cultural features of a place. More recently, creative tourism has gained popularity as a form of cultural tourism, drawing on active participation by travelers in the culture of the host communities they visit. Several countries offer examples of this type of tourism development, including the United Kingdom, the Bahamas, Jamaica, Spain, Italy and New Zealand.

Dark Tourism

One emerging area of special interest has been identified by Lennon and Foley (2000) as "dark" tourism. This type of tourism involves visits to "dark" sites, such as battlegrounds, scenes of horrific crimes or acts of genocide, for example: concentration camps. Dark tourism remains a small niche market, driven by varied motivations, such as mourning, remembrance, education, macabre curiosity or even entertainment. Its early origins are rooted in fairgrounds and medieval fairs.

Doom Tourism

Also known as "Tourism of Doom," or "Last Chance

Tourism" this emerging trend involves traveling to places that are environmentally or otherwise threatened (the ice caps of Mount Kilimanjaro, the melting glaciers of Patagonia, The coral of the Great Barrier Reef) before it is too late. Identified by travel trade magazine TravelAge West editor-in-chief Kenneth Shapiro in 2007 and later explored in The New York Times, this type of tourism is believed to be on the rise. Some see the trend as related to sustainable tourism or ecotourism due to the fact that a number of these tourist destinations are considered threatened by environmental factors such as global warming, over population or climate change. Others worry that travel to many of these threatened locations increases an individual's carbon footprint and only hastens problems threatened locations are already facing.

Growth

The World Tourism Organization (UNWTO) forecasts that international tourism will continue growing at the average annual rate of 4 %. With the advent of e-commerce, tourism products have become one of the most traded items on the internet. Tourism products and services have been made available through intermediaries, although tourism providers (hotels, airlines, etc.) can sell their services directly. This has put pressure on intermediaries from both on-line and traditional shops.

It has been suggested there is a strong correlation between tourism expenditure per capita and the degree to which countries play in the global context. Not only as a result of the important economic contribution of the tourism industry, but also as an indicator of the degree of confidence with which global citizens leverage the resources of the globe for the benefit of their local economies. This is why any projections of growth in tourism may serve as an indication of the relative influence that each country will exercise in the future.

Space tourism is expected to "take off" in the first

quarter of the 21st century, although compared with traditional destinations the number of tourists in orbit will remain low until technologies such as a space elevator make space travel cheap.

Technological improvement is likely to make possible air-ship hotels, based either on solar-powered airplanes or large dirigibles. Underwater hotels, such as Hydropolis, expected to open in Dubai in 2009, will be built. On the ocean, tourists will be welcomed by ever larger cruise ships and perhaps floating cities.

Sports Tourism

Since the late 1980s, sports tourism has become increasingly popular. Events such as rugby, Olympics, Commonwealth games, Asian Games and football World Cups have enabled specialist travel companies to gain official ticket allocation and then sell them in packages that include flights, hotels and excursions.

Latest Trends

As a result of the late-2000s recession, international arrivals suffered a strong slowdown beginning in June 2008. Growth from 2007 to 2008 was only 3.7% during the first eight months of 2008. The Asian and Pacific markets were affected and Europe stagnated during the boreal summer months, while the Americas performed better, reducing their expansion rate but keeping a 6% growth from January to August 2008. Only the Middle East continued its rapid growth during the same period, reaching a 17% growth as compared to the same period in 2007. This slowdown on international tourism demand was also reflected in the air transport industry, with a negative growth in September 2008 and a 3.3% growth in passenger traffic through September. The hotel industry also reports a slowdown, as room occupancy continues to decline. As the global economic situation deteriorated dramatically during September and October as a result of the global financial crisis, growth of international tourism is expected to slow even further for the remaining of 2008, and this slowdown in demand growth is forecasted to continue into 2009 as recession has already hit most of the top spender countries, with long-haul travel expected to be the most affected by the economic crisis. This negative trend intensified as international tourist arrivals fell by 8% during the first four months of 2009, and the decline was exacerbated in some regions due to the outbreak of the influenza AH1N1 virus.

TOURIST ATTRACTION

A tourist attraction is a place of interest where tourists visit, typically for its inherent or exhibited cultural value, historical significance, natural or built beauty, or amusement opportunities. Some examples include historical places, monuments, zoos, aquaria, museums and art galleries, botanical gardens, buildings and structures (e.g., castles, libraries, former prisons, skyscrapers, bridges), national parks and forests, theme parks and carnivals, living history museums, ethnic enclave communities, historic trains and cultural events. Many tourist attractions are also landmarks. Tourist attractions are also created to capitalise on legends such as a supposed UFO crash site near Roswell, New Mexico and the alleged Loch Ness monster sightings in Scotland. Ghost sightings also make tourist attractions. Ethnic communities may become tourist attractions, such as Chinatowns in the United States and the black British neighborhood of Brixton in London, England. In the US, owners and marketers of attractions advertise tourist attractions on billboards along the side of highways and roadways, especially in remote areas. Tourist attractions often provide free promotional brochures and flyers in information centres, fast food restaurants, hotel and motel rooms or lobbies, and rest areas.

While some tourist attractions provide visitors a memorable experience for a reasonable admission charge or even for free, others can have a tendency to be of low quality and to overprice their goods and services (such as admission, food, and souvenirs) in order to profit from tourists excessively. Such places are commonly known as tourist traps.

Novelty Attraction

Novelty attractions are oddities such as the "biggest ball of twine" in Cawker City, Kansas, the Corn Palace in Mitchell, South Dakota, or Carhenge in Alliance, Nebraska where old cars serve in the place of stones in a replica of Stonehenge. Novelty attractions are not limited to the American Midwest, but are part of Midwestern culture.

ROADSIDE ATTRACTION

A roadside attraction is a feature along the side of a road, that is frequently advertised with billboards to attract tourists. In general, these are places one might stop on the way to somewhere else, rather than being a final or primary destination in and of themselves. The modern tourist-oriented highway attraction originated as a U.S. and Western Canadian phenomenon in the 1940s to 1960s, and subsequently caught on in Australia.

History

When long-distance road travel became practical and popular in the late 1930s, entrepreneurs began building restaurants, motels, coffee shops, and more unusual businesses to attract travelers. Many of the buildings took the form of common objects of enormous size, often advertising the items sold there, and became attractions in themselves. Some other types of Roadside Attractions include monuments and pseudo-scientific amusements such as the Santa Cruz Mystery Spot.

With the building of the U.S. interstate highway system in the mid-1950s, most roadside attractions were by-passed and quickly went out of business. But the most famous remained attractive enough to travelers to make them leave the comfort of the interstate highway for a brief time and thus keep the attraction in business.

TOURIST DESTINATION

A tourist destination is a city, town, or other area that is dependent to a significant extent on the revenues accruing from tourism. It may contain one or more tourist attractions and possibly some "tourist traps." These tourist destinations are represented in the United States by Convention and Visitor Bureaus (CVB's), which are paid by bed taxes to market the destinations to travelers.

In Australia, most destinations are found on the official government tourism website .

TOURIST TRAP

A tourist trap is an establishment, or group of establishments, that has been created with the aim of attracting tourists and their money. Tourist traps will typically provide services, entertainment, souvenirs and other products for tourists to purchase.

While the term may have negative connotations for some, such establishments may be viewed by tourists as fun and interesting diversions.

Tourist traps in the US

Activities

In some areas like Ishpeming, Michigan, Flush toilets may be a sufficient draw to entice tourist to stop as they are not readily available at many tourist facilities in Michigan's Upper Peninsula. Wall Drug, in South Dakota, began its tourist trade simply by offering ice water.

Size

Tourist traps range significantly in size, from a single tree to the city of Las Vegas, Nevada.

Term "Tourist Trap"

A few establishments take pride in the term and embody it into their names, such as "Da Yoopers Tourist Trap" in Michigan's Upper Peninsula, and "The TOURIST TRAP" at Deep Creek Lake, Maryland. Other establishments like The "Trees of Mystery" in Klamath, California avoid the phrase.

HOLIDAY

A holiday is a day designated as having special significance for which individuals, a government, or a religious group have deemed that observation is warranted. It is generally an official (more common) or unofficial observance of religious, national, or cultural significance, often accompanied by celebrations or festivities.

Etymology

The word *holiday* derived from the notion of "Holy Day", and gradually evolved to its current form.

The word *holiday* comes from the Old English word *hâligdᵻg*. The word originally referred only to special religious days. In modern use, it means any special day of rest or relaxation, as opposed to normal days away from work or school.

Regional Meaning

The usage of the word *holiday* varies in different parts of the English-speaking world.

Australia, Canada, UK

In Australia, Canada, and the UK, all usage of the word holiday means time away from normal employment or education. The meaning is further subdivided into two major sub-categories:

1. Public holiday, a day decreed by government as a day when the bulk of the population is not normally

expected to be at work, such as Australia Day, Anzac Day, Bank Holiday or Christmas Day.

2. A non-working trip or stay away from one's normal home. This is similar to what is described elsewhere as a vacation, but that word is rarely used in Australia or the UK. Canadians variously use either the term *vacation* or the word *holiday*.

Days referred to as holidays in other places but which do not involve formally decreed time away from work especially for that day, such as Valentine's Day and Mother's Day, are not described as holidays in Australia or the UK.

U.S.A.

In the U.S.A. *holiday* may refer to a day set aside by a nation or culture (in some cases, multiple nations and cultures) for commemoration, celebration, or other observance. Schools and businesses often close for certain holidays. The term "holiday" is also commonly used to refer to the December gift-giving season; businesses may announce, for example, that a product will be available "for Holiday 2011", meaning that it will be available in time for Christmas shopping.

India

In India holidays are days in which mainly schools or small firms get a free day because of some regional or religious reason.The term "Bank Holiday" in India is referred as a day when majority of the people get a leave due to National,International or major Cultural reason.

Types of Holiday (Observance)

Religious Holidays

Many holidays are linked to faiths and religions. Christian holidays are defined as part of the liturgical year. The Catholic patronal feast day or 'name day' are celebrated in each place's patron saint's day, according to the Calendar of saints. In Islam, the largest holidays are

Eid ul-Fitr (immediately after Ramadan) and Eid al-Adha (at the end of the Hajj). Hindus, Jains and Sikhs observe several holidays, one of the largest being Diwali (Festival of Light). Japanese holidays contain references to several different faiths and beliefs. Celtic, Norse, and Neopagan holidays follow the order of the Wheel of the Year. Some are closely linked to Swedish festivities. The Bahá'í Faith observes holidays as defined by the Bahá'í calendar. Jews have two holiday seasons: the Spring Feasts of Pesach (Passover) and Shavuot (Weeks, called Pentecost in Greek); and the Fall Feasts of Rosh Hashanah (Head of the Year), Yom Kippur (Day of Atonement), Sukkot (Tabernacles), and Shemini Atzeret (Eighth Day of Assembly).

Northern Hemisphere Winter Holidays

Winter in the Northern Hemisphere features many holidays that involve festivals and feasts. The Christmas and holiday season surrounds the winter solstice, Christmas and Holiday, and is celebrated by many religions and cultures. Usually, this period begins near the start of November and ends with New Year's Day. *Holiday season* is, somewhat, a commercial term that applies, in the US, to the period that begins with Thanksgiving and ends with New Year's Eve. Some Christian countries consider the end of the festive season to be after the feast of Epiphany.

National Holidays

Sovereign nations and territories observe holidays based on events of significance to their history. For example, Australians celebrate Australia Day.

Secular Holidays

Several secular holidays are observed, such as Earth Day or Labour Day, both internationally, and across multi-country regions, often in conjunction with organizations such as the United Nations. Many other days are marked to celebrate events or people, but are not strictly holidays as time off work is rarely given.

Unofficial Holidays

These are holidays that are not traditionally marked on calendars. These holidays are celebrated by various groups and individuals. Some promote a cause, others recognize historical events not officially recognized, and others are "funny" holidays celebrated with humorous intent. For example, Monkey Day celebrated on December 14, and International Talk Like a Pirate Day observed on September 19.

Opposition

Jehovah's Witnesses do not celebrate certain holidays, such as Christmas, Halloween, and Easter, because they believe these holidays are pagan. They also reject national holidays as well, because they believe that, by celebrating these holidays, they are giving honor to man's governments and not God's Kingdom.

REFERENCES

Barbara Klebanow and Sara Fischer (2005). *American Holidays: Exploring Traditions, Customs, and Backgrounds.* Pro Lingua Associates. ISBN 0-86647-196-0.

Beaver, Allan (2002). *A Dictionary of Travel and Tourism Terminology.* Wallingford: CAB International. p. 313.

Lucille Recht Penner and Ib Ohlsson (September 1993). *Celebration: The Story of American Holidays.* MacMillan Publishing Company. ISBN 0-02-770903-5.

Spode, Hasso (1998). "Geschichte der Tourismuswissenschaft". In Haedrich, Günther (in German). *Tourismus-management: Tourismus-marketing Und Fremdenverkehrsplanung.* Berlin: [u.a.] de Gruyter.

Susan E. Richardson (July 2001). *Holidays & Holy Days: Origins, Customs, and Insights on Celebrations Through the Year.* Vine Books. ISBN 0-8307-3442-2.

Theobald, William F. (1998). *Global Tourism* (2nd ed.). Oxford [England]: Butterworth–Heinemann. pp. 6–7.

6

Focus on Relevance of Couch Surfing, Hospitality Service and Social Networks

COUCHSURFING

CouchSurfing is a hospitality exchange network and website. With almost 2.7 million members in 246 countries and territories, CouchSurfing has an Alexa Traffic Rank of about 2,500.

Etymology

Couchsurfing is a neologism referring to the practice of moving from one friend's house to another, sleeping in whatever spare space is available, floor or couch, generally staying a few days before moving on to the next house.

Membership

Free to register, members have the option of providing information and pictures of themselves and of the sleeping accommodation they offer, if any. More information provided by a member, and other members, improves the chances that someone will find the member trustworthy enough to be his host or guest. Security is often measured in the reference established by networking. Volunteers may verify names and addresses. Members looking for accommodation can search for hosts using several parameters such as age, location, gender and activity level.

Homestays are consensual between the host and guest, and the duration, nature, and terms of the guest's stay are generally worked out in advance. No monetary exchange takes place except for compensation of incurred expenses (e.g. food).

CouchSurfing provides editable travel guides and forums where members may seek travel partners or advice. CouchSurfing's main focus is "social networking" and members organize activities such as camping trips, bar crawls, meetings, and sporting events.

The website features a searchable database of hundreds of upcoming events organized by CouchSurfing members, including the annual "Berlin Beach Camp" which draws over 1,000 attendees, the annual "WinterCamp," and a New Year's Eve party hosted in a different city in Europe every year. Famous Couchsurfers include Julian Assange and Daniel Bedingfield.

Security Verification

There are three methods designed to increase security and trust, which are all visible on member profiles for potential hosts and surfers:

1. Personal references, which hosts and surfers have the option to leave after having used the service.

2. An optional credit card verification system, allowing members to "lock in" their name and address by making a credit card payment and entering a code that CouchSurfing mails to an address of their choice. This also allows CouchSurfing to recoup some costs by requiring a fee for verification. For fairness, the verification fee is based on a sliding scale, taking into account the Purchasing Power Parity and Human Development Index of the country of residence.

3. A personal vouching system, whereby a member that had been vouched for three times — originally

starting with the founders of the site — might in turn vouch for any number of other members he knew or had met through CouchSurfing, and trusts.

Ambassadors

Members who wished to volunteer for various tasks on the site and help spread the word about CouchSurfing in general were able to become ambassadors. Ambassadors must be role-models and actively promote the CouchSurfing spirit among members and to the public. In addition to promoting use of the site, they greet new members, help with questions and perform other administrative tasks, all on a volunteer basis. No new ambassadors are being created at this time.

Demographics

As of January 2011, there were over 2.4 million persons who were registered with Couchsurfing, a population comparable in size to Latvia or Jamaica.

As of January 2011, couchsurfers represents more than 80,000 unique towns in 245 states and territories. Around 20% of the couchsurfers had registered their country as being the United States, with Germany, France, Canada and England also registering large numbers of participants. The city with the largest number of resident couchsurfers was Paris.

English was spoken by nearly 74% of registered Couchsurfers. French (20%), Spanish (17%) and German (16%) were also spoken.

The average age of participants was 28 years of age.

History

Casey Fenton

The CouchSurfing project was conceived by Casey Fenton in 1999. According to Fenton's account, the idea arose after finding an inexpensive flight from Boston to Iceland.

Fenton randomly e-mailed 1,500 students from the University of Iceland asking if he could stay. He ultimately received more than 50 offers of accommodation. On the return flight to Boston, he began to develop the ideas that would underpin the CouchSurfing project.

Fenton developed the code intermittently over the next few years. The site was launched with the cooperation of Dan Hoffer, Sebastien Le Tuan, and Leonardo Silveira as a beta in January 2003. The project became a public website in January 2004.

Initial growth of the site was slow. By the end of 2004 the site had just over 6,000 members. In 2005, growth accelerated and by the end of the year, membership stood at just under 45,000. As of 29 January 2011, CouchSurfing has almost 2.5 million members and is the most popular free accommodation site. As of April 2011, the site has an Alexa Traffic Rank of 2,434.

2006 Database Loss and Relaunch

In June 2006, the project experienced a number of computer problems resulting in much of the database being irrevocably lost. Due to the volume of critical data that had been lost, Casey Fenton was of the opinion that the project could not be resurrected. On 29 June 2006, he sent an e-mail to all members: "It is with a heavy heart that I face the truth of this situation. CouchSurfing as we knew it doesn't exist anymore."

Fenton's e-mail was met with vocal opposition to the termination of the project and considerable support for its recreation. A CouchSurfing Collective was underway in Montreal at the time and those in attendance committed to fully recreating the original site, with users to re-enter their profile data. "CouchSurfing 2.0" was announced early in July 2006, with the intent to be operational within 10 days. The initial implementation of CouchSurfing 2.0 actually launched after only four days with the current CouchSurfing slogan *"Participate in Creating a Better World,*

One Couch At A Time". Since the site relaunch, the project has received international media coverage.

2009 Leeds Incident

On 5 March 2009 in Leeds, UK, a man named Abdelali Nachet raped a woman from Hong Kong who stayed at his place through the CouchSurfing project. Nachet was sentenced to 10 years in prison.

Organization

Mission

The mission statement of CouchSurfing is *Create Inspiring Experiences*:

> "At CouchSurfing International, we envision a world where everyone can explore and create meaningful connections with the people and places they encounter. Building meaningful connections across cultures enables us to respond to diversity with curiosity, appreciation and respect. The appreciation of diversity spreads tolerance and creates a global community."

CouchSurfing Collectives

Since June 2006, development of the website has been run in large part by CouchSurfing Collectives: events which may last days or weeks, bringing groups of CouchSurfers together in a chosen city, to develop and improve CouchSurfing. Previous Collectives took place in Montreal, Vienna, New Zealand, Rotterdam, Thailand, Alaska, Costa Rica and Istanbul.

HOSPITALITY SERVICE

The concept of hospitality exchange, also known as "accommodation sharing", "hospitality services" (short "hospex"), and "home stay networks", "home hospitality" ("hoho"), refers to centrally organized social networks of individuals, generally travelers, who offer or seek accommodation without monetary exchange. These services generally connect users via the internet.

History

In 1949, Bob Luitweiler founded the first hospitality service called Servas Open Doors as a cross national, non-profit, volunteer run organization advocating interracial and international peace. In 1965, John Wilcock set up the Traveler's Directory as a listing of his friends willing to host each other when traveling. In 1988, Joy Lily rescued the organization from imminent shutdown, forming Hospitality Exchange. In 1970 Jimmy Carter (then US President) announced the formation of Friendship Force International which has chapters in 57 countries today. In 2000, Veit Kuhne founded Hospitality Club, the first Internet-based service. In 2004, Casey Fenton started CouchSurfing, now the largest hospitality exchange organization.

How They Work

Generally, after registering, members have the option of providing very detailed information and pictures of themselves and of the sleeping accommodation being offered, if any. The more information provided by a member improves the chances that someone will find the member trustworthy enough to be their host or guest. Names and addresses may be verified by volunteers. Members looking for accommodation can search for hosts using several parameters such as age, location, sex, and activity level. Home stays are entirely consensual between the host and guest, and the duration, nature, and terms of the guest's stay are generally worked out in advance to the convenience of both parties. No monetary exchange takes place except under certain circumstances (e.g. the guest may compensate the host for food). After using the service, members can leave a noticeable reference about their host or guest.

Instead of **or** in addition to accommodation, members

also offer to provide guide services or travel-related advice. The websites of the networks also provide editable travel guides and forums where members may seek travel partners or advice. Many such organizations are also focused on "social networking" and members organize activities such as camping trips, bar crawls, meetings, and sporting events.

Some networks cater to specific niche markets such as students, activists, religious pilgrims, and even occupational groups like police officers.

Benefits

Monetary Savings

As these networks provide accommodation at no charge, monetary savings can be significant.

Local Contact

Hospitality exchange gives travelers the chance to experience what life is like for people living in other places. In addition, making interpersonal connections and fostering understanding of different cultures may in the long run also be important to international relations. During hospitality exchanges, hosts may show off their local knowledge and exciting places "off the tourist map". Not only may travelers get a distinct experience, but they will also get a feel for the everyday lives of local residents.

Reciprocity

The concept behind Hospitality services is based on the pay it forward philosophy, gift economy, and reciprocal altruism.

Drawbacks

Lack of Guarantee

There is no contractual agreement between users in these systems. Reservations are made, but if they are for some reason broken, there is no higher authority to which one could plead for a refund or other compensation. The only repercussion will be the poor rating you give that user and your only consolation will be that your warning will deter others from visiting or hosting them. For those who feel insecure unless their travel arrangements are written in stone before departure, this system will not be comforting.

Potential Interpersonal Conflict or Awkwardness

There is a chance that guest and host will not get along. Perhaps there will be scheduling or ideological conflicts. Maybe you will find that hosts or visitors have misrepresented themselves. Perhaps the experience will not live up to your expectations. Intense interpersonal communications in advance and a flexibility once you have arrived is your best bet. These experiences require additional planning and courtesy towards the demands of your host. Thus, your living conditions, length of stay, and overall experience will be circumscribed by the living conditions you enter into.

Digital Divide and Demographic Segregation

As use of these services generally requires access to the internet and knowledge of the English language, the sample population found in searches of these databases is really much less diverse than a geographical representation of worldwide users might suggest.

Security

Staying in someone's house, or inviting people into your house leaves open the possibility of being taken advantage of.

Home Hospitality in Scouting

In the Scout Movement, home hospitality (hoho) refers to Scouts living for a few days with a host Scouting family to experience everyday life in that community. This often takes place before or after a jamboree and is usually organized by the organization running the jamboree.

Example Networks

There are countless websites that serve the idea of hospitality service, with new ones appearing as this phenomenon becomes more popular. While this page is not intended to be a directory listing, here is a small sample of the well-established and long-standing networks:

- CouchSurfing - A very active network with over 2 million members in more than 200 countries
- Friendship Force International A network of chapters worldwide which concentrates on building understanding across cultures.
- Hospitality Club - A very active network with over 550,000 members in more than 200 countries
- Servas International - human rights and global peace oriented since 1949. A relatively small network now with over 15,000 members(?) with a very long history.
- Tripping - A global network of travelers with the motto "For Travelers, Not Tourists"
- BeWelcome

Specialized Networks

Some networks offer specialised hospitality services.

- Lesbian and Gay Hospitality Exchange International
- Warm Showers - Hospitality network for touring cyclists
- Dachgeber - Hospitality network for touring cyclists in Germany with about 3000 members
- Pasporta Servo - for Esperanto speakers
- WWOOF - "Worldwide Opportunities on Organic Farms", help on the property is exchanged for food, accommodation, education and cultural interaction

- Freagle "Free Camping, worldwide!" - Uniting Outdoor Lovers Through Hospitality and Mutual Help.
- HelpX - "Help Exchange", help is exchanged for food, accommodation, experience and cultural interaction
- Homeshare International - charitable organization providing exchange of housing for help in the home
- Ridester - ride sharing for travelers in USA
- Jewgether - a hospitality network that connects Jewish people from all around the world and helps Jewish travelers find a place to stay.

SOCIAL NETWORK

A social network is a social structure made up of individuals (or organizations) called "nodes", which are tied (connected) by one or more specific types of interdependency, such as friendship, kinship, common interest, financial exchange, dislike, sexual relationships, or relationships of beliefs, knowledge or prestige.

Social network analysis views social relationships in terms of network theory consisting of *nodes* and *ties* (also called *edges*, *links*, or *connections*). Nodes are the individual actors within the networks, and ties are the relationships between the actors. The resulting graph-based structures are often very complex. There can be many kinds of ties between the nodes. Research in a number of academic fields has shown that social networks operate on many levels, from families up to the level of nations, and play a critical role in determining the way problems are solved, organizations are run, and the degree to which individuals succeed in achieving their goals.

In its simplest form, a social network is a map of specified ties, such as friendship, between the nodes being studied. The nodes to which an individual is thus connected are the social contacts of that individual. The network can also be used to measure social capital – the value that an individual gets from the social network. These concepts are often displayed in a social network diagram, where nodes are the points and ties are the lines.

Social Network Analysis

Social network analysis (related to *network theory*) has emerged as a key technique in modern sociology. It has also gained a significant following in anthropology, biology, communication studies, economics, geography, information science, organizational studies, social psychology, and sociolinguistics, and has become a popular topic of speculation and study.

People have used the idea of "social network" loosely for over a century to connote complex sets of relationships between members of social systems at all scales, from interpersonal to international. In 1954, J. A. Barnes started using the term systematically to denote patterns of ties, encompassing concepts traditionally used by the public and those used by social scientists: bounded groups (e.g., tribes, families) and social categories (e.g., gender, ethnicity). Scholars such as S.D. Berkowitz, Stephen Borgatti, Ronald Burt, Kathleen Carley, Martin Everett, Katherine Faust, Linton Freeman, Mark Granovetter, David Knoke, David Krackhardt, Peter Marsden, Nicholas Mullins, Anatol Rapoport, Stanley Wasserman, Barry Wellman, Douglas R. White, and Harrison White expanded the use of systematic social network analysis.

Social network analysis has now moved from being a suggestive metaphor to an analytic approach to a paradigm, with its own theoretical statements, methods, social network analysis software, and researchers. Analysts reason from whole to part; from structure to relation to individual; from behaviour to attitude. They typically either study *whole networks* (also known as *complete networks*), all of the ties containing specified relations in a defined population, or *personal networks* (also known as *egocentric networks*), the ties that specified people have, such as their "personal communities". In the latter case, the ties are said to go from *egos*, who are the focal actors who are being analyzed, to their *alters*.

The distinction between whole/complete networks and personal/egocentric networks has depended largely on how analysts were able to gather data. That is, for groups such as companies, schools, or membership societies, the analyst was expected to have complete information about who was in the network, all participants being both potential egos and alters. Personal/egocentric studies were typically conducted when identities of egos were known, but not their alters. These studies rely on the egos to provide information about the identities of alters and there is no expectation that the various egos or sets of alters will be tied to each other. A *snowball network* refers to the idea that the alters identified in an egocentric survey then become egos themselves and are able in turn to nominate additional alters. While there are severe logistic limits to conducting snowball network studies, a method for examining *hybrid networks* has recently been developed in which egos in complete networks can nominate alters otherwise not listed who are then available for all subsequent egos to see.

The hybrid network may be valuable for examining whole/complete networks that are expected to include important players beyond those who are formally identified. For example, employees of a company often work with non-company consultants who may be part of a network that cannot fully be defined prior to data collection.

Several analytic tendencies distinguish social network analysis:

> There is no assumption that groups are the building blocks of society: the approach is open to studying less-bounded social systems, from nonlocal communities to links among websites.

Rather than treating individuals (persons, organizations, states) as discrete units of analysis, it focuses on how the structure of ties affects individuals and their relationships.

In contrast to analyses that assume that socialization into norms determines behaviour, network analysis looks to see the extent to which the structure and composition of ties affect norms.

The shape of a social network helps determine a network's usefulness to its individuals. Smaller, tighter networks can be less useful to their members than networks with lots of loose connections (weak ties) to individuals outside the main network. More open networks, with many weak ties and social connections, are more likely to introduce new ideas and opportunities to their members than closed networks with many redundant ties. In other words, a group of friends who only do things with each other already share the same knowledge and opportunities. A group of individuals with connections to other social worlds is likely to have access to a wider range of information. It is better for individual success to have connections to a variety of networks rather than many connections within a single network. Similarly, individuals can exercise influence or act as brokers within their social networks by bridging two networks that are not directly linked (called filling structural holes).

The power of social network analysis stems from its difference from traditional social scientific studies, which assume that it is the attributes of individual actors—whether they are friendly or unfriendly, smart or dumb, etc.—that matter. Social network analysis produces an alternate view, where the attributes of individuals are less important than their relationships and ties with other actors within the network. This approach has turned out to be useful for explaining many real-world phenomena, but leaves less room for individual agency, the ability for individuals to influence their success, because so much of it rests within the structure of their network.

Social networks have also been used to examine how organizations interact with each other, characterizing the many informal connections that link executives together, as well as associations and connections between individual employees at different organizations. For example, power within organizations often comes more from the degree to which an individual within a network is at the center of many relationships than actual job title. Social networks also play a key role in hiring, in business success, and in job performance. Networks provide ways for companies to gather information, deter competition, and collude in setting prices or policies.

History of Social Network Analysis

A summary of the progress of social networks and social network analysis has been written by Linton Freeman.

Precursors of social networks in the late 1800s include Émile Durkheim and Ferdinand Tönnies. Tönnies argued that social groups can exist as personal and direct social ties that either link individuals who share values and belief (*gemeinschaft*) or impersonal, formal, and instrumental social links (*gesellschaft*). Durkheim gave a non-individualistic explanation of social facts arguing that social phenomena arise when interacting individuals constitute a reality that can no longer be accounted for in terms of the properties of individual actors. He distinguished between a traditional society – "mechanical solidarity" – which prevails if individual differences are minimized, and the modern society – "organic solidarity" – that develops out of cooperation between differentiated individuals with independent roles.

Georg Simmel, writing at the turn of the twentieth century, was the first scholar to think directly in social network terms. His essays pointed to the nature of network size on interaction and to the likelihood of interaction in ramified, loosely-knit networks rather than groups (Simmel, 1908/1971).

After a hiatus in the first decades of the twentieth century, three main traditions in social networks appeared. In the 1930s, J.L. Moreno pioneered the systematic recording and analysis of social interaction in small groups, especially classrooms and work groups (sociometry), while a Harvard group led by W. Lloyd Warner and Elton Mayo explored interpersonal relations at work. In 1940, A.R. Radcliffe-Brown's presidential address to British anthropologists urged the systematic study of networks. However, it took about 15 years before this call was followed-up systematically.

Social network analysis developed with the kinship studies of Elizabeth Bott in England in the 1950s and the 1950s–1960s urbanization studies of the University of Manchester group of anthropologists (centered around Max Gluckman and later J. Clyde Mitchell) investigating community networks in southern Africa, India and the United Kingdom. Concomitantly, British anthropologist S.F. Nadel codified a theory of social structure that was influential in later network analysis.

In the 1960s-1970s, a growing number of scholars worked to combine the different tracks and traditions. One group was centered around Harrison White and his students at the Harvard University Department of Social Relations: Ivan Chase, Bonnie Erickson, Harriet Friedmann, Mark Granovetter, Nancy Howell, Joel Levine, Nicholas Mullins, John Padgett, Michael Schwartz and Barry Wellman. Also independently active in the Harvard Social Relations department at the time were Charles Tilly, who focused on networks in political and community sociology and social movements, and Stanley Milgram, who developed the "six degrees of separation" thesis. Mark Granovetter and Barry Wellman are among the former students of White who have elaborated and popularized social network analysis.

Significant independent work was also done by scholars

elsewhere: University of California Irvine social scientists interested in mathematical applications, centered around Linton Freeman, including John Boyd, Susan Freeman, Kathryn Faust, A. Kimball Romney and Douglas White; quantitative analysts at the University of Chicago, including Joseph Galaskiewicz, Wendy Griswold, Edward Laumann, Peter Marsden, Martina Morris, and John Padgett; and communication scholars at Michigan State University, including Nan Lin and Everett Rogers. A substantively-oriented University of Toronto sociology group developed in the 1970s, centered on former students of Harrison White: S.D. Berkowitz, Harriet Friedmann, Nancy Leslie Howard, Nancy Howell, Lorne Tepperman and Barry Wellman, and also including noted modeler and game theorist Anatol Rapoport.In terms of theory, it critiqued methodological individualism and group-based analyses, arguing that seeing the world as social networks offered more analytic leverage.

Research

Social network analysis has been used in epidemiology to help understand how patterns of human contact aid or inhibit the spread of diseases such as HIV in a population. The evolution of social networks can sometimes be modeled by the use of agent based models, providing insight into the interplay between communication rules, rumor spreading and social structure.

SNA may also be an effective tool for mass surveillance – for example the Total Information Awareness programme was doing in-depth research on strategies to analyze social networks to determine whether or not U.S. citizens were political threats.

Diffusion of innovations theory explores social networks and their role in influencing the spread of new ideas and practices. Change agents and opinion leaders often play major roles in spurring the adoption of innovations, although factors inherent to the innovations also play a role.

Robin Dunbar has suggested that the typical size of an egocentric network is constrained to about 150 members due to possible limits in the capacity of the human communication channel. The rule arises from cross-cultural studies in sociology and especially anthropology of the maximum size of a village (in modern parlance most reasonably understood as an *ecovillage*). It is theorized in evolutionary psychology that the number may be some kind of limit of average human ability to recognize members and track emotional facts about all members of a group. However, it may be due to economics and the need to track "free riders", as it may be easier in larger groups to take advantage of the benefits of living in a community without contributing to those benefits.

Mark Granovetter found in one study that more numerous weak ties can be important in seeking information and innovation. Cliques have a tendency to have more homogeneous opinions as well as share many common traits. This homophilic tendency was the reason for the members of the cliques to be attracted together in the first place. However, being similar, each member of the clique would also know more or less what the other members knew. To find new information or insights, members of the clique will have to look beyond the clique to its other friends and acquaintances. This is what Granovetter called "the strength of weak ties".

Guanxi is a central concept in Chinese society (and other East Asian cultures) that can be summarized as the use of personal influence. It is loosely analogous to "clout" or "pull" in the West. Guanxi can be studied from a social network approach.

The small world phenomenon is the hypothesis that the chain of social acquaintances required to connect one arbitrary person to another arbitrary person anywhere in the world is generally short. The concept gave rise to the famous phrase six degrees of separation after a 1967 *small world experiment* by psychologist Stanley Milgram. In

Milgram's experiment, a sample of US individuals were asked to reach a particular target person by passing a message along a chain of acquaintances. The average length of successful chains turned out to be about five intermediaries or six separation steps (the majority of chains in that study actually failed to complete). The methods (and ethics as well) of Milgram's experiment were later questioned by an American scholar, and some further research to replicate Milgram's findings found that the degrees of connection needed could be higher. Academic researchers continue to explore this phenomenon as Internet-based communication technology has supplemented the phone and postal systems available during the times of Milgram.

A recent electronic small world experiment at Columbia University found that about five to seven degrees of separation are sufficient for connecting any two people through e-mail. Collaboration graphs can be used to illustrate good and bad relationships between humans. A positive edge between two nodes denotes a positive relationship (friendship, alliance, dating) and a negative edge between two nodes denotes a negative relationship (hatred, anger). Signed social network graphs can be used to predict the future evolution of the graph.

In signed social networks, there is the concept of "balanced" and "unbalanced" cycles. A balanced cycle is defined as a cycle where the product of all the signs are positive. Balanced graphs represent a group of people who are unlikely to change their opinions of the other people in the group. Unbalanced graphs represent a group of people who are very likely to change their opinions of the people in their group. For example, a group of 3 people (A, B, and C) where A and B have a positive relationship, B and C have a positive relationship, but C and A have a negative relationship is an unbalanced cycle. This group is very likely to morph into a balanced cycle, such as one where B only has a good relationship with A, and both A and B have a negative relationship with C. By using the concept of balances and unbalanced cycles, the evolution of signed social network graphs can be predicted. One study has found that happiness tends to be correlated in social networks. When a person is happy, nearby friends have a 25 percent higher chance of being happy themselves. Furthermore, people at the center of a social network tend to become happier in the future than those at the periphery. Clusters of happy and unhappy people were discerned within the studied networks, with a reach of three degrees of separation: a person's happiness was associated with the level of happiness of their friends' friends' friends.

Some researchers have suggested that human social networks may have a genetic basis. Using a sample of twins from the National Longitudinal Study of Adolescent Health, they found that in-degree (the number of times a person is named as a friend), transitivity (the probability that two friends are friends with one another), and betweenness centrality (the number of paths in the network that pass through a given person) are all significantly heritable. Existing models of network formation cannot account for this intrinsic node variation, so the researchers propose an alternative "Attract and Introduce" model that can explain heritability and many other features of human social networks.

Metrics (Measures) in Social Network Analysis

Betweenness

The extent to which a node lies between other nodes in the network. This measure takes into account the connectivity of the node's neighbors, giving a higher value for nodes which bridge clusters. The measure reflects the number of people who a person is connecting indirectly through their direct links.

Bridge

An edge is said to be a bridge if deleting it would cause its endpoints to lie in different components of a graph.

Centrality

This measure gives a rough indication of the social power of a node based on how well they "connect" the network. "Betweenness", "Closeness", and "Degree" are all measures of centrality.

Centralization

The difference between the number of links for each node divided by maximum possible sum of differences. A centralized network will have many of its links dispersed around one or a few nodes, while a decentralized network is one in which there is little variation between the number of links each node possesses.

Closeness

The degree an individual is near all other individuals in a network (directly or indirectly). It reflects the ability to access information through the "grapevine" of network members. Thus, closeness is the inverse of the sum of the shortest distances between each individual and every other person in the network. The shortest path may also be known as the "geodesic distance".

Clustering Coefficient

A measure of the likelihood that two associates of a node are associates themselves. A higher clustering coefficient indicates a greater 'cliquishness'.

Cohesion

The degree to which actors are connected directly to each other by cohesive bonds. Groups are identified as 'cliques' if every individual is directly tied to every other individual, 'social circles' if there is less stringency of direct contact, which is imprecise, or as structurally cohesive blocks if precision is wanted.

Degree

The degree a respondent's ties know one another/

proportion of ties among an individual's nominees. Network or global-level density is the proportion of ties in a network relative to the total number possible (sparse versus dense networks).

Efficient Immunization Strategy

The acquaintance immunization strategy, propose to immunize friends of randomly selected nodes. It is found to be very efficient compared to random immunization.

Flow Betweenness Centrality

The degree that a node contributes to sum of maximum flow between all pairs of nodes (not that node).

Eigenvector Centrality

A measure of the importance of a node in a network. It assigns relative scores to all nodes in the network based on the principle that connections to nodes having a high score contribute more to the score of the node in question.

Influential Spreaders

A method to identify influential spreaders is described by Kitsak et al.

Local Bridge

An edge is a local bridge if its endpoints share no common neighbors. Unlike a bridge, a local bridge is contained in a cycle.

Path Length

The distances between pairs of nodes in the network. Average path-length is the average of these distances between all pairs of nodes.

Prestige

In a directed graph prestige is the term used to describe a node's centrality. "Degree Prestige", "Proximity Prestige", and "Status Prestige" are all measures of Prestige. See also degree (graph theory).

Radiality

Degree an individual's network reaches out into the network and provides novel information and influence.

Reach

The degree any member of a network can reach other members of the network.

Second Order Centrality

It assigns relative scores to all nodes in the network based on the observation that important nodes see a random walk (running on the network) "more regularly" than other nodes.

Structural Cohesion

The minimum number of members who, if removed from a group, would disconnect the group. The relation between fragmentation (Structural cohesion) and percolation theory is discussed by Li et al.

Structural Equivalence

Refers to the extent to which nodes have a common set of linkages to other nodes in the system. The nodes don't need to have any ties to each other to be structurally equivalent.

Structural Hole

Static holes that can be strategically filled by connecting one or more links to link together other points. Linked to ideas of social capital: if you link to two people who are not linked you can control their communication.

Network Analytic Software

Network analytic tools are used to represent the nodes

(agents) and edges (relationships) in a network, and to analyze the network data. Like other software tools, the data can be saved in external files. Additional information comparing the various data input formats used by network analysis software packages is available at NetWiki. Network analysis tools allow researchers to investigate large networks like the Internet, disease transmission, etc. These tools provide mathematical functions that can be applied to the network model.

Visualization of Networks

Visual representation of social networks is important to understand the network data and convey the result of the analysis. Many of the analytic software have modules for network visualization. Exploration of the data is done through displaying nodes and ties in various layouts, and attributing colors, size and other advanced properties to nodes.

Typical representation of the network data are graphs in network layout (nodes and ties). These are not very easy-to-read and do not allow an intuitive interpretation. Various new methods have been developed in order to display network data in more intuitive format (e.g. Sociomapping).

Especially when using social network analysis as a tool for facilitating change, different approaches of participatory network mapping have proven useful. Here participants / interviewers provide network data by actually mapping out the network (with pen and paper or digitally) during the data collection session. One benefit of this approach is that it allows researchers to collect qualitative data and ask clarifying questions while the network data is collected. Examples of network mapping techniques are Net-Map (pen-and-paper based) and VennMaker (digital).

Patents

There has been rapid growth in the number of US

patent applications that cover new technologies related to social networking. The number of published applications has been growing at about 250% per year over the past five years. There are now over 2000 published applications. Only about 100 of these applications have issued as patents, however, largely due to the multi-year backlog in examination of business method patents.

FRIENDSHIP FORCE INTERNATIONAL

Friendship Force International is a non-profit organization founded in Atlanta, Georgia, United States, and introduced on March 1, 1977, by President Jimmy Carter at a White House gathering of state governors. First Lady Rosalynn Carter served as Honorary Chairperson until 2002. In 1992, Friendship Force International was nominated for the Nobel Peace Prize.

Friendship Force International (FFI), is an international cultural exchange programme, founded in 1977 by Wayne Smith, a Presbyterian minister and former U.S. missionary to Brazil. For the first five years, it used chartered airplanes to shuttle delegations of 150 to 400 visitors between partner cities. The first exchange involved 762 travelers from Newcastle-upon-Tyne, England, and Atlanta, Georgia, United States. Staying in private homes is a central feature of the programme.

In 1982, the plan was changed from large simultaneous exchanges to smaller one-way visits using scheduled airlines, but retaining the basic homestay theme, supported by local clubs in the host countries. Expanding from a few large simultaneous exchanges annually in the early years, Friendship Force now organizes 250-300 smaller exchanges of 20 to 25 visitors each year. It has active clubs in more than 50 countries. In 2007, 5763 visitors, called "friendship ambassadors," traveled between 58 countries, with thousands of club members hosting visitors in their homes.

BEWELCOME

BeWelcome is a hospitality exchange service that is run by a non-profit organization. The site was founded in February of 2007 by volunteers from another hospitality exchange website Hospitality Club. As of July 2010, the organization has approximately 9,100 members from all over the world who offer free accommodation and help during travels. It is the first such service to provide a truly multilingual environment with multilingual profiles. Joining is free and the software behind the site, the BW-rox platform, is free and open-source software.

REFERENCES

A.R. Radcliffe-Brown (1940). "On Social Structure," *Journal of the Royal Anthropological Institute:* 70: 1–12.

Baker, Vicky (22 January 2011). "How to stay with a local". *The Guardian.* January 2011.

Freeman, Linton (2006). *The Development of Social Network Analysis.* Vancouver: Empirical Pres, 2006; Wellman, Barry and S.D. Berkowitz, eds., 1988. *Social Structures: A Network Approach.* Cambridge: Cambridge University Press.

Hansen, William B. and Reese, Eric L. (2009). Network Genie User Manual. Greensboro, NC: Tanglewood Research.

Linton Freeman (2006). *The Development of Social Network Analysis.* Vancouver: Empirical Press.

M. Kitsak, L. K. Gallos, S. Havlin, F. Liljeros, L. Muchnik, H. E. Stanley, H.A. Makse (2010). "Identification of influential spreaders in complex networks". *Nature Physics* 6: 888.

Mark Granovetter, "Introduction for the French Reader," *Sociologica* 2 (2007): 1–8; Wellman, Barry. 1988. "Structural Analysis: From Method and Metaphor to Theory and Substancem" pp. 19-61.

Moody, James, and Douglas R. White (2003). "Structural Cohesion and Embeddedness: A Hierarchical Concept of Social Groups." *American Sociological Review* 68(1):103–127. Online: (PDF file).

Nadel, S.F. (1957). *The Theory of Social Structure.* London: Cohen and West.

Romuald Bokëj (2008). "Apsikeitimas svetingumu" (PDF). *Žalioji Lietuva* Nr. 6 (298).

Wasserman, Stanley, and Faust, Katherine (1994). *Social Network Analysis: Methods and Applications.* Cambridge: Cambridge University Press.

Wellman, Barry and S.D. Berkowitz, eds. (1988). *Social Structures: A Network Approach.* Cambridge: Cambridge University Press.

7

Related Elements of Guest Management with Focus on Role of Hotel Manager, General Manager and Receptionist

HOTEL MANAGER

A hotel manager or hotelier is a person who holds a management occupation within a hotel, motel, or resort establishment. Management titles and duties vary by company. In some hotels the title hotel manager or hotelier may solely be referred to the General Manager of the hotel. Small hotels may have a small management team consisting of only two or three managers while larger hotels may often have a large management team consisting of various departments and divisions.

Typical Full Service Hotel Management Structure

A typical organizational chart for a mid-scale to large hotel:

- General Manager
  - o Deputy General Manager
    - Director of Revenue & Rooms Division
    - Front Of House Manager
    - Front Desk / Front Office Manager (s)
    - PBX Supervisor

- Reservations Manager (may report to Sales in some hotels)
- Guest Services Manager
- Bell Captain
- Concierge Supervisor
- Executive Housekeeper
- Housekeeping Manager(s)
- Laundry Supervisor
- Custodial Supervisor
- Director of Sales & Marketing
- Senior Sales Manager
- Sales Manager(s)
- Sales Coordinator (s)
- Catering Manager
- Marketing Manager
- Convention Services Manager(s)
- Event Manager (s)
- Director of Food & Beverage
- Restaurant Manager(s)
- Room Service Manager
- Bar Manager
- Director of Catering
- Assistant General Manager(s) / Duty Manager(s)
- Chief Engineer
- Director of Human Resources
- Director of Security
- Spa & Recreation Manager
- Director of Finances / Controller
- Director of Information Technology

Typical Qualifications for a Hotel Manager

Background and training required varies by management title and duties involved. Industry experience has proven to be an essential qualification for nearly any management occupation within the lodging industry. Basic qualifications for a management occupation within a hotel usually consist of the following:

- Industry Experience is the main factor
- Education
    - o A high school diploma is a required qualification for any management occupation.
    - o A degree in Hospitality management studies or equivalent Business degree is often required or strongly preffered
    - o A graduate degree may be desired for a General Manager position but is often not required with sufficient management experience and tenure.

Working Conditions

Hotel managers are generally exposed to long shifts that include late hours, weekends, and holidays due to the 24 hour operation of a hotel. The common workplace in hotels is a fast-paced environment, with high levels of interaction with guests, employees, investors, and other managers.

Upper management consisting of senior managers, department heads, and General Managers may sometimes enjoy a more desirable work schedule consisting of a more traditional business day including weekdays and days off on holidays.

In Popular Culture

The occupation of a hotel manager has appeared in many Hollywood films including the film Hotel Rwanda and other media outlets.

GENERAL MANAGER

General manager (sometimes abbreviated GM) is a descriptive term for certain executives in a business operation. It is also a formal title held by some business executives, most commonly in the hospitality industry.

Generic Usage

A manager may be responsible for one functional area, but the general manager is responsible for all areas. Sometimes, most commonly, the term *general manager* refers to any executive who has overall responsibility for managing both the revenue and cost elements of a company's income statement. This is often referred to as profit & loss (P&L) responsibility. This means that a general manager usually oversees most or all of the firm's marketing and sales functions as well as the day-to-day operations of the business. Frequently, the general manager is also responsible for leading or coordinating the strategic planning functions of the company.

In many cases, the general manager of a business is given a different formal title or titles. Most corporate managers holding the titles of chief executive officer (CEO) or president, for example, are the general managers of their respective businesses. More rarely, the chief financial officer (CFO), chief operating officer (COO), or chief marketing officer (CMO) will act as the general manager of the business. Depending on the company, individuals with the title managing director, regional vice president, country manager, product manager, branch manager, or segment manager may also have general management responsibilities.

In consumer products companies, general managers are often given the title brand manager or category manager. In professional services firms, the general manager may hold titles such as managing partner, senior partner, or managing director.

In non-profit enterprises, the general manager is often given the title executive director.

Industry-Specific Usages

Hotels

In hotels, the General Manager is the executive manager responsible for the overall operation of a hotel establishment. The General Manager holds ultimate authority over the hotel operation and usually reports directly to a corporate office or hotel owner. Common duties of a General Manager include hiring and management of a management team, overall management of hotel staff, budgeting and financial management, creating and enforcing business objectives and goals, managing projects and renovations, management of emergencies and other major issues involving guests, employees, or the facility, public relations with the media, local governments, and other businesses, and many additional duties. The extent of duties of a hotel General Manager vary significantly depending on the size of the hotel and company; for example, General Managers of smaller hotels may have additional duties such as accounting, human resources, payroll, purchasing, and other duties that would usually be handled by other managers or departments in a larger hotel.

Sports Teams

In most professional sports, the general manager is a team executive responsible for acquiring the rights to player personnel, negotiating their contracts, and reassigning or dismissing players no longer desired on the team. The general manager may also have responsibility for hiring the head coach of the team.

For many years in U.S. professional sports, coaches often served as general managers for their teams as well, deciding which players would be kept on the team and which ones dismissed, and even negotiating the terms of their contracts in cooperation with the ownership of the team. In fact, many sports teams in the early years of U.S. professional sports were coached by the owner of the team, so in some cases the same individual served as owner, general manager and head coach.

As the amount of money involved in professional sports increased, many prominent players began to hire agents to negotiate contracts on their behalf. The intensified contract negotiations that resulted, as well as the overall increased need for professional business management, drove many sports teams to separate the positions of coach and general manager. Some coaches, however, still insist on being allowed to fill both positions as a condition of employment.

In some sports leagues salary caps have been adopted to maintain a competitive balance and in these leagues it is one of the functions of the general manager to ensure all player contracts are in accordance with these caps, as well as consistent with the desires of the ownership and its ability to pay.

General managers are usually responsible for the selection of players in player drafts and work with the coaching staff and scouts to build a strong team. In sports with developmental or minor leagues, the general manager is usually the team executive with the overall responsibility for "sending down" and "calling up" players to and from these leagues, although the head coach may also have significant input into these decisions.

Some of the most successful sports general managers have been former players and coaches, while others have backgrounds in ownership and business management.

The term is not commonly used in Europe, especially in soccer, where the position of manager or coach is used instead to refer to the managing/coaching position. The position of director of football might be the most similar position on many European football clubs.

RECEPTIONIST

A receptionist is an employee taking an office/administrative support position. The work is usually performed in a waiting area such as a lobby or front office desk of an organization or business. The title "receptionist" is attributed to the person who is specifically employed by an organization to receive or greet any visitors, patients, or clients and answer telephone calls.

The business duties of a receptionist may include answering visitors' inquiries about a company and its products or services, directing visitors to their destinations, sorting and handing out mail, answering incoming calls on multi-line telephones or, earlier in the 20th century, a switchboard, setting appointments, filing, records keeping, keyboarding/data entry and performing a variety of other office tasks, such as faxing or emailing. Some receptionists may also perform bookkeeping or cashiering duties. Some, but not all, offices may expect the receptionist to serve coffee or tea to guests, and to keep the lobby area tidy.

A receptionist may also assume some security guard access control functions for an organization by verifying employee identification, issuing visitor passes, and observing and reporting any unusual or suspicious persons or activities.

A receptionist is often the first business contact a person will meet at any organization. It is an expectation of most organizations that the receptionist maintains a calm, courteous and professional demeanor at all times regardless of the visitor's behaviour. Some personal qualities that a receptionist is expected to possess in order to do the job successfully include attentiveness, a well-groomed appearance, initiative, loyalty, maturity, respect for confidentiality and discretion, a positive attitude and dependability. At times, the job may be stressful due to interaction with many different people with different types of personalities, and being expected to perform multiple tasks quickly.

Depending upon the industry, a receptionist position can be considered a low-ranking, dead-end or servile position, or it could be perceived as having a certain veneer of glamor with opportunities for networking in order to advance to other positions within a specific field. Some people may use this type of job as a way to familiarize themselves with office work, or to learn of other functions or positions within a corporation. Some people use receptionist work as a way to earn money while pursuing further educational opportunities or other career interests such as in the performing arts or as writers.

While many persons working as receptionists continue in that position throughout their careers, some receptionists may advance to other administrative jobs, such as a customer service representative, dispatcher, interviewers, secretary, production assistant, personal assistant, or executive assistant. In smaller businesses, such as a doctor's or a lawyer's office, a receptionist may also be the office manager who is charged with a diversity of middle management level business operations. For example, in the hotel industry, the night-time receptionist's role is almost always combined with performing daily account consolidation and reporting, more particularly known as night auditing.

When receptionists leave the job, they often enter other career fields such as sales and marketing, public relations or other media occupations.

A few famous people were receptionists in the beginning, such as Betty Williams, a co-recipient of the 1976 Nobel Peace Prize. A number of celebrities had worked as receptionists before they became famous, such as singer/songwriter Naomi Judd and the late entrepreneur/Beatle wife Linda McCartney. Other famous people who began their careers as receptionists or worked in the field include civil rights activist Rosa Parks and former Hewlett-Packard CEO Carly Fiorina.

The advancement of office automation has eliminated

some receptionists' jobs. For example, a telephone call could be answered by an Automated attendant. However, a receptionist who possesses strong office/technical skills and who is also adept in courtesy, tact and diplomacy is still considered an asset to a company's business image, and is still very much in demand in the business world.

With the recent development in optical fiber technology, some small-to-medium-sized business owners hire a live remote receptionist in lieu of a full-time, in-house receptionist. As the phrase itself suggests, a live remote receptionist deals with phone calls for a company in another location using telephony private branch exchange (PBX) servers. Often, the responsibilities of a live remote receptionist include, but are not limited to live phone answering, live call screening/forwarding, appointment scheduling, customized greetings, flexible call routing, email and fax services, order taking, voicemail services, and message taking.

Appendix

GUEST SATISFACTION INDEX: THE NEXT BIG MEASURE OF HOTEL PERFORMANCE?

Traditionally, hotels have made pricing decisions based on a combination of demand forecasts, supply, operating costs, competitor activity, and gut feel. Market performance is measured in terms of indexes of occupancy, rate, and revPAR from data provided by companies like PKF Consulting and STR Global.

In terms of guest satisfaction, however, hotels have known little about how they fare against competitors. Social media has changed that by bringing reviews and feedback into the open, enabling an important new measure of market performance: the Guest Satisfaction Index (GSI).

Why important? Increasingly, travel shoppers are bypassing traditional sources of information and advice and turning to other travelers on review sites and in social networks. "Online reputation management is becoming hugely important to hotels because reviews have a direct correlation with demand, the holy grail of revenue management," Corin Burr, Director of Bamboo Revenue in London.

But how easy is it to rank guest satisfaction among hotels?

With over 45 million reviews to draw from, TripAdvisor's Popularity Index probably provides the most comprehensive ranking system. The index is derived from a proprietary algorithm that takes into account the quantity, quality, and timeliness of reviews, among other factors. Hoteliers can drill down further in the Owners' Center, where they can compare performance to competitors and the destination as a whole via the Customer Satisfaction Index (CSI), a Market Metrix 0-to-100 scoring system derived from seven key review components. Recently, online travel agencies beefed up efforts to amass reviews, likely motivated by SEO benefits and conversion rates. A 2010 PhoCusWright survey found that OTA shoppers who visited hotel review pages were twice as likely to book.

But so far OTA reviews hardly represent the wisdom of the crowds. In recent searches of London hotels by Guest Rating on Expedia and Hotels.com, none of the top ten hotels listed had more than a handful of reviews. The number one hotel on Hotels.com had just one review—in a foreign language. A similar search on Orbitz produced no more than five reviews of each of the top ten hotels, some of them several years old. Only Booking.com offered anything resembling a representative sample, with between 68 and 824 reviews of the top ten hotels ranked by Review Score.

Of course, the priority of OTAs is to sell rooms, not to rank hotels. Yet on TravelPost, which doesn't sell rooms, a search of London hotels sorted by User Rating produced three reviews or less of each of the top ten hotels. The number one hotel had only one review—from 2004. Google Places, which also doesn't sell rooms, lists up to thousands of reviews per property aggregated from a variety of sites. That positions it nicely to offer the ultimate ranking of guest satisfaction, but at present it doesn't offer the option to sort hotels by review score.

Meanwhile, the top ten hotels on TripAdvisor's Popularity Index feature from 102 to 802 reviews per property, each with a handful of reviews posted in the past week.

To make sense of reviews, hotels are turning to reputation monitoring tools like Revinate and Synthesio that aggregate, organize, and score review data from across the web. The information has typically not been made available to travelers, although that's beginning to change.

Barcelona-based ReviewPro offers a Quality Seal for hotels to post to their website that displays the Global Review Index™ (GRI), a 0-to-100 score derived from a proprietary algorithm that aggregates reviews from more than 60 travel review sites in eight languages. Munich-based TrustYou Analytics offers a similar seal. But few hotels display these seals—unlike TripAdvisor badges, which are becoming ubiquitous, at least among properties with rankings to brag about.

Recently, ReviewPro published a list of "Top 10 Hotels in Berlin According to Online Guest Satisfaction" ranked by the GRI. Said CEO R. J. Friedlander, "For the first time the hotel sector has an independent online reputation benchmark that takes into account reviews from reviews sites and online travel agencies from around the world." The company intends to roll out rankings for other cities in the coming months.

Meanwhile, San Francisco-based Revinate is about to introduce an internal measure for hotel clients called the Guest Satisfaction Comp Index (GSCI). "The GSCI is straightforward and doesn't use any algorithm or black box analytics," explains Michelle Wohl, VP of Marketing and Client Services. "We take a property's average rating across the leading review sites and OTAs and compare it to its competitive set to provide a score. It allows hotels to see how they are doing against their comp set in terms of guest satisfaction."

  ‚ Revinate's index will be particularly helpful to hoteliers because it's measured in the same format as occupancy, rate, and revPAR indexes, with a score of 100 being fair market share. The availability of such data paves the way for hoteliers to use reputation metrics to guide revenue decisions, a topic I'll explore further in my next post.

Glossary

Attendance Building. Marketing and promotional programs designed to increase attendance at conventions, trade shows, meetings, and events.

Attraction. Any visitor service or product which tourists would enjoy visiting or using. An attraction may not be an "attractor" but can still be an attraction. To be considered an attraction, a product must be: A. Findable (clearly located on maps and street addresses, and directions provided). If tourists can't find the facility, it is not a tourist attraction. B. Hours of operation clearly denoted in any and all promotional materials (if a tourist arrives only to find the attraction closed, it is not an attraction). Examples of attractions include everything from a theme park that attracts over a million visitors a year, to a produce stand by the side of the road. General all-inclusive term travel industry marketers use to refer to products that have visitor appeal, like museums, historic sites, performing arts institutions, preservation districts, theme parks, entertainment and national sites.

Attractor. A significant tourist attraction, which compels visitation. The primary "must sees" in an area. The top reasons a tourist would choose to visit this area.

AVHRM. Association of Vacation Home Rental Managers.

Bed Tax (Transient Occupancy Tax of TOT). City or county tax added to the price of a hotel room.

Benchmarking. The process of comparing performance and processes within an industry to assess relative position against either a set industry standard or against those who are "best in class" (Synergy, 2000).

Best Practice(s). A term used to designate highest quality, excellence, or superior practices in a particular field by a tourism operator.

Blocked rooms. Hotel rooms held without a deposit.

Blocked. (1) Hotel rooms held without deposit. (2) Hotel rooms, airline tickets or other travel services held for a specific client.

Booking. Term used to refer to a completed sale by a destination, convention center, facility, hotel or supplier (i.e. convention, meeting, trade show or group business booking).

Brigade. French term used to describe all the staff working on the floor of the restaurant or the kitchen.

Business Travel. Travel for commercial, governmental or educational purposes with leisure as a secondary motivation.

Business Travel. Travel for commercial, governmental or educational purposes with leisure as a secondary motivation.

Buyer. A member of the travel trade who reserves room blocks from accommodations or coordinates the development of a travel product.

BYO. Bring Your Own. A restaurant which allows patrons to bring their own alcohol.

Carrier. Any provider of mass transportation, usually used in reference to an airline.

Chambers of Commerce. Typically, a Chamber of Commerce will specialize in local economic development that can include tourism promotion.

Charter Group. Group travel in which a previously organized group travels together, usually on a custom itinerary.

Commissions. A percent of the total product cost paid to travel agents and other travel product distributors for selling the product to the consumer.

Consumer Show. A product showcase for the general public. Differs from a "Trade Show" as a trade show generally targets industry professionals. Consumer Shows target the consumer. Often there is a charge to get into the show.

Convention and Visitors Bureau. These organizations are local tourism marketing organizations specializing in developing conventions, meetings, conferences and visitations to a city, county or region.

Conventions and Trade Shows. Major segment of travel industry business. Trade shows differ from conventions in that they have exhibit space that provides product exhibition and sales opportunities for suppliers, as well as information gathering and buying opportunities for customers.

Conversion Study. Research study to analyze whether advertising respondents actually were converted to travelers as a result of advertising and follow-up material.

Co-op Advertising. Advertising funded by two or more destinations and /or suppliers.

Cooperative Marketing. Marketing programs involving two or more participating companies, institutions or organizations.

Cooperative Partner. An independent firm or organization which works with a tourism office by providing cash or in-kind contributions to expand the marketing impact of the tourism officeÕs program.

Country of Residence. Consists of the country where she/he has lived for most of the past year (12 months), or for a shorter period if she/he intends to return within 12 months to live there.

Cover. Each diner at a restaurant.

CRS. Central Reservation System

CTRLA. Car and Truck Rental and Leasing Association.

Cultural tourism. Travel for the purpose of learning about cultures or aspects of cultures (NEAP, 2000).

CVB. Convention and Visitors Bureau.

Day visitors. Visitors who arrive and leave the same day for leisure, recreation and holidays, visiting friends and relatives, & business and professional.

Destination Marketing Organization (DMO). A company or other entity involved in the business of increasing tourism to a destination or improving its public image. Local tourism marketing organizations, such as convention and visitors bureaus or chambers of commerce.

Destination Marketing. Marketing a city, state, country, area or region to consumers and trade.

Destination. A hotel, resort, attraction, city, region, or state.

Discounted Fare. Negotiated air fare for convention, trade show, meeting, group and corporate travel.

Discover America. Theme used by the Travel Industry Association and its marketing partners to market travel within the United States.

Ecotourism. "Responsible travel to natural areas that conserves the environment and improves the welfare of local people," according to The International Ecotourism Society.

Fam Tours. Organized trips for travel agents, tour operators, tour wholesalers or other members of the travel trade for the purpose of educating and "familiarizing" them with tourism destinations. By seeing the destinations where they are sending travelers, the travel trade is better prepared to answer customer questions and promote travel to the location. Also called "fams" or "familiarization tours."

Familiarization Trip. A complimentary or reduced-rate travel program for travel agents, airline or rail employees or other travel buyers, designed to acquaint participants with specific destinations or suppliers and to stimulate the sale of travel. Familiarization tours, also called fam tours, are sometimes offered to journalists as research trips for the purpose of cultivating media coverage of specific travel products.

Feeder Airport/City. An outlying city which feeds travelers to hubs or gateway cities.

FIT (Free Independent Travel). Individual travel in which a tour operator has previously arranged blocks of rooms at various destinations in advance for use by individual travelers. These travelers travel independently, not in a group, usually by rental car or public transportation.

Foreign Independent Travel or Foreign Individual Travel (FIT). An international pre-paid unescorted tour that includes several travel elements such as accommodations, rental cars and sightseeing. A FIT operator specialises in preparing FITs documents at the request of retail travel agents. FITs usually receive travel vouchers to present to on-site services as verification of pre-payment.

Frequency. The number of times an advertisement appears during a given campaign.

Fulfillment. Servicing consumers and trade who request information as a result of advertising or promotional programs. Service often includes an 800 number, sales staff and distribution of materials.

Function. Term used to for specialty catering such as weddings, meetings, birthdays, dances and product launches etc.

Gateway or Gateway City. A major airport, seaport, rail or bus center through which tourists and travelers enter from outside the region.

GDS. Global Distribution System, such as Sabre and Worldspan

GIT (Groups Independent Travel). Group travel in which

individuals purchase a group package in which they will travel with others along a pre-set itinerary.

Gourmet. French term, originally and still used to describe a person who is a critic of food and beverage. Also used to describe establishments that provide sophisticated food and beverage.

Gross lettings. This refers to all room lettings, i.e. both paid & complimentary listings are included

Group Rate. Negotiated hotel rate for convention, trade show, meeting, tour or incentive group.

Group Tour and Group Leader - Group Tour. A travel agent type company which plans motor coach trips. Group Leader: A small, informal group, such as a church group, scout troop, or social group. Usually one person plans the activities for the group. Some travel shows target these planners such as GLAMER.

Head in Beds. Industry slang referring to the primary marketing objective of accommodations and most destinations. increasing the number of overnight stays.

Hospitality Industry. Another term for the travel industry.

Hospitality. A general term used in travel & tourism describing the "hospitality industry"; Refers to the general greeting, welcoming, food service, etc

Hotel Package. A package offered by a hotel, sometimes consisting of no more than a room and breakfast; sometimes, especially at resort hotels, consisting of (ground) transportation, rooms, meals, sports facilities and other components.

Hub and Spoke. Air carriers use of selected cities as "hubs" or connected points for service on their systems to regional destinations.

Hub. An airport or city which serves as a central connecting point for aircraft, trains or buses from outlying feeder airports or cities.

Icon. A facility or landmark which is visually synonymous with a destination.

IDS. Internet Distribution System

Incentive Tour. A trip offered as a prize, usually by a company to stimulate employee sales or productivity.

Incentive Travel. Travel offered as a reward for top performance and the business that develops, markets and operates these programs.

Inclusive Tour. A tour program that includes a variety of feature for a single rate (airfare, accommodations, sightseeing, performances, etc.)

Inclusive Tour. A tour program that includes a variety of feature for a single rate (airfare, accommodations, sightseeing, performances, etc.)

Inquiry. A request for more information about an attraction or destination.

International Marketing. Marketing a destination, product or service to consumers and the trade outside the of the United States.

IPU. Interface Processing Unit

Itinerary. A travel schedule provided by a travel agent for his/her customer. A proposed or preliminary itinerary may be rather vague or specific. A final itinerary however provides all details (flight numbers, departure times, reservation confirmation numbers) and describes planned activities.

Joint venture. A form of strategic alliance or co-operative arrangement where ownership is shared and a separate enterprise formed. This may strengthen existing businesses through shared expertise, capital, removal of competition and creation of economies of scale. International tourism joint ventures between foreign organisations and local partners facilitate introduction of foreign products into local markets.

Jungle tourism. Jungle tours have become a major component of green tourism in tropical destinations. A jungle is a subclimax tropical forest consisting of a tangled growth of lianas, trees and scrub which may form an almost impenetrable barrier to the tourist. Jungle tours are a relatively recent phenomenon of Western international tourism.

Key-informant Survey. This involves interviewing people who are likely to have some insight into a problem: operating managers; sales staff; managers; suppliers; and consultants.

Keying. A social convention by which social 'reality' is transformed and seen as something else, such as the presentation of a fight as mere horseplay. In tourism, a peculiar, inverted variety of keying is frequently employed: the 'as if' situation in which participants are induced to playfully make believe that presented settings, activities or events are 'real', when as tourists they may be well aware that such occurences are contrived.

Leisure Tourist. Leisure tourists, in contrast with business travellers, travel for pleasure and thus are not under any obligations to frequent specific destinations or facilities. They tend to be price and fashion conscious, concentrate their touristic activities to specific (vacation) times, and are influenced by marketing and publicity. Leisure tourism is heavily influenced by living standards, discretionary income levels and vacation entitlements.

Leisure Travel. Travel for recreational, educational, sightseeing, relaxing and other experiential purposes.

Length of Stay. This refers to the period of time which people spend in a destination. Many definitions require that visitors to a destination stay at least 24 hours or overnight, and less than one year, to be considered a tourist. Destination areas often look for means to extend tourists' length of stay in order to increase positive economic impacts.

Limited Bar. Restricted service of alcoholic beverages at a function. For example, $1000 limit for beer, wine and soft drinks, or unlimited beer wine and soft drinks for four hours. In both cases spirits would incur additional costs.

maîtred'. Full term is 'maître d' hôtel'. Literally 'master of the hotel'. In English we sometimes call this position the headwaiter, but the French term is frequently used.

Market Share. The percentage of business within a market category.

Market Volume. The total number of travelers within a market category.

Maximum Room Nights. This is calculated based on the total room inventory for all gazetted hotels.

Mise en place. Literally this means to 'put in place' and generally refers to pre-service preparation, including setting the tables and stocking up the stations. Also used in the kitchen, where it refers to the pre-preparation before cooking takes place.

Mission (Sales). A promotional and sales trip coordinated by a state travel office, conventional and visitors bureau or key industry member to increase product awareness, sales and to enhance image. Target audiences may include tour operators, wholesales, incentive travel planners, travel agents, meeting planners, convention and trade show managers and media. Missions often cover several international or domestic destinations and include private and public sector participants. Mission components can include receptions, entertainment representatives of the destination, presentations and pre- scheduled sales and media calls.

Motorcoach. Deluxe equipment used by most tour operators in group tour programs. Amenities include reclining seats, bathrooms, air conditioning, good lighting and refreshment availability.

Nature Tourism. Travel to unspoiled places to experience and enjoy nature.

Net Rate. The rate provided to wholesalers and tour operators that can be marked up to sell to the customer.

No Show. A customer with a reservation at a restaurant, hotel, etc. who fails to show up and does not cancel.

NTA. National Tour Association, comprised of domestic tour operators.

Occupancies. A percentage indicating the number of bed nights sold (compared to number available) in a hotel, resort, motel or destination.

Occupancy Rate. A tourism business occupancy rate refers to the number of airline seats or the units of hotel room space sold. This demand is usually measured as a percentage of available seats or space occupied for a given period of time. It is calculated by dividing the number of occupied rooms/seats by the total number available for sale during the same period.

Open Bar. unrestricted service of alcoholic beverages at a function. plated food presentation of food on plates by kitchen staff.

Outbound. Outbound tourism is defined as tourism involving residents of a country travelling to another country. Outbound tour operators offer package tours abroad. They either operate the tours themselves, or they commission the services of an inbound operator to handle local arrangements at the destination. The country from which the tourists originate is known as the generating market or country.

Package Tour. A saleable travel product offering an inclusive price with several travel elements that would otherwise be purchased separately. Usually has a predetermined price, length of time and features but can also offer options for separate purchase.

Package. A fixed price salable travel product that makes it easy for a traveler to buy and enjoy a destination or several destinations. Packages offer a mix of elements like transportation, accommodations, restaurants, entertainment, cultural activities, sightseeing and car rental.

Paid Lettings. This refers to room lettings that are paid for by hotel guests

Peaks and Valleys. The high and low end of the travel season. Travel industry marketers plan programs to build consistent year-round business and event out the "peaks and valleys."

Person Trip Visit. Every time a person travels more than 100 miles (round-trip) in a day or stays overnight away from their primary domicile, whether for business or leisure purposes, they make one "person trip visit."

Pow Wow. The largest international travel marketplace held in the United States, sponsored by the Travel Industry Association of America.

Press Trips. Organized trips for travel writers and broadcasters for the purpose of assisting them in developing stories about tourism destinations. Often, journalists travel independently, though with the assistance of a state's office of tourism of a DMO.

Press/Publicity Release. A news article or feature story written by the subject of the story for delivery and potential placement in the media.

Property. A hotel, motel, inn, lodge or other accommodation facility.

Quality. In tourism, the product is often intangible and quality is not apparent until after it is consumed. Quality has been defined as zero defects or defections, but still may be defined by the customer. The International Organisation for Standardisation defines quality as 'the totality of features and characteristics of a product or service that bear on its ability to satisfy stated or implied needs'. Others believe that quality is a combination of outcome and processes, including internal and external conditions, and is obtained when the expectations and needs of customers are met.

Rack Card. The typical tourism brochure sized 4" x 9" and used primarily in tourism racks. Also known as a "teaser."

Rack Rate. The official cost posted by a hotel, attraction or rental car, but not used by tour operators. The rate accommodations quote to the public. Group rates, convention, trade show, meeting and incentive travel rates are negotiated by the hotel and program organizers.

Reach. The percentage of people within a specific target audience reached by an advertising campaign.

Receptive Operator. Specialists in handling arrangements for incoming visitors at a destination including airport transfers, local sightseeing, restaurants, accommodations, etc. Receptive operators can be a travel agent or tour operator.

Repeat Business. Business that continues to return, thereby generating increased profits.

Reservation Systems (Automation Vendors). Computerized systems leased to travel agencies offering airline, hotel, car rental and selected tour availability and bookings. Systems are affiliated with major carriers, including American (Sabre), United (Apollo), Eastern (System One), TWA (PARS), and Delta (DATAS II) and feature flight schedules of the sponsoring and other carriers, plus additional travel products.

Resident. A person living in a given country, whether he is a national or not.

Retail Agent. A travel agent. **Retailer.** Another term for travel agents who sell travel products directly to consumers.

Retailer. Another term for travel agents who sell travel products directly to consumers.

Room Block. Several rooms held for a group.

Room. Double: No guarantee of two beds; Double Double:

Two double beds (or two queens or kings); Twin: Two twin beds (or two doubles or queens)

Sales Mission. Where suppliers from one DMO travel together to another state of country for the purpose of collectively promoting travel to their area. Sales missions may include educational seminars for travel agents and tour operators.

Sales Seminar. An educational session in which travel agents, tour operators, tour wholesales or other members of the travel trade congregate to receive briefings about tourism destinations.

Shells. A marketing and sales promotional piece that depicts a destination, accommodation or attraction on the cover and provides space for copy to be added at a later date. Usually shells fit a #10 envelope.

Site Inspection. An assessment tour of a destination or facility by a meeting planner, convention or trade show manager, site selection committee, tour operator, wholesaler or incentive travel manager to see if it meets their needs and requirements prior to selecting a specific site for an event. After site selection, a site inspection may be utilized to make arrangements.

Spouse Program. Special activities planned for those who accompany an attendee to a convention, trade show or meeting. Note that programs today are not simply for women, but rather for men and women, spouses and friends. Programs must be creatively designed to interest intelligent and curious audiences.

Station. The preparation, or worktable allocated to dining room staff. It also serves as limited storage for crockery, cutlery and table linen in the restaurant or dining room.

Supplier. Those businesses that provide industry products like accommodations, transportation, car rentals, restaurants and attractions.

Sustainable tourism. This is, according to the World

Tourism Organisation, "envisaged as leading to management of all resources in such a way that economic, social and aesthetic needs can be fulfilled with maintaining cultural integrity, essential ecological processes, biological diversity, and life support systems."

Table d'hôte menu. Set menu of two or more courses and maybe one or more choices within each course. The price is pre-set for this style of meal.

Target Audience/Market. A specific demographic, sociographic target at which marketing communications are directed.

Target Rating Points. TRPŌs are a statistical measurement which allows one to evaluate the relative impact of differing advertising campaigns.

Tariff. Rate of fare quoted and published by a travel industry supplier (i.e. hotels, tour operators, etc.) Usually an annual tariff is produced in booklet form for use in sales calls at trade shows.

TIA. Travel Industry Association of America.

TOT. Transient Occupancy Tax.

Tour Operator. Develops, markets and operates group travel programs that provide a complete travel experience for one price and includes transportation (airline, rail, motorcoach, and/or ship), accommodations, sightseeing, selected meals and an escort. Tour operators market directly to the consumer, through travel agents and are beginning to be listed on computerized reservation systems.

Tour Wholesaler. An individual or company that sells tour packages and tour product to travel agents. Tour wholesalers usually receive a 20% discount from accommodations, transportation companies and attractions and pass on a 10 to 15% discount to the retail agent.

Tourism Receipts. Tourism Receipts (TR) measures the

total revenue received by Singapore from tourism activity. It includes all payments and prepayments for goods and services made by visitors, transit passengers, air & sea crew and foreign students (staying for one year or less) during their stay in Singapore. Visitors' payments to our national carriers (SIA & Silk Air) for international transport are also included.

Tourism. The business of providing and marketing services and facilities for pleasure travellers. Thus, the concept or tourism is of direct concern to governments, carriers, and the lodging, restaurant and entertainment industries and of indirect concern to virtually every industry and business in the world.

Tourist. Temporary visitor staying at least twenty-four hours in the country visited for a purpose classified as either holiday (recreation, leisure, sport and visit to family, friends or relatives), business, official mission, convention, or health reasons.

Tourist/Visitor/Traveler. Any person who travels either for leisure or business purposes more than 100 miles (round-trip) in a day or who stays overnight away from his/her primary domicile.

Tourist/Visitor/Traveler. Any person who travels either for leisure or business purposes more than 100 miles (round-trip) in a day or who stays overnight away from his/her primary domicile.

Trade Show. A product showcase for a specific industry. Generally it is not open to the public. Differs from a "Consumer Show" in that a trade show targets the professional industry, while a consumer show targets consumers.

Transient Occupancy Tax. TOT or bed tax is a locally set tax on the cost of commercial accommodations and campgrounds.

Travel Agent. (1) An individual who arranges travel for

individuals or groups. Travel agents may be generalists or specialists (cruises, adventure travel, conventions and meetings.) The agents receive a 10 to 15% commission from accommodations, transportation companies and attractions for coordinating the booking of travel. They typically coordinate travel for their customers at the same or lower cost than if the customer booked the travel on his/her own. (2) The individual who sells travel services, issues tickets and provides other travel services to the travel services to the traveller sat the retail level.

Travel Product. Refers to any product or service that is bought by or sold to consumers of trade including accommodations, attractions, events, restaurants, transportation, etc.

Travel Seasons. Travel industry business cycles including: *Peak:* Primary travel season *Off Peak:* Period when business is slowest *Shoulder:* Period between peak and off peak periods when business is stronger, but has room for growth.

Travel Trade. The collective term for tour operators, wholesalers and travel agents.

Travel. Leisure and other travel including travel for business, medical care, education, etc. All tourism is travel, but not all travel is tourism.

Traveler. (1) Definitions very, but in general a traveler is someone who leaves their own economic trade area, (usually going a distance of a minimum of fifty to one hundred miles) and stays overnight. (2) Someone who leaves his or her own economic trade area, (usually going a distance of a minimum of fifty to one hundred miles) and stays overnight.

Underdevelopment. Within development theory, the concept of underdevelopment suggests that wealthy capitalist countries have held back the development of so-called Third World countries. Tourism in Third World destinations is controlled for the economic benefit of foreign owners, reinforces dependency, lacks involvement of local decision makers, leads to negative sociocultural impacts, and results in the promotion of staged attractions to capture an international tourism market.

Urban recreation. The concept of urban recreation covers recreational activity that takes place in an urban environment in contrast to a rural setting. Participants in such activities are either urban residents themselves, day visitors from rural areas, or tourists. The major activities are shopping, visits to heritage sites, museums, movie theatres, operas, sport and music events, and indoor sports activities.

VFR. Visiting friends and relatives

Visitor Arrivals. Includes all who go through immigration clearance regardless of length of stay. This excludes the following: (a) All Malaysian citizens arriving by land, (b) Returning Singapore citizens residing abroad, (c) Non-resident air and sea crew (except for sea crew flying in to join ship), (d) All visitors arriving and leaving Singapore on the same ship/vessel and stayed in Singapore for less than 24 hours are not required to complete Disembarkation / Embarkation (D/E) cards, if passenger manifest is submitted, (e) All organised tour groups leaving Singapore for Johor Bahru, Batam and Bintan, returning on the same day are not required to complete Disembarkation / Embarkation (D/E) cards, if passenger manifest is submitted, (f) Air transit passengers

Visitor Expenditure. Includes expenditure incurred during a visitor's stay in Singapore, or prepayment by non-package tour visitors (this took effect from 1995). This excludes: (a) international air and sea fare. It is made up of the following components: (a) Shopping, (b) Accommodation, (c) Entertainment, (d) Sightseeing, (e) Food & beverage (f) Local transportation, (g) Medical/dental treatment, (h) Miscellaneous

Visitor. Any person visiting a country other than that in which he has his usual place of residence for any reason other than following an occupation remunerated from within the country visited.

Visitors Center. Travel information center located at a destination to make it easier for visitors to plan their stay; often operated by a convention and visitors bureau, chamber of commerce or tourism promotion organization.

Vouchers. Forms or coupons provided to a traveler who purchases a tour that indicate that certain tour components have been prepaid. Vouchers are then exchanged for tour components like accommodations, meals, sightseeing, theater tickets, etc. during the actual trip.

World Tourism Organisation (WTO). The World Tourism Organisation, a UN-related institution based in Madrid that collects data on tourism and lobbies on behalf of the industry.

World Travel and Tourism Council (WTTC). The WTTC is made up of chief executives from all sectors of the tourism industry, including accommodation, catering, cruises, entertainment, recreation, transportation and travel-related services. Its central goal is to work with governments to realise the full economic impact of tourism. Its millennium vision is to make tourism a strategic economic and employment priority, to move towards open and competitive markets, to pursue sustainable development, and to eliminate barriers to growth.

Xenophobia. Xenophobia is an irrational fear or contempt of strangers or foreigners. This ancient cultural and political phenomenon is also present in contemporary tourism, mainly manifesting itself in the hostile attitudes of residents towards tourists. Xenophobia should be considered in domestic and international tourism in terms of economic, social and cultural distance, which is accentuated by the type and the number of tourists and the rate of tourism development.

Yield Management. The concept of maximising the revenue by raising or lowering prices in respect to demand is known as yield management. The necessary conditions for a successful application of yield management include a fairly fixed capacity, high fixed costs, low variable costs, fluctuations in demand and similarity of inventory capacity. Yield management was popularised with the deregulation of the US airline industry and it is extensively used by this and other tourism sectors.

Yield Percentage. To demonstrate the variable effect of both average price rates and occupancy rates, tourism managers develop a comparison focusing upon the yield rates during a given period of time. Managers can increase the yield rate (see yield management) by raising rates when demand is high.

Bibliography

Adams, D.J. (1991), "Do corporate failure prediction models work?", *International Journal of Contemporary Hospitality Management*, Vol. 3 No.4, pp. 25-9.

Alexander, N., McKenna, A. (1999), "Rural tourism in the heart of England", *International Contemporary Hospitality Management*, Vol. 10 No.5, pp. 203-7.

Almanza, B.A., Jaffe, W., Lin, L. (1994), "Use of the service attribute matrix to measure consumer satisfaction", *Hospitality Research Journal*, Vol. 17 No.2, pp. 63-75.

Amoah, V., Baum, T. (1997), "Tourism education: policy versus practice", *International Journal of Contemporary Hospitality Management*, Vol. 9 No.1, pp. 5-12.

Arnaldo, M.J (1981), "Hotel general managers: a profile", *The Cornell Hotel and Restaurant Administrative Quarterly*, Vol. 22 No.3, pp. 53-6.

Ayala, H. (1996b), "Resort ecotourism: a master plan for experience management", *Cornell Hotel and Restaurant Administration Quarterly*, Vol. 37 No.5, pp. 54-61.

Barrows, C.W. (1999), "Introduction to hospitality education", in Barrows, C.W., Bosselman, R.H. (Eds), *Hospitality Management Education*, Haworth Hospitality Press, New York, NY, pp. 1-20.

Barrows, C.W., Bosselman, R.H. (1999), *Hospitality Management Education*, Haworth Hospitality Press, New York, NY.

Barsky, J.D. (1996), "Building a program for world-class service", *Cornell Hotel and Restaurant Administration Quarterly*, Vol. 37 No.1, pp. 17-27.

Barton, D. (1999), "It takes two to make a relationship", *Brandweek*, Vol. 40 No.1, pp. 14-15.

Barton, L., Eichelberger, J. (1994), "Sexual harassment:

assessing the need for corporate policies in the workplace", *Executive Development*, Vol. 7 No.1, pp. 24-8.

Basker, A.J. (1985), "Presentation skills: a vital experience for trainee managers", *International Journal of Hospitality Management*, Vol. 4 No.2, pp. 77-8.

Bateson, J.E.G. (1977), "Do we need service marketing?", *Marketing Consumer Services: New Insights*, Marketing Science Institute, Cambridge, MA.

Baum, T. (1996), "Managing cultural diversity in tourism", *Tourism Insights*, November, British Tourist Authority/ English Tourist Board, pp. A77-A84.

Bawden, R. (1991), "Towards action research systems", in Zuber-Skerritt, O. (Eds), *Action Research for Business Development*, Avebury, Aldershot.

Becker-Suttle, C.B., Weaver, P., Crawford-Welch, S. (1994), "A pilot study utilizing conjoint analysis in the comparison of age-based segmentation strategies in the full service restaurant market", *Journal of Restaurant and Food Service Marketing*, Vol. 1 No.2, pp. 71-.

Bell, C., Newby, H. (1976), "Husbands and wives: the dynamics of the deferential dialectic", in Barker, D.L., Allen, S. (Eds),*Dependence and Exploitation in Work and Marriage*, Longman, London

Bennett, R., Krebs, G. (1993), "Chambers of Commerce in Britain and Germany: the Challenges of the Single Market", in Bennett, R.J., Krebs, G., Zimmermann, H. (Eds),*Chambers of Commerce in Britain and Germany and the Single European Market*, Anglo-German Foundation, London, pp. 1-38.

Berkeley Scott (1991), *The Hotel, Catering and Leisure Business Review*, Berkeley Scott and Marketpower, London

Berry, L.L. (1981), "The employee as customer", *Journal of Retail Banking*, Vol. 11 No.1, pp. 33-40.

Bian, Y., Ang, S. (1997), "Guanxi networks and job mobility in China and Singapore", *Social Forces*, Vol. 75 No.3, pp. 981-1005.

Bonn, M.A, Forbringer, L.R. (1992), "Reducing turnover in the hospitality industry: an overview of recruitment, selection and retention", *International Journal of Hospitality Management*, Vol. 11 No.1, pp. 47-63.

Bosselman, R.H. (1996), "Current perceptions of hospitality accreditation", *FIU Hospitality Review*, Vol. 14 No.2, pp. 77.

Bowen, D.E. (1990), "Interdisciplinary study of service: some progress, some prospects", *Journal of Business Research*, Vol. 2 No.1, pp. 71-9.

Bradley, A., Ingold, A. (1993), "An investigation of yield management in Birmingham hotels", *International Journal of Contemporary Hospitality Management*, Vol. 5 No.2, pp. 13-16.

Brander-Brown, J., McDonnell, B. (1995), "The balanced score-card: short-term guest or long-term resident?", *International Journal of Contemporary Hospitality Management*.

Breiter, D., Tyink, S.A., Corey-Tuckwell, S. (1995), "Bergstrom Hotels: a case study in quality", *International Journal of Contemporary Hospitality Management*, Vol. 7 No.6, pp. 14-18.

Brewer, K.P., Hurley, R.E. (1994), "The staying power of hospitality corporations in the continuing care industry: issues from the front lines", Vol. 17 No.2, pp. 107-16.

Brotherton, B., Wood, R. (2000), "Hospitality and hospitality management", in Lashley, C., Morrison, A. (Eds), *In Search of Hospitality: Theoretical Perspective and Debates*, Butterworth-Heinemann, Oxford, pp. 134-54.

Brotherton, R., Coyle, M. "Managing instability in the hospitality operations environment: part three: variance", *International Journal of Contemporary Hospitality Management*, Vol. 3 No.1, pp. 26-31.

Brown, D. (1996), "Team rewards: lessons from the coal-face", *Team Performance Management*, Vol. 2 No.2, pp. 6-12.

Brown, T.S., Churchill, G.A., Peter, J.P. (1993), "Research note: More on improving service quality measurement", *Journal of Retailing*, Vol. 69 pp. 127-39.

Brownell, J., Jameson, D. (1996), "Getting quality out on the street: a case of show and tell", *Cornell Hotel and Restaurant Administration Quarterly*, Vol. 37 No.1, pp. 28-33.

Brymer, R.A. (1991), "Employee empowerment: a guest driven

258   *Guest Management*

leadership strategy", *The Cornell Hotel and Restaurant Quarterly*, Vol. 32 No.1, pp. 58-68.

Buhalis, D. (1993), "RICIRMS as a strategic tool for small and medium tourism enterprises", *Tourism Management*, pp. 366-78.

Bull, A.O. (1994), "Pricing a motel's location", *International Journal of Contemporary Hospitality Management*, Vol. 6 No.6, pp. 10-15.

Burgess, C. (1996), "A profile of the hotel financial controller in the United Kingdom, United States and Hong Kong", International Journal of Hospitality Management, Vol. 15 No.1, pp. 19-28.

Burgess, J. (1982), "Perspectives on gift exchange and hospitable behaviour", *International Journal of Hospitality Management*, Vol. 1 No.1, pp. 49-57.

Business Council of Australia (1989), "Time for the next industrial relations bill", *BCA Bulletin*, pp. 4-6.

Buttle, F. (1986), *Hotel and Foodservice Marketing*, Holt, Eastbourne.

Buttle, F., Bok, B. (1996), "Hotel marketing strategy and the theory of reasoned action", *International Journal of Contemporary Hospitality Management*, Vol. 8 No.3, pp. 5-10.

Cahill, D.J. (1995), "The managerial implications of the learning organization: a new tool for internal marketing", *Journal of Services Marketing*, Vol. 9 No.4, pp. 43-51.

Cai, L., Ninemeier, J.D. (1993), "Food service styles in Chinese hotels: tradition and tourism pressures merge", Vol. 11 No.2, pp. 33-40.

Callan, R.J. (1989), "Small country hotels and hotel award schemes as a measurement of service quality", *Service Industries Journal*, Vol. 9 No.2, pp. 223-46.

Callus, R, Morehead, A, Cully, M, Buchanan, J (1991), *Industrial Relations at Work*, AGPS, Canberra.

Calver, S. (1994), " Innovation in FE and HE tourism courses", *Transitions in European Tourism Education*, University of Exeter, No.July.

Calver, S., Vierich, W. , Phillips, J. (1993), "Leisure in later life ", *International Journal of Contemporary Hospitality Management*, Vol. 5 No.1, pp. 4-9.

Camp, R.C. (1989), *Benchmarking: The Search for Industry Best Practices that Leads to Superior Performance*, ASQC Quality Press, Milwaukee, WI.

Campbell, I (1993), "Labour market flexibility in Australia: enhancing management prerogative?", *Labour and Industry*, Vol. 5 No.3, pp. 1-32.

Campbell, M, Baldwin, S (1993), "Recruitment difficulties and skill shortages: an analysis of labour market information in Yorkshire and Humberside", *Regional Studies*, Vol. 27 pp. 271-80.

Campbell, M. (1999), *Learning Pays and Learning Works*, Prolog, Ipswich, NACETT.

Canina, L. (1996), "Underpricing and overperformance: initial public offerings in the hospitality industry", *Cornell Hotel and Restaurant Administration Quarterly*, Vol. 37 No.5, pp. 18-25.

Carper, J (1993), "The painful truth: operations is no longer King", *Hotels*, Vol. 50.

Carvalho, C.L. (1998), "Desenvolvimento do turismo no Brasil", São Paulo, Vol. 33 No.4, pp. 26-9.

Cassee, E.H., Reuland, R. (1983), "Hospitality in hospitals", in Cassee, E.H., Reuland, R. (Eds), *The Management of Hospitality*, Pergamon, Oxford, pp. 143-63.

Charlton, C. (1999), *Euro Impact and Reality*, Pitman, London.

Chartered Institute of Personnel and Development (CIPD) (1999), *The Impact of the Working Time Regulations on UK PLC*, IPD Survey Report, CIPD, available at: www.cipd.co.uk/NR/rdonlyres/F1AE52BB-7221-460C-97D4-1B53A8E7E5F3/0/Wrk_Time_Full.pdf.

Chen, X.P., Chen, C.C. (2004), "On the intricacies of the Chinese Guanxi: a process model of Guanxi development", *Asia Pacific Journal of Management*, Vol. 21 No.3, pp. 305-24.

Chervenak, L. (1993), "Hotel technology at the start of the new millennium", Vol. 17 No.1, pp. 113-20.

Chittium, R. (2004), "Budget hotels to get a makeover: in bid for business travelers; major chains plan boutiques, area rugs and glassed-in showers", *Wall Street Journal*, 8 June, pp. D1.

260 *Guest Management*

Cho, B.H. (1996), "An analysis of the Korean youth tourist market in Australia", *Australian Journal of Hospitality Management*, Vol. 3 No.2, pp. 15-26.

Choi, J.G., Woods, R.H., Murrmann, S.K. (2000), "International labor markets and the migration of labor forces as an alternative solution for labor shortages in the hospitality industry", *International Journal of Contemporary Hospitality Management*, Vol. 12 No.1, pp. 61-7.

Chon, K.S., Whelihan, W.P. (1992), "Changing guest preferences and marketing challenges in the resortindustry", Vol. 10 No.2, pp. 9-16.

Chorengel, B., Teare, R. (1991), "Hyatt style and personality: an investment in quality", *International Journal of Contemporary Hospitality Management*, Vol. 3 No.1, pp. i-ii.

Chow, I.H.S., Ng, I. (2004), "The characteristics of Chinese personal ties (Guanxi): evidence from Hong Kong", *Organization Studies*, Vol. 25 No.7, pp. 1075-93.

Choy, D. (1995), "The quality of tourism employment", *Tourism Management*, Vol. 16 No.2, pp. 129-37.

Christou, E. (2000), "Revisiting competencies for hospitality management: contemporary views of the stakeholders", *Journal of Tourism and Hospitality Education*, Vol. 14 No.1, pp. 25-32.

Chung, K.Y. (2000), "Hotel management curriculum reform based on required competencies of hotel employees and career success in the hotel industry", *Tourism Management*, Vol. 21 No.5, pp. 473-87.

Church, I., Lincoln, G. (1998), "Quality management", in Thomas, R. (Eds),*The Management of Small Tourism and Hospitality Firms*, Cassell,, London, pp. 138-55.

Churchill, N.C., Lewis, V.L. (1983), "The five stages of small business growth", *Harvard Business Review*, Vol. 61 No.3, pp. 30-50.

Clark, J.D., Price, C.H., Murrmann, S.K. (1996), "Buying centers: who chooses convention sites?", *Cornell Hotel and Restaurant Administration Quarterly*, Vol. 37 No.4, pp. 72-6.

Clarke, S (1992), "What in the f—'s name is Fordism?", in

Burrows, R, Gilbert, N, Pollert, A (Eds),*Fordism and Flexibility: Divisions and Change*, St Martin Press, New York, NY.

Clifton, W.J., Johnson, K. (1994), "A structural analysis of the European hotel sector: a simple case of déjà-vu?", *International Journal of Contemporary Hospitality Management*, Vol. 6 No.4, pp. vii-viii.

Close, A., Teare, R. (1990), "Effective management development", *International Journal of Contemporary Hospitality Management*, Vol. 2 No.4, pp. i-ii.

CNAA (1992), *CNAA Tourism Degree Review*, CNAA, London.

Collins, G. (1995), "Information technology trends: impact on hotel corporations", *FIU Hospitality Review*, Vol. 13 No.1.

Comen, T. (1989), "Making quality assurance work for you", *The Cornell Hotel and Restaurant Administration Quarterly*, No.November, pp. 23-30.

Connell, J. (1992), "Branding hotel portfolios", *International Journal of Contemporary Hospitality Management*, Vol. .4 No.1, pp. 26-32.

Connelly, F.M., Clandinin, D.J. (1988), Teachers as Curriculum Planners: Narratives of Experience, Teachers' College Press, New York, NY.

Conroy, P.A., Lefever, M.M.,, Withiam, G. (1996), "The value of college advisory boards", *Cornell Hotel and Restaurant Administration Quarterly*, Vol. 37 No.4, pp. 85-9.

Cooper, C.L., Payne, R. (1988), *Causes, Coping and Consequences of Stress at Work*, John Wiley & Sons, Chichester.

Cornelius, M (1991), "Graduate numeracy", *Teaching Mathematics and its Applications*, Vol. 10 No.4, pp. 151-3.

Cornelius, M (1992), "The numeracy needs of new graduates in employment", Durham University, unpublished.

Corsun, D.L, Young, C.A., Enz, C.A. (1996), "Should NYC's restaurateurs lighten up? Effects of the city's smoke-free-air act", *Cornell Hotel and Restaurant Administration Quarterly*, Vol. 37 No.2, pp. 25-33.

Countryman, C., DeFranco, A. (2002), "Compensation and benefits survey 2002", *The Bottomline*, Vol. 17 No.7, pp. 11-32.

Countryman, C., DeFranco, A., Venegas, T. (2004), "2004 compensation and benefits survey", *The Bottomline*, Vol. 19 No.7, pp. 6-33.

Crafts, D. (1993), "Managers' perceptions of alcohol service training programs", Vol. 11 No.1, pp. 1-10.

Crompton, R., Sanderson, K. (1989), *Gendered Jobs and Social Change*, Unwin Hyman, London

Crosby, L.A., Evans, K.R., Cowles, D. (1990), "Relationship quality in services selling: an interpersonal influence perspective", *Journal of Marketing*, Vol. 54 No.3, pp. 68-81.

Cross, R., Leonard, P. (1994), "Benchmarking: a strategic and tactical perspective", in Dale, B.G. (Eds), *Managing Quality*, 2d ed, Prentice-Hall, Englewood Cliffs, NJ, pp. 497-513.

Cross, R., Smith, J. (1995), "Customer bonding and the information core", *Direct Marketing*, Vol. 57 pp. 28-31.

Crouch, G.I. (1994), "Price elasticities in international tourism", Vol. 17 No.3, pp. 27-40.

Damitio, J.W., Schmidgall, R.S. (2001), "The value of professional certifications for hospitality financial experts", *Cornell Hotel & Restaurant Administration Quarterly*, Vol. 42 No.1, pp. 66-70.

Davies, H. (1995), *China Business: Context and Issues*, Longman Asia Ltd, Hong Kong.

Davis, D.J. (1990), " Demographic change: the role of the hospitality manager", *International Journal of Contemporary Hospitality Management*, Vol. 2 No.2, pp. 33-5.

Day, A., Peters, J. (1994), "Rediscovering standards: static and dynamic quality", *International Journal of Contemporary Hospitality Management*, Vol. 6.

De George, R. T. (1999), Business Ethics, 5th ed., Prentice Hall, Englewood Cliffs, NJ.

de Souza, A.R, Stutz, F.P (1994), *The World Economy: Resource, Location, Trade, and Development*, Macmillan College Publishing Company, New York, NY.

Deakins, D. (1996), *Entrepreneurs and Small Firms*, McGraw-Hill, London.

Dean, R.A. (1983), "Reality shock: the link between socialisation and organisational commitment", *Journal of Management and Development*, Vol. 2 No.4, pp. 55-65.

Deery, M, Iverson, R (1995), "Enhancing productivity: intervention strategies for employee turnover", *Proceedings of IAHMS Spring Conference*, Norwich Hotel School, Norwich.

Dex, S (1991), *Life and Work History Analyses: Qualitative and Quantitative Developments*, Routledge, London.

Ditmer, L., Xiaobo, L. (1996), "Personal politics in the Chinese Danwei under reform", *Asian Survey*, Vol. 36 No.3, pp. 246-67.

Dittman, D.A. Dodrill, K., Riley, M. (1992), "Hotel workers' orientations to work: the question of autonomy and scope", *International Journal of Contemporary Hospitality Management*, Vol. 4 No.1 , pp. 23-5.

Dodwell, S., Simmons, P. (1994), "Trials and tribulations in the pursuit of quality improvement", *International Journal of Contemporary Hospitality Management*, Vol. 6 No.1/2, pp. 14-18.

Dodwell, S., Simmons, P. (1994), "Trials and tribulations in the pursuit of quality improvement", *International Journal of Contemporary Hospitality Management*, Vol. 6 pp. 14-18.

Dube, L., Renaghan, L.M., Miller, J.M. (1994), "Measuring customer satisfaction for strategic management", *The Cornell Hotel and Restaurant Quarterly*, Vol. 35 No.1, pp. 39-47.

Dube, L., Renaghan, L.M., Miller, J.M. (1994), "Measuring customer satisfaction for strategic management", *Cornell Hotel & Restaurant Administration Quarterly*, Vol. 35 No.1, pp. 39-47.

Dwyer, F.R., Schurr, P.H., Oh, S. (1987), "Developing buyer-seller relationships", *Journal of Marketing*, Vol. 51 No.2, pp. 11-27.

Dwyer, L., Forsyth, P. (1994), "Foreign ownership and leakages from tourist expenditure: a framework for analysis", *Australian Journal of Hospitality Management*, Vol. 1 No.2, pp. 1 -10.

Elliott, A. (1999), "Introduction", in Elliott, A. (Eds), *Contemporary Social Theory*, Blackwell, Oxford, pp. 1-32.

Elloy, D., McCombs, T (1996), "Application of open systems theory in a manufacturing plant", *Team Performance Management*, Vol. 2 No.3, pp. 15-22.

Eloranta, E., Crom, S. (1995), "Performance indicators", in Rolstadas, A. (Eds), *Benchmarking: Theory and Practice*, Chapman & Hall, London, pp. 391-6.

Evans, J. (1993), "Tourism graduates: a case of over-production", *Tourism Management*, Vol. 14 No.4, pp. 243-6.

Farquhar, P.H. (1990), "Managing brand equity", *Journal of Advertising Research*, Vol. 30 pp. RC7-RC12.

Farrar, A.L., Murrmann, S.K., Vest, J.M. "Profiling managerial entrants to the hospitality industry", Vol. 18 No.1994, pp. 65-76.

Fasone, P. (1994), "How Holiday Inn puts out welcome mat for in-house customers", *Communications News*, Vol. 31 No.10, pp. 27-9.

Fender, D., Litteljohn, D. (1992), "Forward planning in uncertain times", *International Journal of Contemporary Hospitality Management*, Vol. 4 No.3, pp. i-iv .

Fenich, G.G. (1996), "The uses and abuses of multipliers: a current case", *Hospitality Research Journal*, Vol. 20 No.1, pp. 101-8.

Ferreira, R. (1998), "A comparison of the response rates, return times, return methods and costs for surveys faxed and mailed in clubs", *Journal of Hospitality & Tourism Research*, Vol. 21 No.3, pp. 81-91.

Getz, D., Carlsen, J. (2000), "Characteristics and goals of family and owner-operated businesses in the rural tourism and hospitality sectors", *Tourism Management*, Vol. 21 No.6, pp. 547-60.

Ghiselli, R., Hiemstra, S., Almanza, B. "Reducing school foodservice waste through the choice of serviceware", Vol. 18 No.3.

Gilmore, A., Carson, D. "Ferry travel: a case of comparative services", *International Journal of Contemporary Hospitality Management*, Vol. 4 No.4, pp. 16-20 .

Gilmore, S. (1992), "Effectiveness of class discussion in the case method of instruction", Vol. 16 No.1, pp. 93-108.

Goldman, K. (1993), "Concept selection for independent restaurants", *The Cornell Hotel and Restaurant Quarterly*, Vol. 34 No.6, pp. 59-72.

Graves, N.S. (1996), "Personality traits in successful managers as perceived by food and beverage human resources executives and recruiters", *Hospitality Research Journal*, Vol. 20 No.2, pp. 95-112.

Gray, W.S., Ligouri, S.C. (1980), *Hotel and Motel Management Operations*, Prentice-Hall, Englewood Cliffs, NJ.

Greathouse, K.R., Gergoire, M.B., Shanklin, C.W., Tripp, C. (1996), "Factors considered important in hotel accommodations by travelers stopping at visitor information centers", *Hospitality Research Journal*, Vol. 19 No.4, pp. 129-40.

Gregoire, M., Sneed, J., Martin, J. "School foodservice: a look to the future", Vol. 17 No.1993, pp. 175-94.

Griffin, R.K. (1995), "A categorization scheme for critical success factors of lodging yield management systems", *International Journal of Hospitality Management*, Vol. 14 No.3, pp. 325-38.

Gronroos, C. (1984), "A service quality model and its marketing implications", *European Journal of Marketing*, Vol. 18 No.4, pp. 36-44.

Gruen, T.W. (1997), "Relationship marketing: the route to marketing efficiency and effectiveness", *Business Horizons*, Vol. 40 No.6, pp. 32-8.

Harrison, L.C., Husbands, W. (1996), *Practicing Responsible Tourism*, John Wiley & Sons, Inc., Toronto, pp. 1-15.

Harrison, M. (1993), *Operations Management Strategy*, Pitman, London.

Hart, C.W.L. (1991), "Hampton Inns.guests satisfied with satisfaction guarantee", *Marketing News*, Vol. 25 No.3.

Hartline, M.D., Jones, K.C. (1996), "Employee performance cues in a hotel service environment: influence on perceived service quality, value, and word-of-mouth intentions", *Journal of Business Research*, Vol. 35 No.3, pp. 207-15.

Harwood, C., Pieters, G. (1990), "How to Manage Quality Improvement", *Quality Progress*, No.March.

Hasek, G. (1992), "Country lodging seeks perfection", *Hotel & Motel Management*, Vol. 207 No.5, pp. 1.

Hassmiller, B. (2000), "Compensation and benefits survey 2000", *The Bottomline*, Vol. 15 No.7, pp. 6-25.

Hawke, A (1998), "An indigenous worker's guide to the Workplace Relations Act – an alternative view", *Journal Of Industrial Relations*, Vol. 40 No.2, pp. 304-9.

Haywood, K.M (1987), "Thoughts on thinking: a critical human resource skill", *The Cornell Hotel and Restaurant Administrative Quarterly*, Vol. 28 No.2, pp. 51-5.

Haywood, K.M. (1991), "A strategic approach to managing costs", Vol. 14 No.3, pp. 73-84.

HCITB (1983), *Manpower Changes in the Hotel and Catering Industry*, Hotel and Catering Industry Training Board, Wembley.

Head, J., Lucas, R. (2004), "Employee relations in the non-union hotel industry: a case of determined opportunism?", *Personnel Review*, Vol. 33 No.6, pp. 693-710.

Head, T.C., Sorenson, P.F. Jr., Pincus, L.B. (1995), "Sexual harassment in the eye of the beholder: but what focuses that eye?", *Mid American Journal of Business*, Vol. 10 No.1, pp. 47-54.

Heal, R. (1990), *Hospitality in Early Modern England*, Clarendon Press, Oxford.

Heide, J.B., John, G. (1990), "Alliances in industrial purchasing: the determinants of joint action in buyer-supplier relationships", *Journal of Marketing Research*, Vol. 27 No.1, pp. 24-36.

Heizer, J., Render, B. (1992), *Production and Operations Management*, 3rd, Allyn and Bacon, Boston, MA, pp. 2.

Hellinger, F.J. (1993), "The lifetime cost of treating a person with HIV", *Journal of the American Medical Society*, Vol. 270 No.4, pp. 474-8.

Hendry, C. *International Small Business Journal*, Vol. 10 pp. 68-72.

Henley Centre (1996), *Hospitality into the 21st Century. A Vision for the Future*, Henley Centre.

Hepple, J., Kipps, M., Thomson, J. (1990), "The concept of hospitality and an evaluation of its applicability to the experience of hospital patients", *International Journal of Hospitality Management*, Vol. 9 No.4, pp. 305-17.

Herzberg, F. (1966), *Work and the Nature of Man*, World Publishing Company, Chicago, IL..

Heskett, J.L., Jones, T.O., Loveman, G.W., Sasser, W.E. Jr, Schlesinger, L.A. (1994), "Putting the service profit chain to work", *Harvard Business Review*, No.March-April, pp. 164-74.

Heymann, K. (1992), "Quality management: a ten-point model", *The Cornell Hotel and Restaurant Quarterly*, Vol. 33 No.5, pp. 51-60.

Hiemstra, S., Kosiba, S., 'Recession, tax impacts on the U.S. restaurant industry", Vol.17 No. 2, 1994, pp. 17-23.

Higgs, M. (1996), "Overcoming the problems of cultural differences to establish success for international management teams", *Team Performance Management*, Vol. 2 No.1, pp. 36-43.

Hill, T. (1993), *The Essence of Operations Management*, Prentice-Hall International, New York, NY, pp. 2.

Hing, N. (1996), "An empirical analysis of the benefits and limitations for restaurant franchisees", International Journal of Hospitality Management, Vol. 15 No.2, pp. 177-87.

Hinkin, T.R., Tracey, B. (1994), "Transformational leadership in the hospitality industry", Vol. 18 No.1, pp. 49-64.

Hirst, M. "Creating a service-driven culture globally", *International Journal of Contemporary Hospitality Management*, Vol. 4 No.1, pp. i-iii.

HM Treasury (1991), *Competing for Quality: Buying Better Public Services*, HMSO, London.

Hochschild, A. (1983), *The Managed Heart*, University of California Press, Berkeley.

Hodges, L. (1998), "Welcome to the new world of Disney degrees", *Independent Education Section*, pp. 9.

Hogan, R., Hogan, J., Busch, C. (1984), "How to measure service orientation", *Journal of Applied Psychology.*, Vol. 69 No.1, pp. 104-26.

Holden, L. (1991), "European trends in training and development", *International Journal of Human Resource Management*, Vol. 2 No.2, pp. 113-31.

Holland, M.A., McCool, A.C. (1994), "Cross-culture cuisine: long-term trend or short lived fad", Vol. 12 No.1, pp. 17-30.

Holloway, J.C. (1985), *The Business of Tourism*, Macdonald and Evans, Plymouth.

Honey, P., Mumford, A. (1982), *The Manual of Learning Styles*, Maidenhead, Berkshire.

Hoque, K. (2000), *Human Resource Management in the Hotel Industry: Strategy, Innovation and Performance*, Routledge, London.

Horwath Consulting (1995), *Worldwide Hotel Industry 1995*, New York, NY.

Hotel and Catering International Management Association (1993), *The Hospitality Year Book*.

Howey, R.M., Savage, D.S. (1995), "Information processing: coordination and control in large hotels", *FIU Hospitality Review*, Vol. 13 No.1, pp. 51-62.

Hsu, C.H.C. (1993), "Management development activities and learning interests of university residence hall foodservice managers", Vol. 16 No.2, pp. 3-16.

Hu, C., Hiemstra, S. (1996), "Hybrid conjoint analysis as a research technique to measure meeting planners' preferences in hotel selection", *Journal of Travel Research*, Vol. 35 No.2, pp. 62-9.

Huang, S.E., Brown, N.E. (1996), "First-Choice international graduate students in hospitality programs: school choice, career expectations, and academic adjustment", *Hospitality Research Journal*, Vol. 20 No.1, pp. 109-18.

Ingold, T., Worthington, T. (1994), "Prophylaxis, not diagnosis and cure ", *International Journal of Contemporary Hospitality Management*, Vol. 6 No.1/2, pp. 46-52.

Ingram, H. (1998), *The IJCHM Millennium Issue*, Millennium Internet Conference.

Jacoby, J., Kyner, D.B. (1973), "Brand loyalty versus repeat purchasing", *Journal of Marketing Research*, Vol. 10 pp. 1-9.

Jaffe, W.F., Almanza, B.A., Min, C-H.J. (1993), "Solid waste disposal: independent food service practices", Vol. 11 No.1, pp. 69-78.

Jahoda, M. (1985), *Current Concepts of Positive Mental Health*, Basic Books, New York, NY.

Jarvis, L.P., Mayo, E.J. (1986), "Winning the market-share game", *The Cornell Hotel and Restaurant Administration Quarterly*, pp. 73-9.

Jayawardena, C. (2000), "International hotel manager", *International Journal of Contemporary Hospitality Management*, Vol. 12 No.1, pp. 67-9.

Jeffrey, D., Hubbard, N.J. (1994), "A model of hotel occupancy performance for monitoring and marketing in the hotel industry", *International Journal of Hospitality Management*, Vol. 13 No.1, pp. 57-71.

Jenkins, A.K. (2001), "Making a career of it? Hospitality students' future perspectives: an Anglo-Dutch study", *International Journal of Contemporary Hospitality Management*, Vol. 13 No.1, pp. 13-20.

Jensen, G.L. (1994), "Outsourcing information services in the hospitality industry", *FIU Hospitality Review*, Vol. 12 No.1, pp. 31-6.

Jienpetivate, M. (1995), "The management of service encounters", University of Surrey, Guildford., MSc dissertation.

Johns, N. (1993), " Productivity management through design and operation: a case study", *International Journal of Contemporary Hospitality Management*, Vol. 5 No.2, pp. 20-24.

Johns, N., Chesterton, J. (1994), "ICL Kidsgrove: engineering a quality culture", *International Journal of Contemporary Hospitality Management*, Vol. 6 No.1/2, pp. 25-9.

Johnson, G., Scholes, K (1999), *Exploring Corporate Strategy*, Prentice-Hall, Hemel Hempstead.

Kanter, R., Corn, R. (1994), "Do cultural differences make a business difference?", *Journal of Management Development*, Vol. 13 No.2, pp. 5-23.

Kaplan, R.S., Norton, D.P (1992), "The balanced scorecard –

270 *Guest Management*

measures that drive performance", *Harvard Business Review*, Vol. 70 No.1, pp. 71-9.

Kapoor, S. (1990), "Mandatory fast food labeling: support by twelfth graders", Vol. 13 No.2, pp. 23-30.

Karlof, B., Ostblom, S. (1994), *Benchmarking: A Signpost Excellence in Quality and Productivity*, John Wiley, West Sussex.

Karmarkar, U. (2004), "Will you survive the services revolution?", *Harvard Business Review*, Vol. 82 No.6, pp. 100-8.

Kaufman, D. (1998), "Regulation of the employment relationship: the 'old' institutionalist perspective", *Journal of Economic Behaviour and Organisation*, Vol. 34 pp. 349-85.

Kavanaugh, R.R., Ninemeier, J.D. (1991), "Interactive video instruction: a training tool whose time has come", Vol. 9 No.2, pp. 1-6.

Kay, C., Russette, J. (2000), "Hospitality management competencies: identifying manager's essential skills", *The Cornell Hotel and Restaurant Administration Quarterly*, Vol. 41 No.2, pp. 52-63.

Keiser, J. (1998), "Hospitality and tourism: a rhetorical analysis and conceptual framework for identifying industry meanings", *Journal of Hospitality and Tourism Research*, Vol. 22 No.2, pp. 115-28.

Kelley, C.L., Marquette, R.P. (1996), "A tax primer for bed and breakfasts", *Cornell Hotel and Restaurant Administration Quarterly*, Vol. 37 No.4, pp. 34-42.

Kent, W.E. (1992), "Vanguard management: an emerging new paradigm", Vol. 10 No.1, pp. 53-64.

Kim, C., Mauborgne, R. (2000), "Value innovation: the strategic logic of high growth", *Harvard Business Review*, Vol. 75 No.1, pp. 102-13.

Kimble, D. (1996), "Barriers and opportunities in Singapore", *Cornell Hotel and Restaurant Administration Quarterly*, Vol. 37 No.3, pp. 50-4.

King, A.R., Brownell, J. (1966), *The Curriculum and the Disciplines of Knowledge*, John Wiley, New York, NY.

Kipps, M., Middleton, V.T.C. (1990), "Achieving quality and

choice for the customer in hospital catering", *International Journal of Hospitality Management*, Vol. 9 No.1, pp. 69-83.

Kirzner, I. (1980), "The primacy of entrepreneurial discovery", in Seldon, A. (Eds), *Prime Mover of Progress: The Entrepreneur in Capitalism and Socialism*, Institute of Economic Affairs, London, pp. 101-16.

Kittrell, A. (1), "Employers lack AIDS strategy: study", *Business Insurance*.

Kivela, J (1996), "Marketing in the restaurant business", *Australian Journal of Hospitality Management*, Vol. 3 No.1, pp. 1-12.

Koontz, H., O'Donnell, C., Weihrich, H. (1980), *Management*, 7th ed., McGraw-Hill, New York, NY.

Kornhauser, A.W. (1965), *Mental Health of the Industrial Worker*, Wiley, New York, NY.

Kreck, L.A., Rutherford, D.G. "Measuring of foodservice operational success: entrepreneurs vs. executives".

Kriegl, U. (2000), "International hospitality management. identifying important skills and effective training", *Cornell Hotel and Restaurant Administration Quarterly*, Vol. 41 No.2, pp. 64-71.

Krol, C. (1999), "Web becomes crucial to relationship efforts", *Advertising Age*, Vol. 70 No.22, pp. 52.

Ladkin, A, Riley, M (1996), "Mobility and structure in the career paths of UK hotel general managers: a labour market hybrid of the bureaucratic model?", *Tourism Management*, Vol. 17 No.6, pp. 443-52.

Lago, D., Poffley, J.K. (1993), "The aging population and the hospitality industry in 2010: important trends and probable services", Vol. 17 No.1, pp. 29-26.

Landry, D. (1996), "Franchise opportunities abound with new and established brands", *FIU Hospitality Review*, Vol. 14.

Langeard, E., Eiglier, P. (1983), "Strategic management of service development", in Berry, L.T., Shostack, G.L., Upah, G.D. (Eds), *Emerging Perspectives on Services Marketing*, American Marketing Association, Chicago, IL, Proceedings Series, pp. 68-72.

Laudadio, D.M. (1988), "Sexual and gender Harassment: assessing the current climate", *Hospitality Education and Research Journal*, Vol. 2 No.2, pp. 411-15.

Laws, E. (1999), "Two ways of serving pizza – a comparative study of low and high contact services using blueprinting techniques", University of Surrey, Brighton, paper presented at the CHME Research Conference.

Learning and Teaching Support Network (2004), "Accepted students and applicants 1996-2003 in hospitality, leisure, sport and tourism", based on data provided by UCAS. Learning and Teaching Support Network, available at: www.hlst.ltsn.ac.uk/resources/ucas.pdf.

Ledingham, J.A., Bruning, S.D. (1998), "Relationship management in public relations: dimensions of an organization-public relationship", *Public Relations Review*, Vol. 24 No.1, pp. 55-65.

Lee, Y.L., Hing, N. (1995), "Measuring quality in restaurant operations: an application of SERVQUAL instrument", *International Journal of Hospitality Management*, Vol. 14 No.3, pp. 293-310.

Leidner, R. (1993), *Fast Food, Fast Talk*, University of California Press, Berkeley

Lenckus, D. (1993), "A quality solution to improving service", *Business Insurance*, Vol. 27 No.50, pp. 19-20.

Lewis, R.C. (1990), "Advertising your hotel's position", *The Cornell Hotel and Restaurant Quarterly*, Vol. 31 No.2, pp. 84-91.

Lin, M-F. (1997), *Feasibility Planning in Budget Hotel Development*, University of Buckingham, unpublished MSc thesis.

Litvan, L.M. (1996), "Increasing revenue with repeat sales", *Nation's Business*, Vol. 84 pp. 36-8.

Lockwood, A., Jones, P. (1990), "Applying value engineering to rooms management ", *International Journal of Contemporary Hospitality Management*, Vol. 2 No.1, pp. 27-32.

Louviere, J.J., Timmermans, H. (1990), "Stated preference and choice models applied to recreation research: a review", *Leisure Sciences*, Vol. 12 pp. 9-32.

Lucas, R., Laycock, J. (1991), "An interactive personnel function for managing budget hotels", *International Journal of Contemporary Hospitality Management*, Vol. 3 No.3, pp. 33-6.

MacKinnon, C. (1979), "Sexual harassment of working women", *New Haven CT*, Yale University Press.

Makens, J.C., Bowen, J.T. (1996), "Increasing restaurant profits with product merchandising", *Cornell Hotel and Restaurant Administration Quarterly*, Vol. 37 No.1, pp. 72-9.

Margerison, J. (1998)), "Business planning", in Thomas, R. (Eds),*The Management of Small Tourism and Hospitality Firms*, Cassell, London, pp. 101-16.

Marsh, C.J. (1997), Perspective, Key Concepts for Understanding Ccurriculum, Falmer Press, London.

Martin, L.J. (1998), "Integrating ethics into hospitality curriculum", *Journal of Hospitality and Tourism Education*, CHRIE, Washington DC, Vol. 10 No.2, pp. 22-5.

Maylor, H. (1999), *Project Management*, Financial Times Management, London.

McCulloch, J. (1992), "The Youth Hostels Association: precursors and contemporary achievements", *Journal of Tourism Studies*, Vol. 3 No.1, pp. 22-7.

McKenna, S. (1990), "The business ethic in public sector catering", *The Service Industries Journal*, Vol. 10 No.2, pp. 377-98.

Mennel, S., Murcott, A., van Otterloo, A. (1992), *The Sociology of Food: Eating, Diet and Culture*, Sage, London.

Meyer, R.A. (1996), "Waikiki faces major problems: does new master plan hold solutions?", *FIU Hospitality Review*, Vol. 14 No.1, pp. 7-18.

Miller, A., Watts, A.G., Jamieson, I. (1991), *Rethinking Work Experience*, Falmer, for the School of Curriculum Industry Partnership, London.

Mok, C., Armstrong, R.W. (1994), "Perception of Australia as a holiday destination: a case of Hong Kong and Taiwanese tourists", *Australian Journal of Hospitality Management*, Vol. 1 No.2, pp. 25-8.

Moos, R.H. (1994), *Work Environment Scale Manual*, 3rd edition, Consulting Psychologists Press, Palo Alto, CA.

Morcos, S.H., Tak, J., Gregoire, M.B. (1992), "Customer perceptions of drive-thru service", Vol. 10 No.2, pp. 17-24.

Morrison, A. (1996), "Guesthouses and small hotels", in Jones, P. (Eds),*Introduction to Hospitality Operations*, Cassell,, London, pp. 73-85.

Muhlmann, W.E. (1932), "Hospitality", in Seligman, E.R.A. (Eds), *Encyclopaedia of Social Sciences*, Macmillan, New York, NY.

Mulhern, A. (1993), "The Policies of the European Commission, Small and Medium-sized Enterprises and the Single Market", Small Businesses and Small Business Development Conference, Leicester, No.April.

Muller, C., Campbell, D. (1995), "The attributes and attitudes of multiunit managers in a national quick service restaurant chain", *Hospitality Research Journal*, Vol. 19 No.2, pp. 3-18.

Mullins, L., Meudell, K. , Scott, H. (1993), "Developing culture in short-life organizations", *International Journal of Contemporary Hospitality Management*, Vol. 5 No.4 , pp. 15-19.

Murphy, J., Forrest, E., Wotring, C.E. (1996a), "Restaurant marketing on the world wide web", *Cornell Hotel and Restaurant Administration Quarterly*, Vol. 37 No.1, pp. 61-71.

Murrmann, S.K., Murrmann, K.F. (1993), "Employee attitudes toward a nonunion grievance procedure and their influence on unionization", Vol. 16 No.1, pp. 41-53.

Nailon, P. (1982), "Theory in hospitality management", *International Journal of Hospitality Management*, Vol. 1 No.3, pp. 135-42.

Namasivayam, K., Enz, C.A., Siguaw, J.A. (2000), "How wired are we?", *Cornell Hotel and Restaurant Administration Quarterly*, Vol. 41 No.6, pp. 40-8.

Nassikas, J.A. (1991), " Words of warning, words of encouragement", *Hotels*, No.March, pp. 46-7.

Nebel, E.C. III, Braunlich, C.G., Zhang, Y. (1994), "Career

paths in American luxury hotels: hotel food and beverage directors", *International Journal of Contemporary Hospitality Management*, Vol. 6 No.6, pp. 3-9.

Nelson, A.A., Dopson, L. (1999), "Future of hotel education: required skills and knowledge for graduates of US hospitality programs beyond the year 2000 – part one", *Journal of Tourism and Hospitality Education*, Vol. 13 No.5, pp. 58-67.

Nibblelink, A., Teare, R. (1991), "Hotel services for the international business traveller", *International Journal of Contemporary Hospitality Management*, Vol. 3 No.2, pp. iv-vi.

Nicholls, J.A.F., Roslow, S. (1989), "Segmenting the hotel market", Vol. 7 No.1, pp. 39-47.

Nicholls, L., Nystuen, C. (1993), "Future foodservice waste management", Vol. 17 No.1, pp. 231-44.

Nightingale, M. (1985), " The hospitality industry: defining quality for a quality assurance programme – a study in perceptions", *Service Industries Journal*, Vol. 5 No.1, pp. 9-22.

Northern Ireland Tourist Board *Corporate Plan 1992-1995*.

Norusis, M.J. (1992), Chicago, II, SPSS for Windows, Advanced Statistics-Release 5. SPSS Inc.

Novarra, V. (1981), *Men's Work, Women's Work*, Marion Boyars, London

Nowlis, S.M., Simonsen, I. (1996), "The effect of new product features on brand choice", *Journal of Marketing Research*, Vol. 33 pp. 36-46.

Nurmi, R. (1996), "Teamwork and team leadership", *Team Performance Management*, Vol. 2 No.1, pp. 9-13.

Oberoi, U., Hales, C. (1990), "Assessing the quality of the conference hotel service product: towards an empirically based model", *Service Industries Journal*, Vol. 10 No.4, pp. 700-2.

Oh, H., Jeong, M. (1996), "Improving marketers' predictive power of customer satisfaction on expectation-based target market levels", *Hospitality Research Journal*, Vol. 19 No.4, pp. 65-85.

Olsen, M., Murphy, B., Teare, R.E. (1994), "CEO perspectives on scanning the global hotel business environment", International Journal of Contemporary Hospitality Management, Vol. 6 No.4, pp. 3-9.

Olsen, M.D. (1996), "Events shaping the future and their impact on the multinational hotel industry", *Tourism Recreation Research*, Vol. 21 No.2, pp. 7-14.

Olsen, M.D., Connolly, D.J. (2000), "Experience-based travel", *Cornell Hotel and Restaurant Administration Quarterly*, Vol. 41 No.1, pp. 30-40.

OMT (1999), *Tourism Highlights 1999*, Relatório do World Tourism Organization.

Palmer, A. (1994), "Relationship marketing: back to basics?", *Journal of Marketing Management*, Vol. 10 pp. 571-9.

Pannell Kerr Forster Associates (1993), "Factors influencing the design of hotels", *International Journal of Contemporary Hospitality Management*, Vol. 5 No.2, pp. 17-19.

Parsa, H.G. (1996), "Franchisor-franchisee relationships in quick-service-restaurant systems", *Cornell Hotel and Restaurant Administration Quarterly*, Vol. 37 No.3, pp. 42-9.

Parsons, D. (1992), "Developments in the UK tourism and leisure labour market", in Lindley, R. (Eds),*Women's Employment: Britain in the Single European Market*, Equal Opportunities Commission, HMSO, London

Partlow C.G., Gregoire, M.B. (1993), "Activities of hospitality management program administrators", Vol. 16 No.3, pp. 17-23.

Payne, R.L., Hartley, J. (1987), "A test of a model for explaining the affective experience of unemployed men", *Journal of Occupational Psychology* , Vol. 60 pp. 31-47.

Peacock, M. (1993), "A question of size", *International Journal of Contemporary Hospitality Management*, Vol. 5 No.4, pp. 29-32.

Pearce, J.A.I., Robinson, R.B. Jr (2000), "Cultivating Guanxi as a foreign investor strategy", *Business Horizons*, Vol. 43 No.1, pp. 31-8.

Perkins, J., Cummings, P. (1994), "A community economic development survey of part-time labor: implications for the hospitality industry", Vol. 17 No.3, pp. 111-18.

Pfeifer, Y. (1983)), "Small business management", in Cassee, E.H., Reuland, R. (Eds), *The Management of Hospitality*, Pergamon, Oxford, pp. 189-202.

Phillips, P.A. (1994), " Welsh hotel: cost-volume-profit analysis and uncertainty", *International Journal of Contemporary Hospitality Management*, Vol. 6 No.3, pp. 31-6 .

Pickering, J., Greenwood, J., Hunt, D. (1971), *The Small Firm in the Hotel and Catering Industry (Committee of Inquiry on Small Firms: Research Report 14)*, HMSO, London.

Pickert, M.J., Miller, J. (1996), "Food production forecasting in six commercial foodservice operations: a pilot study", *Hospitality Research Journal*, Vol. 20 No..2, pp. 137-44.

Pickworth, J.R. (1987), " Minding the Ps and Qs", *The Cornell Hotel and Restaurant Administration Quarterly*, Vol. 28 No.May , pp. 40-7.

Porter, M. E. (1990), *The Competitive Advantage of Nations*, The Free Press, New York, NY.

Powers, T.F. (1992), "The standard world of 2005: a surprise-free scenario", Vol. 16 No.1, pp. 1-22.

Pratt, R., Whitney, D. (1991), "Attentional and interpersonal characteristics of restaurant general managers in comparison with other groups of interest", Vol. 15 No.1, pp. 9-24.

Price, F. (1986), *Right First Time – Using Quality Control for Profit*, Wildwood House.

Prichard, M. (1981), *Guests and Hosts*, Oxford University Press, Oxford.

Prideaux, B., Dunn, A. (1995), "Tourism and crime—how can the tourism industry respond?", *Australian Journal of Hospitality Management*, Vol. 2 No.1, pp. 7-16.

Purcell, K. (1989), "Gender at work", in Gallie, D. (Eds),*Employment in Britain*, Blackwell, Oxford

Ralston, C.E. (1993), "Manager-customer relationship in food service commissary operations", Vol. 11 No.2, pp. 61-72.

Rao, C.P., Kelkar, M.M. (1997), "Relative impact of performance and importance ratings on measurement of service quality", *Journal of Professional Services Marketing*, Vol. 15 No.2, pp. 69-86.

278 *Guest Management*

Raymond, M.A., Tanner, J.F. Jr (1994), "Maintaining customer relationships in direct sales: stimulating repeat purchase behavior", *Journal of Personnel Selling and Sales Management*, Vol. 14 No.3, pp. 67-76.

Reardon, K.K., Enis, B. (1990), "Establishing a company-wide customer orientation through persuasive internal marketing", *Management Communication Quarterly*, Vol. 3 No.February, pp. 376-87.

Records, H.A., Glennie, M.F. (1991), "Service management and quality assurance...a systems approach", *Cornell Hotel & Restaurant Administration Quarterly*, Vol. 32 No.1, pp. 26-35.

Reich, A.Z. (1994), "Comprehensive strategic planning as a capstone course in hospitality education", *Hospitality and Tourism Educator*, Vol. 6 No.2, pp. 67-70.

Reichheld, F.F., Sasser, W.E. Jr (1990), "Zero defections: quality comes to services", *Harvard Business Review*, Vol. 68 No.5, pp. 105-11.

Reilly, B., DiAngelo, J. (1987), "Entrepreneurial behaviour in large organisations", *SAM Advanced Management Journal*, pp. 24-31.

Reisenger Y., Waryszak, R.Z. (1994), "Assessment of service quality for international tourists in hotels: an exploratory study of Japanese tourists in Australia", *Australian Journal of Hospitality Management*, Vol. 1 No.2, pp. 11-16.

Rejowski, M. (1996), *Turismo e Pesquisa Científica*, Papirus Editora, São Paulo.

Remington, J., Escoffier, M. (1996), "Tourism: who needs it?", *FIU Hospitality Review*, Vol. 14 No.1, pp. 19-26.

Riley, M (1990), "The role of age distributions in career path analysis", *Tourism Management*, Vol. 11 No.1, pp. 38-44.

Rimmer, M (1991), "Enterprise awards: are they more flexible?", *Asia Pacific Human Resource Management*, Vol. 29 No.1, pp. 71-81.

Rita, P., Moutinho, L. (1992), "Allocating a promotion budget", *International Journal of Contemporary Hospitality Management*, Vol. 4 No.3, pp. 3-8.

Roberts, J. (1995), *Human resource Practices in the Hospitality Industry*, Hodder and Stoughton, London.

Robson, D. (1995), "Nettforce and training—the challenge begins", *Australian Journal of Hospitality Management*, Vol. 2 No.1, pp. 49-51.

Roh, Y.S., Andrew, W. (1994), "U.S. hospitality investment in six potential Eastern European markets", Vol. 17 No.3, pp. 41-50.

Roper, A. (1995), "The emergence of hotel consortia as transorganizational forms", *International Journal of Contemporary Hospitality Management*, Vol. 7 No.1, pp. 4-9.

Rotter, J.B. (1966), " Generalised expectancies for internal versus external control of reinforcement", *Psychological Monographs*, Vol. 80 No.1.

Ruddy, J. (1989), "Career development of hotel managers in Hong Kong", *International Journal of Hospitality Management*, Vol. 8 No.3, pp. 215-25.

Shanklin, C. (1993), "Ecology age: implications for the hospitality and tourism industry", Vol. 17 No.1, pp. 219-25.

Shanklin, C., Petrillose, M., Pettay, A. (1991), "Solid waste management practices in selected hotel chains and individual properties", Vol. 15 No.1, pp. 59-74.

Singh, A., Chon, K.S. (1993), "Teleconferencing technology: recent developments and implications for hotel industry", *FIU Hospitality Review*, Vol. 11 No.2, pp. 1-6.

Singh, A., Gu, Z. (1994), "Diversification, financial performance, and stability of foodservice firms", Vol. 18 No.2, pp. 3-18.

Skinner, W. (1974), "The focused factory", *Harvard Business Review*, Vol. 52 No.3, pp. 113-21.

Slattery, P. (1983), "Social scientific methodology and hospitality management", *International Journal of Hospitality Management*, Vol. 2 No.1, pp. 9-14.

Stevens, B., Fleckenstein, A. (1999), "Comparative ethics: how students and human-resources directors react to real-life situations", *Cornell Hotel and Restaurant Administration Quarterly*, Vol. 40 No.2, pp. 69-75.

Syer, J. (1986), *Team Spirit: The Elusive Experience*, The Kingswood Press, London, pp. 13-14.

Tas, R.E (1988), "Teaching future managers", *The Cornell Hotel and Restaurant Administration Quarterly*, Vol. 29 No.2, pp. 41-3.

Teixeira, R.M., Fletcher, J., Westlake, J. (2000), "Ensino superior em turismo: experiência do reino unido", *Turismo em Análise*, ECA, Universidade de São Paulo, São Paulo., Vol. 11 No.2.

Telfer, E. (1996), *Food for Thought, Philosophy of Food*, Routledge, London.

Templeton, W., Bond, C.A. (1999), "Banking on the euro: changes and challenges", *Managerial Finance*, Vol. 25 No.11, pp. 17-26.

Van Hoof, H.B., Verbeeten, M.J.,, Combrink, T.E. (1996), "Information technology revisited—international lodging industry technology needs and perceptions: a comparative study", *Cornell Hotel and Restaurant Administration Quarterly*, Vol. 37 No.6, pp. 66-91.

Velasquez, M.G. (1998), Business Ethics, Concepts and Cases, 4th ed., Prentice Hall, Englewood Cliffs, NJ.

Verma, R., Iqbal, Z., Plaschka, G. (2004), "Choice drivers and switching inertia in e-financial services", *California Management Review*, Vol. 46 No.4, pp. 43-68.

Warren, P., Ostergren, N.W. (1990), "Marketing your hotel: challenges of the '90s", *The Cornell Hotel and Restaurant Administration Quarterly*, pp. 56-9.

Watkins, E. (1992), "How Ritz-Carlton won the Baldrige Award", *Lodging Hospitality*, Vol. 48 No.11, pp. 22-4.

Watson, S., Brotherton, B. (1996), "Hospitality management development: minimizing conflict - maximising potential", *Management Development Review*, Vol. 9 No.5, pp. 13-22.

Watson, S., D'Annunzio-Green, N. (1996), "Implementing cultural change through human resources: the elusive organization alchemy?", International Journal of Contemporary Hospitality Management, Vol. 8 No.2.

Watson, S., Litteljohn, D. (1992), "Multi and transnational forms: the impact of expansion on corporate structures", in Teare, R., Olsen, M. (Eds),*International Hospitality Management*, Pitman, London, pp. 135-59.

Weatherford, L.R. (1995), "Length of stay heuristics, do they really make a difference", *The Cornell Hotel and Restaurant Quarterly*, Vol. 36 No.6, pp. 70-9.

Weaver, P.A., Oh, H.C. (1993), "Do American business travellers have different hotel service requirements?", *International Journal of Contemporary Hospitality Management*, Vol. 5 No.3 , pp. 16-21.

Weaver, P.A., Oh, H.C. (1993), "Do American travellers have different hotel service requirements?", *International Journal of Contemporary Hospitality Management*, Vol. 5 No.3, pp. 16-21.

West, A., Jameson, S.M. (1990), "Supervised work experience in graduate employment", *International Journal of Contemporary Hospitality Management*, Vol. 2 No.2, pp. 29-32.

Whitney, D. (1990), "Ethics in the hospitality industry", *International Journal of Hospitality Management*, Vol. 9 No.1, pp. 187-92.

Whyte, W.F. (1949), "The social structure of the restaurant", *American Journal of Sociology*, Vol. 54 pp. 302-10.

Wicks, B, Uysal, M., Kim, S. (1994), "The effects of lodging prices on visitors' demand: Everglades National Park", Vol. 17 No.2, pp. 51-62.

Wight, P. (1996), "North American ecotourists: market profile and trip characteristics", *Journal of Travel Research*, Vol. 34 No.4, pp. 2-10.

Wild, R. (1984), *Production and Operations Management. Principles and Techniques*, 3rd, Holt, Rinehart and Winston, London, pp. 276.

Wilks, J., Atherton, T. (1995), "The lifestyle factor: employment practices in the Queensland recreational diving industry", *Australian Journal of Hospitality Management*, Vol. 2 No.1, pp. 23-30.

Williams, A. (2002), *Understanding the Hospitality Consumer*, Butterworth-Heinemann, Oxford.

Williams, C.E. (1996), "The british pub—an industry in transition", *Cornell Hotel and Restaurant Administration Quarterly*, Vol. 37 No.6, pp. 62-73.

Williams, P.W., Hunter, M (1992), "Supervisory hotel employee perceptions of management careers and professional development requirements", *International Journal of Hospitality Management*, Vol. 14 No.4, pp. 359-72.

Williams, P.W., Hunter, M. (1991), "Recruitment and retention insights for the hotel industry", Vol. 9 No.1, pp. 51-8.

Wilson, D.T. (1995), "An integrated model of buyer-seller relationships", *Journal of the Academy of Marketing Science*, Vol. 23 No.4, pp. 335-45.

Wilson, D.T. (2000), "Deep relationships: the case of the vanishing salesperson", *Journal of Personal Selling*, Vol. 20 No.1, pp. 53-61.

Wilson, I., McPhail, J. (1995), "Strategic implications of market orientation and organizational innovativeness on the business performance of hospitality service firms in Australia", *Australian Journal of Hospitality Management*, Vol. 2 No.2, pp. 1-12.

Wilson, M.D.J., Murray, A.E., Black, A.M. (2000), "Contract catering: the skills required for the next millennium", *International Journal of Contemporary Hospitality Management*, Vol. 12 No.1, pp. 75-9.

Wilson, R.H. (1992), "Combining hotel promotions, discount packages, and yield management systems: make sure it's legal", Vol. 15 No.2, pp. 21-30.

Wilson, R.H., Enghagen, L.K., Sharma, P. (1994), "Overbooking: the practice and the law", Vol. 17 No.2, pp. 93-108.

Winer, B.J., Brown, D.R., Michels, K.M. (1991), *Statistical Principles in Experimental Design*, 3rd edition, McGraw-Hill, New York, NY.

Witt, C., Witt, S.F. (1989), "Why productivity in the hotel sector is low", *International Journal of Contemporary Hospitality Management*, Vol. 1 No.2, pp. 28-33.

Wolff, C. (1995), "Days Inn alliances spawn reciprocal payoffs", *Lodging Hospitality*, Vol. 51 No.7.

Wood, R.C. (1995), "Status and hotel and catering work: theoretical dimensions and practical implications", *Hospitality Research Journal*, Vol. 16 No.3, pp. 3-15.

Woods, R.H, Macaulay, J.F (1989), "R for Turnover: retention programs that work", *The Cornell Hotel and Restaurant Administration Quarterly*, Vol. 30 pp. 79-90.

Worsfold, P. (1989), " Management selection in the hospitality industry", *International Journal of Contemporary Hospitality Management*, Vol. 1 No.1, pp. 17-21.

Yavas, U., Yasin, M.M., Wafa, M. (1995), "Front and back-stage strategies in service delivery in the hospitality industry: a conceptual framework", *Marketing Intelligence & Planning*, Vol. 13 No.1, pp. 22-6.

Index

■■■